SUFI BODIES

SUFI BODIES

RELIGION AND SOCIETY IN MEDIEVAL ISLAM

S H A H Z A D   B A S H I R

COLUMBIA UNIVERSITY PRESS
NEW YORK

COLUMBIA UNIVERSITY PRESS

Publishers Since 1893

New York Chichester, West Sussex

Library of Congress Cataloging-in-Publication Data

Bashir, Shahzad, 1968–

Sufi bodies : religion and society in medieval islam / Shahzad Bashir.

p. cm.

Includes bibliographical references and index.

ISBN 978-0-231-14490-2 (cloth: alk. paper) — ISBN 978-0-231-51760-7 (e-book)

1. Sufism.   2. Sufism—Doctrines.   I. Title.

BP189.2.B366 2011

297.409'02—dc22

2011000817

Casebound editions of Columbia University Press books
are printed on permanent and durable acid-free paper.

Printed in the United States of America

c 10 9 8 7 6 5 4 3 2 1

Design by Shaina Andrews

To **NANCY**

For making life beautiful and full of love

CONTENTS

ACKNOWLEDGMENTS

IT IS MY pleasure to acknowledge the institutional and personal support I have received while writing this book. A Charles A. Ryskamp Research Fellowship from the American Council of Learned Societies and a Faculty Fellowship from the National Endowment for the Humanities provided the opportunity to devote myself fully to this project. Small grants from American Academy of Religion and the Associated Colleges of the Midwest enabled me to acquire some necessary materials. At Stanford University, funds from the School of Humanities and Sciences and the department of Religious Studies facilitated the book's production. I am thankful to the libraries of the University of Chicago and the Research Institute for Inner Asian Studies (RIFIAS) at Indiana University for allowing me access to their manuscript microfilm collections.

I am very grateful to the two anonymous reviewers who initially read a partial manuscript for the Press. Subsequently, the great care with which Jamal Elias and Kathryn Babayan commented on the whole manuscript enabled me to clarify significant points and think carefully about how the material should be presented. I have been fortunate to call the congenial environments of Carleton College and Stanford University my academic homes during the period I have worked on this book. At Carleton, the advice, support, and friendship of Adeeb Khalid, Michael McNally, and Lori Pearson were particularly valuable for formulating the project and thinking widely about representing religious history. I would also like to thank Roger Jackson, Michael Kidd, Victoria Morse, Bill North, Cathy Yandell, and Serena Zabin for providing helpful feedback. At Stanford, conversations with Mira Balberg, Jessica Chen, Charlotte Fonrobert, Bob

Gregg, Mohsen Goudarzi, Ariela Marcus-Sells, and Will Sherman were important for clarifying what I wished to say in the book. The friendship of Aishwary Kumar and Parna Sengupta is such that any time spent with them is a great pleasure as well as being a stimulus for thought.

While presenting ideas on this subject at various formal and informal occasions, I have benefited from the comments of Janet Afary, the late Aditya Behl, Sheila Canby, Özgen Felek, Gottfried Hagen, Farooq Hamid, Ahmet Karamustafa, Seyfi Kenan, Bruce Lawrence, Paul Losensky, Ann Matter, Azfar Moin, Sholeh Quinn, and Kishwar Rizvi. It is not a hyperbole to say it would have been impossible for me to write this book without the benefit of Devin DeWeese's many pioneering studies on Sufism in Central Asia and Iran. In addition to his published work, I am deeply grateful to him for his friendship and his generosity of mind. Thanks are also due to Wendy Lochner and Susan Pensak at Columbia University Press for their endorsement of the book's content and for taking care of editorial details.

It is customary to mention the support of family members last, even though they are by far the only people whose love and support is an absolute necessity to make any work possible. I am grateful to my mother and siblings for their love shown in countless ways and for holding my work in esteem. To my regret, my father has not lived long enough to get a satisfactory answer to the question about when the next book would be done. To Zakriya, a quintillion thanks for filling our lives with new passions and for keeping us dreaming about the future. And to Nancy, this book is but a small return for the love I feel fortunate to receive every moment of my life.

NOTES ON TRANSLITERATION

I HAVE OMITTED diacritical marks in the text and notes of this book in order to facilitate the reading of those unfamiliar with them. For readers who would like to see orthographic details, the chronology and bibliography contain full transliteration, according to a system modified slightly from the one used for Persian by the *International Journal of Middle East Studies*.

ABBREVIATIONS

BSOAS	Bulletin of the School of Oriental and African Studies
EI^2	Encyclopedia of Islam, 2d edition
EIr	Encyclopædia Iranica
EQ	Encyclopedia of the Qurʾan
EWIC	Encyclopedia of Women in Islamic Cultures
FIZ	Farhang-i Iran Zamin
HR	History of Religions
IJMES	International Journal of Middle East Studies
JAOS	Journal of the American Oriental Society
JIS	Journal of Islamic Studies
JRAS	Journal of the Royal Asiatic Society
MW	Muslim World
RSO	Rivista degli Studi Orientali
SI	Studia Islamica
ZDMG	Zeitschrift der Deutschen Morgenländischen Gesellschaft

CHRONOLOGY

SUFI BODIES

INTRODUCTION: SHAKING HANDS

In a short Persian work composed in the early sixteenth century of the common era, an author named Hafiz Sultan ʿAli Awbahi tells of one of the most important handshakes of his life. His counterpart for this event on a Wednesday in the month of Rajab, 879 AH (November/December 1474), was a certain Shihab ad-Din ʿAbd al-Ghaffar, who bore the distinction of being able to connect himself to the Prophet Muhammad through a chain of handshakes between living men. What made the event extraordinary was that Awbahi considered this chain to consist of only five links, even though it extended over a period of more than eight centuries separating him from Muhammad's death. As Awbahi describes on the basis of previous authorities, this was possible because of a long-lived companion of the Prophet named Saʿid Habashi who had actually begun his life in the days of Jesus. He once heard Jesus predict the future coming of Muhammad and asked to be given the boon of an unnaturally long life that would allow him to meet the last Prophet. This was granted, and his lease on life was extended further by centuries when he met Muhammad and shook his hand.

As Awbahi explains, Habashi's longevity was of particular significance in the context of a statement attributed to Muhammad: "Whoever shakes my hand, I will shake his hand on the day of resurrection and will be obligated to intercede on his behalf. Likewise, anyone who shakes the hand of someone who shook my hand—up to seven subsequent links—I will shake his hand on the day of resurrection and will be obligated to intercede on his behalf." Habashi could therefore guarantee one's access to Muhammad's intercession, which turned his home in Ethiopia (Habasha) into a place of pilgrimage for religious seekers over the course of his elongated lifespan. Awbahi states that Habashi eventually died about fifty years before the event of the author's own momentous handshake, which assured him salvation through Muhammad's intercession because it fell within the stipulated limit of seven links.[1]

My objective in this book is to present an interpretive history of the people whose lives are reflected in stories such as this tale of handshakes. Awbahi and ʿAbd al-Ghaffar are relatively obscure characters, but the cultural imagination at work here is a pervasive presence in the very considerable mass of literature and art left behind by Muslims from Persianate societies of Central Asia and Iran during the later medieval period (ca. 1300–1500). I aim to reconstruct this imagination by asking questions about the relationships between literary and other works and the human agents who produced and utilized them. The materials I have consulted raise methodological questions that have so far not received adequate analytical attention in academic literature on Sufism, Islam, or religions more generally. While the specific topics I discuss relate to one period in the history of a particular Islamic form, my greater aim in this book is to offer a wide-ranging reconceptualization of the way we treat religious materials that claim to represent history but are often dismissed as mere myth and miracle-mongering with little value for understanding the past.

Premodern religious texts marked by appeals to the extraordinary present a particularly acute challenge to the limitations of traditional historical readings that condition us to fixate on matters that conform to our sense of empirically verifiable reality. For the story of handshakes, an empiricist assessment would suggest that the only things of value in Awbahi's report are the names, a date, and evidence for some beliefs. Such a reading would discount, fundamentally, the historiographic value of the actual claim made by the author, namely, that he had participated in the corporeal act of shaking hands with someone whom he believed to be connected to Muhammad through a chain with only five links. Some historians are likely to scoff at the claim as a figment of the author's fancy resulting from his superstitious religious beliefs. Others may suspend judgment on the claim, seeing it as beyond the job of a historian to assess its truth-value. In either case, the claim made in the text would seem to be the equivalent of historiographic waste matter that is jettisoned once the text's useful content has been absorbed.

I aim to show that, contrary to received wisdom, the details of extraordinary events in religious texts constitute a historiographic treasure trove. Religiously motivated historical writing has received a prejudicial hearing because of our tendency to measure all representations of the past according to our own unstated but highly specific presumptions about the nature of historical writing. However, history is, in all contexts, a subjective ordering of time keyed to events that are deemed worth recording. For the materials that concern me, patterns relating to the narration of miraculous events constitute our most valuable points of access to the societies in which these texts were produced since they reflect on writers' projections regarding relationships between particular actions and experiences and the larger sociocultural context relevant for the situation. Moreover, what appears to us as the improbability of claims such as the one made by Awbahi allows us to see the difference between the determining presumptions of Sufi narratives and the ordering of history we ourselves employ quite often without deliberate consideration. Miracles and other extraordinary events tied to alternative timescales are, therefore, doubly valuable venues to investigate the historiographic process.[2]

While Awbahi's evocation of miraculously long lives may be alien to us, the practice of shaking hands is as customary today as it was in his day. We may not be able to own Awbahi's history, but the physical act he utilizes to convey its concreteness is easily recognizable to us. I believe that this mixture of strangeness and familiarity is critical for allowing us to unlock the historiographic potential of Awbahi's text. However, to do so requires that we keep in mind our sense of the significance of physical touch without presuming the physical act means the same thing for Awbahi that it does for us. We must begin by attempting to situate Awbahi's handshake in the textual context where it occurs.

As reflected in the title I have chosen for this book, I believe Awbahi's emphasis on physicality in the handshake is not an isolated instance but an aspect of the general high valorization of corporeal contact as a marker of social solidarity and transmission of authority in the literature and art that is my subject matter. The mutual apprehension of persons mediated through touch of hands seen here represents, metonymically, the careful and pervasive use of the body as a tableau for mapping social as well as cosmological relations in these materials. The emphasis on the body in Persian Sufi literature from the fourteenth and fifteenth centuries is the thematic core of what I will present in the coming pages. By isolating this theme for analytical purposes, I hope to convey some of the texture of Sufi life as it comes across in the sources.

In my view, Sufi reports about matters such as handshakes and miraculously long lives become invaluable historical data when we subject literary and other materials that contain them to patterned analyses that excavate the correlations between generic and other formalistic features of the sources and their specific sociohistorical contexts. Reflecting an amalgamation of historical, anthropological, and literary methods, this approach involves paying careful attention to textual and other representation as rhetoric tied to the social world of its origins. The reading strategy I am advocating requires us to move away from judging such representations on the basis of probability and instead derive their social import by piecing together their complex functions within the narratives at hand.

This approach to texts and images concentrates on their embeddedness in epistemological paradigms particular to the historical setting in which they were produced. In the location in which such sources were initially heard, read, or seen, their representational content was related to literary, social, and ideological exigencies far removed from what may appear to us as obvious impetuses for their production. Generally, then, treating these works as straightforward descriptions neglects the mutually constitutive relationships that always obtain between narratives and their producers and intended audiences. At a minimum, these can involve deception or lack of self-awareness as readily as direct statements of fact or belief. As advocates of the "linguistic turn" in the writing of history have pointed out, it is problematic to regard texts as transparent windows on the past. Instead, they are better seen as historical objects in and of themselves, holding complex places in the social relations of the times in which they were produced.[3]

HANDSHAKES IN CONTEXT

I would like to exemplify the method I am advocating through a step-by-step unpacking of the story of handshakes with which I began. My argument is that making the best use of materials of this nature requires that we analyze them carefully in multiple dimensions, including intratextual, intertextual, and sociohistorical examinations. That is, we must situate representations within a text or an image 1. next to other elements of the same source, 2. with respect to thematically relevant matters in other sources, and 3. in relation to what else we know about the social milieu surrounding the representations available to us. My interpretations aim to show that many features of Sufi texts and images that appear on the surface to reflect static religious beliefs are in fact critical sources for understanding historically localizable cultural conditions that underlie the production of these sources.

Concentrating now on Awbahi's work on the handshake, it is notable that the text provides evidence of not one but three different chains through which Awbahi can claim himself to have been within the stipulated seven links of the Prophet's hand. Two of these go through the abovementioned Saʿid Habashi, while in the third the mediator is another companion given the sobriquet Muʿammar (long-lived), whom Muhammad is said to have granted the boon of an unnaturally long lifespan at the Battle of the Trench in 627 CE. This occurred because the Prophet saw him work twice as hard as everyone else on the job of digging a trench around the city of Medina that protected the early Muslim community from a Meccan assault. Awbahi states that he became a part of this chain ending in Muhammad upon shaking hands with an important Sufi master, Shams ad-Din Muhammad Tabadkani (d. 1486), at the end of the month of Rajab 879 (December 1474). After providing the details of the various chains that place him in the proximity of the Prophet, Awbahi states that he had shaken hands with Muhammad in a dream as well when the Prophet had certified the veracity of the connections in all the physical chains. He thus felt himself assured of the Prophet's intercession on the Day of Judgment on four different counts.[4]

The original statement attributed to Muhammad requires only one chain to guarantee intercession, making the multiple streams cited by Awbahi appear superfluous. However, I would suggest that what seems to be excess here reflects the idea of increasing intimacy with greater corporeal access: it is as if Awbahi had met and shaken hands with the Prophet four times rather than once, through which he could lay greater claim to having been in his presence.

Awbahi's fourfold access to Muhammad symptomizes his imagination of time, which is clearly not a numerical abstraction measured solely in years and centuries. Instead, the passage of time is indicated through human lifespans whose sequencing together brings one close to the Prophet's body. Such an arrangement of time is well attested in early Islamic textual descriptions of the first few generations of Muslims, who were placed in classes (*tabaqat*) such as Companions (*sahaba*), Followers (*tabiʿun*), and Followers' Followers (*tabʿ tabiʿun*) based on the number of links that connected them to the Prophet.[5] Awbahi can be presumed to be aware of this, and his claim reflects assimilation of the pattern from early Islamic history to the ninth Islamic century. Under this logic, the temporal gap between Muhammad and a fifteenth-century person like Awbahi can be covered through multiple pathways of interlinked human lives governed by the imperative that one is able to place oneself within the stipulated seven links. Instead of being seen as the unstoppable passing of sand through an hourglass, time here is an emphatically subjective stream that one can enter by establishing corporeal contact with the right people at the right moment. I believe this imagination of time, which comes into view when we pay particular attention to the theme of miraculously long lives, is critical for understanding of perspectives to be found in Awbahi's work and other sources utilized in this book.

Although it purports to document the past, Awbahi's treatise is clearly also an invitation to his contemporaries to come to him to shake his hand in order to prepare for their future. By placing himself in the chain, he endows himself with the power to intercede, which he can administer or withhold by shaking or repelling someone's hand. He reminds the reader at the end of the work that, depending on the chain chosen, he forms the fifth or the sixth link in chains going back to Muhammad. Under the overall logic of the prophetic statement, his hand is a proxy for the hand of Muhammad, and touching it can compel the Prophet to intercede on someone's behalf at the time of resurrection. In fact, the handshake he is offering to his contemporary readers collapses the past and the future into the immediate present, with his own hand acting as the instrument that can, on one side, connect people to the Prophet, and on the other, give them access to eternal felicity in paradise.[6]

In addition to being a matter of personal choice, Awbahi's making his hand available to others is subject to precepts of Islamic law and local custom that limit physical contact between men and women to immediate family members. In this textual mode, if physical touch of hands must be the guarantee of intercession, among women he can offer this only to his close female relatives, such as his wives or women he is prevented from marrying by religious taboos (mother, aunts, daughters). His physical contact with men faces no such limitations. The chain of hands that extends forward and backward from him then consists primarily of male hands, with women attached at the sides where they stand in close relationships to men with whom the law allows them to shake hands. Reading Awbahi's work with an eye toward these social restrictions indicates the genderedness of his time. The limitation on cross-gender physical contact underscores women's very narrow access to the time, history, and social world reflected in Awbahi's text.

Now moving outside of Awbahi's treatise into intertextual space, concentrating on the theme of handshakes brings out a religious world put in motion through choices made by authors of interlinked texts. The handshake is a theme echoed in works produced by authors who lived before as well as after Awbahi and were affiliated with the Kubravi-Hamadani Sufi lineage in particular. The earliest citation clearly linked to Awbahi's later representations occurs in a hagiography devoted to the Kubravi master Sayyid ʿAli Hamadani (d. 1385), who is said to have met Saʿid Habashi during his travels. In this work, composed around the end of the fourteenth century CE, Habashi is credited with the quality of constantly changing his outward form so that every time one meets him one presumes him to be a different person. This is, of course, a most useful power since it precludes anyone who has met Habashi from claiming that he could be shown to have grown old and died.[7]

A second hagiography of ʿAli Hamadani, likely compiled around 1450 CE, gives a much more extended account of the meeting between him and Saʿid Habashi. This is said to have occurred when Hamadani was twenty-two years old and Habashi is identified as Muʿammar, who, in Awbahi's work, represents a second long-lived companion of the Prophet. This version of the story is also concerned emphatically with establishing ʿAli Hamadani's authority as Muhammad's definitive universal heir since the author has Habashi tell the young

Hamadani that the sole reason Muhammad had given him the gift of a very long life was so that, 713 years after the Prophet's death, he would have the opportunity to meet Hamadani. This story replicates the trope that connects Jesus and Muhammad and places ʿAli Hamadani at the same level of cosmological significance as the two prophets.[8]

Awbahi's narrations of chains of handshakes rely on stories found in the two earlier hagiographies of ʿAli Hamadani but without replicating either in full. He makes no mention of Habashi's purported ability to change form, cited in the first hagiography, and he regards Saʿid Habashi and Muʿammar as separate companions of Muhammad rather than the latter being a title for Habashi as indicated in the second.[9] The contents of Awbahi's own treatise are cited in two later surviving works produced by members of the Kubravi-Hamadani lineage during the century after Awbahi's momentous handshake. The first of these is a short treatise that cites Awbahi directly and gives the names of three different people who had first shaken Awbahi's hand and then that of the author of this work. This allows the author to place himself within seven links of Muhammad that are assured of the Prophet's intercession.[10] The second source is an extensive Sufi work on the shrines of the city of Tabriz finished in 1567. Its author first relates the general significance of the handshake and the story of Saʿid Habashi as presented in earlier sources and then goes on to describe the links that extend the chain of handshakes to his own hand.[11]

I have now laid out five different texts by authors interconnected through Sufi lineages that narrate the significance of chains of handshakes extending back to Muhammad through the intermediacy of long-lived companions. Seen comparatively, the five texts present an interesting picture of constancy and change: all proceed on the basis of a statement attributed to the Prophet and use the story to substantiate the socioreligious authority of their authors or prime subjects. However, aspects of stories intermediate between these two end points are different in each source. The handshake seems to have been a particular preoccupation in this lineage, but the authors, and presumably other initiates, enjoyed considerable latitude in utilizing the theme, based on the needs of their contexts.

These textual explorations show the handshake to be an act whose quotidian nature masks its value for sociohistorical analysis. Described as a single event in Awbahi's work, it can be interpreted as a corporeal movement concerned with establishing the author's credentials. But, as indicated earlier, its centrality to Awbahi's argument regarding religious authority highlights the author's particular concern with physicality. The presence of similar—but not identical—handshakes in related texts ranging over more than a century and a half indicates a dialectical relationship between a literary motif and the social practice of a particular group in this period. We arrive at greater historical specificity by noting that only sources emanating from certain branches of the Kubravi-Hamadani lineage seem to emphasize shaking hands with people connected to Muhammad via short chains as a means of establishing and conveying authority. However, when we take the hand as a metonym for the body as a whole, the emphasis on the handshake stands for the general salience of corporeal themes in Persian Sufi literature produced during the fourteenth and fifteenth centuries.

To summarize, I hope that my multifaceted examination of the theme of handshakes has established that the types of Sufi materials I will utilize in this book are rich grounds for writing cultural history. In synchronic terms, these works are bounded worlds whose internal elements can be correlated in fruitful ways. They are also products of and responses to factors in the milieus from which they arise. We must see them as parts of larger conversations that need to be excavated from within in order to make sense of the social worlds of their origins. Diachronically, representations made in these texts are reflections of a thoroughgoing intertextuality that must be taken into account in interpreting works that are part of a complex literary tradition. The representations to be found in these sources are closely tied to social worlds, although they are no simple mirrors whose surfaces can reveal the past to us. They are better seen as doorways that can be unlocked only when we pay equal attention to the source material and our own perspective, methodology, and scholarly agenda. Let me then turn to a presentation of the tools that have enabled the excavations you will see reflected in my analyses.

SUFISM AND EMBODIMENT

In this book I concentrate on corporeal themes in literary texts and miniature paintings to present a view of the Persianate social and religious world during the approximate period 1300–1500 CE. The historian Marshall Hodgson recommended the use of the term Persianate to denote Muslim societies in which Persian linguistic and cultural forms were a defining feature of individual and collective identity. It includes not only those societies where Persian was the primary spoken language but also those where Persian forms were marked as prestigious.[12] The Persianate arena in its totality is too large and internally variegated to treat in a single monograph. I use the term here as shorthand to refer to the region now divided between Iran, Afghanistan, and the Central Asian and Caucasian republics of the former Soviet Union that are predominantly Muslim. The full extent of the term would have to include India in the east and Anatolia in the west, both of which were major arenas for the production of materials that could be included in a study such as this book. To be sure, parallel

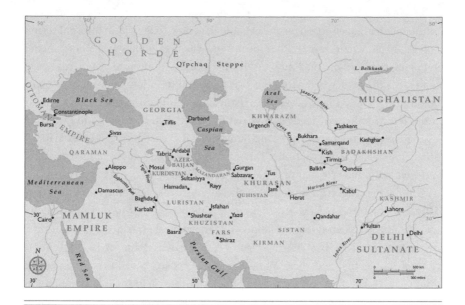

Central Asia and Iran

explorations of materials in these Persianate spheres would complement greatly what I am arguing in this book.[13]

This book's origins lie in my pervious work on Sufism in Central Asia and Iran, which was concerned with explicating the histories and ideologies of specific Sufi movements. My aim here is to be more methodologically self-conscious and to utilize a considerably wider base of sources to present a general account of socioreligious currents that dominated in this context. Notwithstanding this difference, I first noticed the major themes discussed in detail in this book while pursuing work related to the Nurbakhshis and the Hurufis. My overall drive, then and now, has been to work toward historicizing accounts of Sufi intellectual and social concerns. In order to describe the territory I wish to cover, it is necessary to explicate my usage of the terms Sufism, embodiment, and Persianate hagiography.

Sufism and Islamic History

It is notable that while Muslims started using the adjective *Sufi* to describe certain types of religious attitudes quite early in Islamic history, *Sufism* is not, in its origins, an internal term but a descriptor employed by Western observers to refer to a diverse array of intellectual and social phenomena relating to those who have called themselves Sufis.[14] This is to say that the presumption that all things described as being Sufi cohere into a system—becoming an "-ism"—is a modern terminological invention. The closest one can come to Sufism in internal terminology is the Arabic verbal noun *tasawwuf*, whose etymology reflects a meaning along the lines of "making oneself into a Sufi." In internal usage, *tasawwuf* represents the prescribed path Sufis are supposed to follow in order to become better at their religious vocation.[15] Historically, *tasawwuf* demarcates a highly contested domain and is a term invoked by different individuals and groups to legitimate particular ways of being Sufi while also castigating the behavior of others, perceived as corruptions. The term *tasawwuf* equates to Sufism as a prescriptive religious program of a specific group, but it does not encapsulate Sufism as a general descriptor usable for classifying ideas and behaviors from many different times and places. My concern in this book is not *tasawwuf*—which I would describe as an internal Islamic discursive domain concerned with right belief and practice—but Sufism, regarded as an overarching term for a large fund of intellectual and social data. For my purposes, Sufism is to be defined nominally rather than substantively and I consider it to include components such as mystical philosophy, notions of saintly persons invested with miraculous powers, and intellectual lineages built around initiatory rites and distinctive liturgical practices. I do not presume these factors to form a single, fully coherent system that has been a constant through history. Rather, Sufism can be shown to have varied very considerably from context to context and is subject to internal contradiction in equal measure with consistency. I therefore use the term Sufism in this book not to refer to a coherent system but as an analytical horizon that allows me to explore a set of issues in intellectual and social history.[16]

In addition to terminological specificity, it is significant to differentiate historical study of Sufism from what has come to be associated with the term in contemporary popular culture. Today, Sufism is often portrayed as a nonmainstream Islamic perspective that consists mainly of mystical philosophies and lyrical poetry evoking the pleasures and pains of human beings' intimate relationships with the divine. The two most celebrated names in the current public representation of Sufism are the great Andalusian mystical philosopher Ibn al-ʿArabi (d. 1240), whose work is the subject of tens of volumes in many languages and a whole academic society, and Jalal ad-Din Rumi (d. 1273), the Persian poet whose verse is said to be a best seller on the basis of English translations and adaptations.[17] Sufism as a whole is also often glossed as Islamic "mysticism," a term that invokes psychology, individual enlightenment, and liberation from dogmatic and societal constraints far more than a historically specific aspect of religion that needs to be contextualized with respect to times and places.

Those troubled by Islam's potency in contemporary politics sometimes portray Sufism as an improbable but worthy form of Islam since Sufis are thought to shun religious particularity in favor of a broad spiritual universalism akin to heavily romanticized understandings commonly ascribed to forms of Buddhism and Hinduism. Some Americans who identify themselves as Sufis have gone as far as to claim that to be a Sufi one need not be Muslim at all.[18] There is also a long tradition, among Muslims opposed to Sufi ideas as well as in the modern scholarship and popular imagery, that depicts Sufism as an Islamic "heterodoxy" produced from the accretion of alien elements onto a religion thought to be centered on law and jurisprudence in its essence.[19]

Seen from a historical vantage point, understanding Sufism as quaint mysticism or heterodoxy leads to misconceptions that are, at best, based on privileging selective elements in the array of ideas and practices that Muslims have called Sufi. My sense of Sufism is explicitly contrary to these marginalizing and romanticizing associations. As discussed earlier, I see it as an internally variegated array of ideas and practices that, taken together, forms an integral and crucial part of the complex intellectual and sociocultural histories of Islamic societies. Central Sufi personalities and ideas can be placed in the earliest period of Islam's formation, and Sufi actors remain a vital part of the intellectual and sociopolitical landscape of most Islamic societies to the present. Sufism is also not simply the mystical form of Islam that can be regarded as a concentrated repository of spirituality within the tradition—it is relevant not just for making sense of a limited number of religious virtuosi called the mystics. Sufism became a mass phenomenon in the period studied in this book and continues to be the primary mode of religious practice for significant numbers of Muslims in Asia, Africa, and the Middle East to this day. To explore any theme regarding Sufism, then, is to mine a rich vein of material for understanding the functioning and historical evolution of Islamic intellectual and social patterns.

Masters, Disciples, and Networks

Within the history of Sufism, the period that concerns me is most notable for the rise of socioreligious networks that are often referred to as orders due to the fact that they share some features with the great Christian monastic institutions of the medieval period.[20] I prefer to use the term *network* because of its relative neutrality. In my view, the use of *order* has led scholars to misapprehend the type of internal cohesion and discipline than can be attributed to the Sufi communities in question. Resisting this usage opens up the space to try to understand Sufi networks on their own terms as examples of a form of sociality contingent on the particulars of the histories of Islamic societies.

Although Sufi authors and social institutions started becoming influential in Islamic societies from the tenth century, Sufism became a mass phenomenon in the region during the large-scale reconstruction of Islamic social life in the wake of the upheavals brought by Mongol invasions of the twelfth and thirteenth centuries. In overarching terms, the expansion of Sufism was a consequence of the new sociopolitical order that prevailed in the Islamic East during the Mongol and Timurid periods (ca. 1250–1500). Knowing the region's political destiny is significant for understanding the framework within which socioreligious developments unfolded, but to understand how Sufism functioned as the region's paramount religious paradigm we must explore social and intellectual dynamics particular to Sufism as a mode of Islamic religiosity.[21]

For the purposes of the topic of this book, Sufi networks are best understood as religious confraternities held together on the basis of devotion to charismatic exemplars celebrated as God's friends (*awliya*', singular *vali*).[22] As I show in this book, from initiation to becoming acknowledged as great friends, Sufis needed both intellectual understandings and the physical proximity of other Sufis' bodies to acquire spiritual qualities and receive affirmation from others about their special powers. The networks included Sufis, at varying levels of spiritual competence, whose mutual relationships were built on transmission of knowledge within discourse and contacts mediated through the bodily senses. The bodies of the perfected friends—those who were thought to share extraordinary intimacy with God—were of paramount importance in this milieu, and aspiring Sufis' best access to religious authority lay in the degree of corporeal closeness they could demonstrate with those already acknowledged as being saintly. The story of handshakes with which I began this book follows directly from the imperative of such corporeal closeness between masters and disciples.

The question of friendship with God in Sufi thought and practice is, at its heart, an aspect of the construction of religious authority in Islamic societies. Questions about what this friendship is, how it is be attained, and what benefits and responsibilities it bestows on those who have it have been central themes in Sufi discourse in all periods and geographical contexts. Theoretical bases of Sufi understandings of such friendship have received considerable attention in recent academic treatments of specific Sufi individuals or groups.[23] This scholarship has focused mainly on internal Sufi philosophical or theological arguments, with relatively little attention paid to the doctrines' social ramifications. Approaching the topic from hagiographic rather than theoretical literature, I am interested in highlighting how Sufi sources utilize notions regarding friendship with God to argue for the preeminence of particular masters and their communities. I believe that my discussion of this material forms an addition and a necessary complement to the existing academic treatments of the construction of authority in Sufi settings.

In Sufi practice the theory of friendship with God pertained both to internal states and social relationships. It mattered most centrally in the perceived necessity of a master who could lead one along the Sufi path. The Sufi master-disciple relationship was a specific form of sociality that required hierarchically arranged direct contact between two individuals. The relationship was meant to result in the disciple's spiritual maturation through acquiring a kind of intuitive or esoteric knowledge that could not, by definition, be conveyed in a pedagogical relationship limited to rational methods. Most often, the conduction of knowledge in this relationship was mediated in lessons absorbed through the working of the senses of sight, audition, touch, taste, and smell. Even in cases where the contact was displaced to dreams and visions, its description was keyed to the language of the physical senses. The body was, it is fair to say, more central to Sufi practice than the intellect, although how and why this was so is a major subject in the literature Sufis were required to study in order to achieve proper understandings of their spiritual experiences.

In centuries before the period that concerns me, Sufi mystical and pedagogical theorists had elaborated on the powers, prerogatives, and responsibilities that accrued to the two parties when they became a master-disciple dyad. As Sufi ideas rose to social prominence in the Mongol and Timurid periods, the Sufi master-disciple relationship acquired new, grander dimensions in the fourteenth and fifteenth centuries and became one of the primary mechanisms for channeling power in Persianate societies of Central Asia and Iran. The period saw more and more accomplished Sufi masters become acknowledged as great friends of God who mediated between the divine and the earthly realms. The men and women, elite as well as commoners, who thronged around these masters saw them not only as arbiters of the metaphysical world but also as guarantors of material prosperity and crucial mediators of social and political relations. The masters' rise in social prominence, in turn, reconfigured the master-disciple relationship and had a transformative effect on this region's social life in general. This new social world is what we see reflected in depictions of human bodies that form the source base for this book.

Embodiment as an Analytical Tool

My focus on corporeality as the book's thematic center follows from the desire to draw the intellectual and social sides of Persianate Sufism together into a single argument. The texts and paintings that I will cite in the following pages are filled with details about bodily themes that I will treat as "sedimented" forms of corporeal attitudes that prevailed in the societies where these materials were produced. I presume that the producers "inscribed" the body into these materials not out of explicit intention but as a reflection of a socioreligious habitus that was integral to their way of seeing the world. I am more interested in patterns embedded in stories rather than direct theoretical discourse on corporeality, although the latter will be mentioned occasionally. My object is not the retrieval of a coherent philosophy of embodied being that can be attributed to my subjects. Instead, I am concerned with the way we can use representations of the body's display, deployment, and performances to understand the social imagination of this context.

The human body has been an especially generative theme in the humanities and the social sciences in recent decades, leading to numerous pathbreaking publications in religious studies as well as other fields. Embodied human presence was a well-represented topic in anthropology from the very beginning of the modern discipline in the late nineteenth century, but, starting in the 1970s, studies concerned with the body began to proliferate as well in history, religious studies, literature, sociology, political science, and so on. This book is a part of the evolution of the modern study of embodiment. My perspective on the body derives from reading widely across many disciplines in the contemporary study of the body. This literature is too vast to summarize here in any meaningful way, and studies that have aided me in thinking through particular points will be mentioned in the course of detailed discussions. What I would like to offer here is a brief sketch of how I see the body as an object of humanistic inquirty.[24]

I regard the body as an aspect of the human imagination that shifts its parameters through human beings' phenomenological and social experience during a lifetime. The experiencing body is situated at the base of any notion of the human self, although the body is also an aspect of the material world whose shape and texture one comes to know through the bodily senses.[25] All bodies are constantly enmeshed in processes of growth, decay, and movement so that the idea that one has a single body through a lifetime is a kind of illusion. This illusion is necessary for producing a sense of self that allows one to think of oneself as a coherent being moving through the world. Once imagined, the body, whole or in its parts, also constitutes a primary bounded system that human beings utilize to map other systematic phenomena in the cosmos. Through the working of these various processes, the body is found thoroughly interlaced in discursive domains such as the literature and art that constitute my sources for this book.[26]

As to be expected, greater academic scrutiny of the body over the past few decades has led to ever increasing skepticism regarding the very possibility of keeping the body in focus as an object of analysis. However much it may appear to be so instinctively, the body is not the defining feature of the human species that can help us specify universals. As surveys of the field attest, the body is liable to be understood in radically different ways even in a single sociohistorical context. Moreover, the question of meaning pervades the body in such a way as to make it especially resistant to straightforward scrutiny. No matter how hard one tries to stick to the particular limbs and organs that seem to constitute it, the physical body dissolves into webs of symbols, laden with historical and social baggage, from virtually the moment one decides on it as a point of concentration. The body is implicated in all acts of deriving meaning, whether yours, as your eyes read these words or your ears hear it, or that of a medieval author sharpening a reed pen before taking it to inkpot and paper to write a manuscript that I may have read while writing this book. The body's ubiquity renders it vexingly translucent to our ability to observe it as an object.

Philosophical as well as social scientific considerations of corporeality have shown that human bodies—our own as well as of others—always become present to us through social mediation. As human social structures vary between times and places, so does the meaning of what the body is and what it does. This social situatedness of all bodies is starkly evident in considering the body as a "biological" entity. The biological body may, at first sight, appear to be shared by the whole species, but we are faced with the immediate problem that the idea of biology is itself a cultural construct that has a particular history, and speaking about the body as an object of modern biology is premised on metaphors and tropes that are far from universal and elicit different responses based on cultural conditioning.[27] There is no escape from the fact that the body is an artifact that cannot be taken "for granted as a natural, fixed and historically universal datum of human societies."[28]

My use of embodiment as a tool to excavate literary and artistic works derives from a kind of sequencing of phenomenological, sociological, and hermeneutical reflections involving bodies as well as texts. I would like to summarize my composite perspective through reference to the work of Maurice Merleau-Ponty, Pierre Bourdieu, and Gabrielle Spiegel. These three authors can act as stand-ins for larger bodies of interpretive literatures in the humanities and social sciences that I have consulted while considering what best suits the material I wish to scrutinize. I should acknowledge that my usage of these authors is primarily utilitarian; the ideas I am appropriating from them fit into larger analytical schemes that are not engaged directly in my descriptions. My perspective is thus a bricolage that has evolved out of the analytical needs of my own work rather than allegiance to a previously elaborated scheme.

Merleau-Ponty's phenomenology has had a defining influence on the modern philosophical investigation of the body. One of his main arguments is that the human body as it operates in the world has two layers: the "present body" that we see acting in the world and a preceding "habitual body" that "signifies the body as it has been lived in the past, in virtue of which it has acquired certain habitual ways of relating to the world. The 'habitual body' already projects a habitual setting around itself, thereby giving a general structure to the subject's situation. . . . With its 'two layers' the body is the meeting place, so to speak, of past, present, and future because it is the carrying forward of the past in the outlining of a future and the living of this bodily momentum as actual present."[29]

Merleau-Ponty famously exemplified this layered notion of the body through reference to anosognosic amputees who persist in thinking that their severed limbs are still a part of their bodies and can be manipulated. This is because although the anosognosic's "present body" is missing a limb, her habitual body, which is formed from the "sedimentation" of sociocultural effects and prior personal experiences, continues to be there. The dissonance between the two bodies then causes the patient's misapprehension of the phenomenal world.[30] The habitual body casts a kind of aura around the physical body that shapes the subject's feeling of being in the world in the form of expectations regarding what the physical body is to encounter upon extending itself through its limbs and sensory organs. The expectations give the subject the feeling of a concrete self despite the fact that the material world, including the body itself, is continually undergoing change.

Merleau-Ponty's explication of the body is helpful for showing how a dialectical movement between the two layers of the body "ceaselessly carries anonymous biological existence forward into personal existence in a cultural world and conversely, allows the personal and the cultural to become sedimented in general, anonymous structures."[31] The body as a layered artifact allows us to appreciate the predetermined as well as the volitional in the body's action. The experiential and cultural sediments that form the habitual body predispose it to act in certain ways. The body is an agent in itself, independent from language and deliberate thought, that has a crucial function in generating a person's perception of herself and the surrounding world. But the characteristics of this agency are constantly in flux because sedimentation is an ongoing process liable to change the habitual body. Moreover, the present body, which is subject to the person's active consciousness, can interrupt and modify the actions of the habitual body, saving humans from turning into automatons. This understanding makes it possible to see why we may be able to recover sociohistorical understandings from data about bodies. Moreover, as we will see in numerous places in the book, Sufi ideas about human corporeality correspond quite well with some of Merleau-Ponty's theories.

To be serviceable for my purposes, Merleau-Ponty's phenomenology must be complemented by the work of social theorists such as Pierre Bourdieu who make the study of embodiment a central feature in understanding human societies. Bourdieu's analysis is most famous for the notion of habitus, a term signifying a general order of societal practice that is constantly being reproduced by members of a society but is transparent for the practitioners because of its normativity.[32] Habitus is in large part maintained through the functioning of what Merleau-Ponty calls the habitual body. The habitual body is the meeting place of society and the individual, which, moreover, functions instinctually rather than as a result of cognition and active decision making. Habitus becomes coded into bodies from the time of childhood since bodily comportment particular to social settings is relayed "in the form of a pattern of postures" and is internalized by children who are "in all societies . . . particularly attentive to the gestures and postures which, in their eyes, express everything that goes to make an accomplished adult."[33] By paying attention to the body's postures and action, then, an observer can substantiate something about societies that is not recoverable from linguistic representations alone. Since human bodies always exist in social contexts, they can be read to understand unarticulated social norms.

Merleau-Ponty's habitual body and Bourdieu's habitus are suitable for fields such as anthropology and sociology, but the application of these ideas to historical investigations such as the present book may not be obvious. The way human beings carry themselves corporeally can be observed by an eyewitness, but one has to ask if, and how, this can be done with respect to societies that are long dead and from which all that survives for us are highly formalized sources such as genre-bound texts and stylized paintings. This is a question of fundamental importance: any exploration of the type I am attempting in this book must foreground the fact that the proposed arguments stem from scrutinizing formalized representations. It is crucial to query the sources with methodological self-consciousness so that their generic features do not end up being taken as straightforward descriptions.

Utilizing recent theoretical expositions on how premodern texts can be read for historical purposes, I suggest that, in literate societies, texts can be seen to operate in a manner similar to Bourdieu's concept of habitus. Both habitus and formalized texts are societal products and are crucial for shaping and continuing societal practices over time. It is to be granted, of course, that texts convey a small slice of social data in comparison with the scope Bourdieu assigns to habitus. Nevertheless, as Gabrielle Spiegel has argued: "All texts occupy determinate social spaces, both as products of the social world of authors and as textual agents at work in the world, with which they entertain often complex and contestatory relations. In that sense, texts both mirror *and* generate social realities, are constituted by *and* constitute the social and discursive formations which they may sustain, resist, contest, or seek to transform, depending on the case at hand."[34] The job of the historian, then, is to go beyond the surfaces of texts, to reconstitute the social world in question by "looking at the inextricably interrelated nature of social and discursive practices, of the material and linguistic realities that are interwoven into the fabric of the text, whose analysis as a determinate historical artifact in turn grants us access to the past."[35] Spiegel's proposition for what historians must do with texts matches the perspective I have adopted for this project.

While my pursuit of Sufi social worlds in this book is conditioned by the phenomenological, sociological, and hermeneutical ideas I have outlined, I wish to resist the notion that any single interpretive position can provide an exhaustive account of the materials I present in the following pages. The literary and artistic corpus on which this study is based is large and internally variegated, and, even if this were not the case, I am inclined to question universalist claims that tend to undergird social scientific theory. I have endeavored to make this perspective on historiographic practice innate to my discussions by foregrounding contradictions that are part of the record and by deliberately juxtaposing norms and their subversion. As a consequence, the topical discussions in the various chapters have, on occasion, been left deliberately unhemmed and open to alternative interpretations. The Sufi bodies I seek to represent are quite distant objects, made dim in part by the constraints of the nature of my sources. Guided by the work of Michel de Certeau and others, I consider all historiographic operations to reflect a joining of things found interesting in the present with selective marshaling of evidence from the past. The writing of a cultural history such as this book is therefore subject to contingencies pertaining to the evidence as well as methodology that need to remain within sight rather than being obscured behind a pretense of scholarly omniscience.[36]

TEXTS, PAINTINGS, AND THE HAGIOGRAPHIC PROCESS

To approach the history of Sufism through the lens of embodiment requires that we think of the sources not as static representations of the way things were in the past but as elements of a dynamic process that is embedded within them. This kind of analysis necessitates "reading" the materials with respect to their contents as well as issues relating to their forms and the way they were produced and utilized. For Persianate Sufism during the Mongol and Timurid period, hagiography is the literary form tied most closely to the formation of communities and networks as I have discussed earlier. Hagiography is also the genre in which we find authors paying very significant attention to corporeal matters. The term *hagiography* has been used to refer to vastly different types of texts in the study of religions. My use of the term is essentially utilitarian and by it I mean, simply, works that narrate episodes in the lives of Sufi masters. This usage does not intend to imply a deep substantive connection between Sufi texts and other Islamic genres, like lives of prophets or the Shiʿi imams or works on the lives of Christian or Buddhist saints that are written according to different internal exigencies pertaining to generic and ideological concerns. Persianate texts that I include in the category hagiography are known under different names within the context: *manaqib*, *tazkira*, *risala*, or titles that refer to some aspect of internal argument or organization.[37] These texts differ quite considerably from each other on the basis of period and region of composition, generic elements peculiar to specific groups, and personal predilections on the part of authors or compilers.[38] In my presentations I have bracketed these types of distinctions for the most part in order to focus on thematic features that I find central to the narrative patterns that unite the material. Where directly relevant, my notes contain references to secondary studies that clarify the background and contents of specific sources. Other secondary literature on particular groups that contains historical details and has helped me come to my conclusions is included in the bibliography.[39]

In addition to hagiographic texts, I use Persianate painting to substantiate my arguments. When sifting through representations of Sufis generated in the period that concern me, I have found painting to be an indispensible source for identifying patterns central to the vast literary corpus available to us. To be sure, the case of painting in the context of this study is different from texts because these were luxury objects produced for royal and other elites. The social contextualization of these objects raises many questions that remain to be explored in full. For example, what must be the scope of the conclusions we can draw from them? How can we attribute worldviews to the artisans who made these objects given that they were paid servants of the elites? And what can be made, in general, about their place in visual culture and experience given that they remained in books and albums about whose social usage we have very little information?[40]

In my view, putting painting in conjunction with hagiography can provide the basis for addressing some of these questions. The fact that these are elite products signals that Sufi ideas were important for the self-image of the ruling classes. This is a matter easy to demonstrate on the basis of literary evidence as well. Moreover, painting and hagiography share generic and contextual properties in that their forms constitute highly stylized renditions of societal patterns. In both cases, human figures, and details surrounding their interactions, acquire abstract qualities that convey established conventions rather than aspiring to a matter-of-fact realism regarding the lives of the subjects in question. To understand the societies in which these materials were produced, we have to isolate and illuminate the conventions and see them as symptoms of social ideologies that held widespread sway in the period but were not articulated directly in theoretical discourse. Conventional images depicted in both sources ought not to be taken as descriptions on face value. Instead, these images must be collated to establish patterns that, in turn, must be interpreted to arrive at any judgments about the workings of society. In this book, I argue for such a reading of society from the sources using the phenomenological, sociological, and hermeneutical methods I have discussed earlier.

I believe that utilizing miniature painting is particularly helpful for appreciating the performative nature of Persian hagiographic narratives. Both types of sources were produced according to well-established forms and acted as description as well as script for the social contexts in which they mattered. Like paintings no matter how exquisitely "realistic", hagiographies do not provide impartial descriptions of saintly persons' lives. Instead, the hagiographic narrative unites into a dynamic whole the adoring narrator, the great person who is the object of the narrative, and the audience meant to become witness to the friend of God. Understanding the interconnections between the various facets of the system allows us to see the Sufi social world in three dimensions and moving through time. For my purposes, attending to corporeal representations in texts and paintings is the optimal place for appreciating these sources as performances. I term the social mechanism at the root of these performances the "hagiographic process". All my arguments in this book are explorations of this process, aimed at understanding intellectual and social history.

PROGRESSION OF THEMES

My assessments of all the sources I utilize in this book amount to oblique looks at their representations. My principle concern is to see what this material tells us about the social world in which it originated. This is a matter substantially different from reading the works to try to understand the religious worldviews of the specific individuals and groups from whom the texts are derived. The latter approach is exemplified in other recent studies of similar materials, to which my work should be regarded as a complement.[41]

To explore embodiment historically is to examine connections between bodies rather than seeing them in isolation. This book's division into two parts and the progression of chapters exemplifies this perspective by touching upon various facets of corporeal overlap and disjuncture depicted in Persianate hagiographic materials and painting. Part 1 (chapters 1 through 3) is concerned with establishing the frameworks underlying the world of Persianate Sufism. Chapter 1 concentrates on the way representations of the body relate to the foundational Sufi distinction between the *zahir* (exterior or apparent) and *batin* (interior or hidden) aspects of reality. Because of an overarching investment in this duality, Sufi authors never describe the body solely as a material entity. The body is always connected to concomitants such as the spirit (*ruh*), the self (*nafs*), nonmaterial "imaginal" bodies that are tethered to the physical body, and the heart that sits inside the body but gets described as a body onto itself with its special senses. Emphasizing descriptions found in hagiographic narratives, I present the Sufi understanding of the human body as a doorway that stands in the middle between interior and exterior aspects of reality, a placement that speaks to the significance of corporeal themes in any exploration of Sufi materials.

Chapters 2 and 3 address, from two complementary angles, the way Sufi bodies are shown to act religiously in order to generate proper individual selves as well as communities of practitioners joined to each other. Chapter 2 concentrates on normative Islamic rituals, ascetic suppression of corporeal impulses, and specific Sufi practices such as repetitive exercises called *zikr* and *sama*ʿ. These activities feature prominently in hagiographic descriptions of great Sufi masters and are constitutive features of the notion of being God's friend. Chapter 3 attends to the social side of the same phenomenon, showing how the imperative of molding one's body to the habits and practices of renowned Sufis was critical for the rise of large-scale Sufi networks in Persianate societies. My focus in this context is on rules of etiquette, a presumed cosmic hierarchy of God's friends, Sufi lineages, and competition between Sufi masters. I regard these themes as aspects of a religious imagination that contributed to the establishment of communities and the consequent promulgation of internal differentiation.

Part 2 of the book (chapters 4 through 7) is concerned with social dynamics that come across in my materials. Here my foci are bodies in motion rather than the overall structures that seem to define Sufi approaches in the Persianate context. These four chapters divide into pairs that treat the two most pervasive themes in hagiographic materials: the rhetoric of love and desire, and Sufi masters' reputation for performing miracles. Chapters 4 and 5 attend to modulations of affective interpersonal relationships, aspects of human interaction that form the basis for Sufis' becoming connected to each other in hagiographic materials. In chapter 4 I show that the idealized Sufi master-disciple relationship is patterned on poetic rhetoric of interaction between lovers and beloveds and can be described as a cycle with distinguishable phases. The fact that masters and disciples change positions between being lovers and beloveds indicates how this imagination of love acted as the essential cement for the construction of large-scale Sufi communities. Chapter 5 concentrates on representations of disruptive desires, which are acknowledged in the literature as distractions from the idealized love relationships that join male masters and disciples. Here I discuss both the operation of improper desire among male Sufis and ambivalence regarding women that is rooted in presumptions related to desire and sexuality. As to be expected, the primary reason women were marginal characters in this milieu had to do with bodily difference. Persons embodied as female were often perceived to have lesser potential to reach spiritual ends. However, I argue that a more significant element in women's systematic lack of access to this world was that they could not cultivate intimacies with male Sufis that required unrestricted corporeal contact. The corporeal restriction disallowed them from acting as stand-ins and successors to famous male masters, thereby denying them the possibility of becoming prominent nodes in the major lineages. Women's exclusion from the scene was, therefore, related directly to the particular way the male body was inflected as a vehicle for social solidarity in this context.

The last two chapters concentrate on representations of Sufis' ability to perform miracles, the prominent feature of hagiographic narratives that has led most historians to dismiss them as significant sources. My assessment of this theme aims to subvert such negative valuation by showing that miracles can be placed in patterns that illuminate social concerns in a way impossible to substantiate from any other sources. In chapter 6 I concentrate on the fact that the largest number of miracles attributed to Sufi masters have to do with extraordinary production and provision of food. I argue that we should see miracle-working Sufi masters as specialized workers entangled in an economy of exchange in Persianate societies. The linchpin of this economy was the narrativization of miraculous deeds into miracle-working episodes that projected the masters as powerful beings able to mediate with respect to God, nature, and other powerful people in society. In chapter 7 I show the working of a similar process with respect to miraculous bodily protection offered by masters through the means of their religious patronage. The fact that miracles occupy the pride of place in hagiography reflects the thoroughly social nature of these narratives. The miracle story is the cornerstone of the genre because it most directly represents the conjoining of the functions of the saintly figure, the devotee, and the narrator. Chapters 6 and 7 also highlight the significance of the fact that although hagiographic stories portray masters as supremely powerful beings, these personas are disciples' projections rather than masters' own propaganda about themselves. We must see the stories as idealized and wishful portraits of the masters, whose social logic pertains to the interests and concerns of disciples and successors rather than the masters who are proclaimed as heroes. I address the significance of this inversion of roles between masters and disciples in greatest detail when concentrating on narratives about masters' deaths and their commemoration through enshrinement and the production of hagiographic compilations.

My explication of the hagiographic process in this book is predicated on moving back and forth across the frames of the narratives and paintings. To appreciate the social logic of these sources, we have to consider messages projected in their contents that tell us something of the lives of Sufis who lived more than half a millennium ago. When examined in other analytical lights, the same sources convey latent information regarding material and ideological investments on the part of those who produced or sponsored these works. The latter information comes into view when we ask questions about why these materials were produced and by and for whom.

This book highlights the interconnectedness of Sufism's intellectual and social aspects. As I show, this is not a straightforward matter of presuming that instructions found in prescriptive texts can be taken as descriptions of behavior. To see the social significance of Sufi ideas we must contextualize matters with respect to variance and tensions between different ideals as well as the role of sociohistorical circumstances. Exploring representations of Sufi lives generated in a period when Sufi ideas and practices predominated in society takes us into religious and social imaginations integral to Islamic developments over a long stretch during the medieval period. Moreover, although Sufis are not the most talked about Muslims in our own times, the ideas and behaviors described in this book can be observed in abundance in most places where Muslim communities exist in the world today, although with quite different overall ramifications. Observing the world presented in this book provides a venue for considering the unity and diversity that has characterized Islamic ideas and practices over the centuries.

To date, few scholars have mined hagiographic materials systematically for the sake of extracting social worlds. In attempting to do so in this book, I see my work as contributing to a conscious effort to alter the way we think about premodern Islamic societies. The documentary record left behind from premodern Islamic societies is as extensive as that available for medieval Europe, but, unlike historians of the latter, many of us who work on Islamic material do not treat it as a repository of traces of complex social worlds that can be interpreted imaginatively. Due to the philological roots of Islamic studies, we are hesitant to go beyond the surfaces of texts, to reconstitute the social relations that gave rise to the works and are embedded in them. I believe this situation needs a corrective. We should see medieval Islamic materials such as Sufi texts as products of human experience that speak to the categories we use to analyze more familiar societies such as those in which we live. We should attempt to reconstitute the social imagination that underlies medieval Islamic texts, using methods employed in other fields of humanistic inquiry. Our historiographic effort can then be a kind of cross-cultural study that both illuminates the past and highlights cultural alternatives comparable with the patterns that govern our own lives. Coming to understand the logic of Sufi representations may have something to teach us about oddities and absurdities that are a part of our ways of thought but are glossed over because our framework of reality appears natural to us. It is, instead, as much of a construction as a seemingly radically different social imagination such as the world of Persianate Sufism.

I. FRAMING SUFI IDEAS & PRACTICES

1

BODIES INSIDE OUT

Some have said that the master (shaykh) must be able to eat the disciple (murid)
and that a master who is not like this has not reached mastery. This 'eating the
disciple' means the master must be able to work on the interior (batin) of the
disciple. He must be able to eat up his blameworthy habits—meaning annihilate
them—and establish praiseworthy habits in their place. He must be capable of
taking him to the level of [God's] presence (huzur) and awareness (agahi).

— SAFI, *RASHAHAT*

Observed externally, Sufism may fairly be compared to a game of
hide-and-seek. To the extent that such a generalization is possible,
the history of Sufism represents a particular, longstanding evolution of thought
and practice around the idea that the world has apparent or exterior (*zahir*),
and hidden or interior (*batin*) aspects. In Sufi discourse the interior world is
valorized above the exterior, and seeking experiences in the interior is the overarching object of Sufi discussions and the ultimate goal of Sufi practice. There
is, however, no way to get to the interior save through external surfaces: knowledge of the interior is predicated on the ability to understand and interpret the
exterior correctly. Consequently, what we see in Sufi literature is not a world
divided neatly between the interior and the exterior, but the record of transactions across the line that separates these foundational categories. Powerful
masters can reach into disciples' nonmaterial interiors to "eat up" the latter's
habits, which pertain to behaviors in the material world. And disciples wishing
to reach stations of knowledge and experience within the interior need masters
available in the flesh to intrude on fundamental aspects of their beings. The
working of these processes intertwines the interiors and exteriors of masters
and disciples in multiple ways. The rich social worlds inhabited by Sufi actors
we see narrated in Sufi texts are products of this intertwining that is rooted in
particular ways of imagining the place of human beings within the cosmos.[1]

In the Sufi context it is useful to consider human bodies as doorways that
connect the exterior and interior aspects of reality. In material terms, bodies

are objects like any other, subject to generation and corruption and enmeshed in relationships with other material forms of the apparent realm. But bodies are also the instruments that enable human beings to attempt the critical work of excavating through materiality to the interior. Sufi attention to the structure of the human body as a form reflects particular cognizance of the body's double meaning: on one side, the body is seen as the ultimate source of most problems since its instinctive appetites restrict human beings from thinking beyond their immediate desires; on the other side, the body is a vital venue for theorization and investigation because it enables human beings to transcend materiality. The contrast between the two functions endows the body with a thoroughgoing ambiguity that makes corporeality an advantageous lens through which to appraise Sufi ideas and social patterns.

My reading of the extensive collection of sources on which this book is based indicates that Sufi thought and practice in the Persianate context are too heterogeneous to yield a coherent theory of corporeality. Consequently, we must think of the body in this context as an entity suspended in a kind of matrix consisting of varying but interrelated meanings that can be substantiated by surveying the material. My aim in this chapter is to provide an overall skeletal map of this matrix through strategic soundings of literature produced during the fourteenth and fifteenth centuries. I deliberately juxtapose opposing viewpoints in order to keep the heterogeneity of the material in the foreground. The topics I highlight are meant to provide a sense for the intellectual conditioning of the authors whose works are my sources for the book. Presenting this material at the outset offers background information for understanding Sufis' corporeal performances in the socioreligious sphere in Persianate societies. Although the sources I discuss in this chapter pertain to the specific time period that is my focus, the overall tenor of the discussion here is ahistorical since my aim is to lay out the intellectual groundwork for understanding Sufi performances rather than to get into historical specifics.

The chapter has three main sections, each of which highlights a different signification of the apparent-hidden dichotomy in considering Sufi views on corporeality. The first section addresses Sufi understanding of the formation of the human body within the womb as an embryo. The emergence of one body from the interior of another implicates the interior and exterior worlds in multiple ways. The event is seen, simultaneously, as the birth of an animal and the coming into being of a microcosm formed in the image of cosmos.

The second section concentrates on the connection between the body and *ruh* or spirit, the entity seen as the body's animating force. Ideas regarding the two entities show them to be thoroughly interdependent, including notions of spiritual bodies that can experience the internal world through the intermediacy of a place designated the realm of images (*'alam-i misal*). While most Persianate Sufis regarded each body to have one spirit attached to it, some allowed the possibility of multiple spirits pouring into bodies of extraordinary human beings such as prophets and Sufi adepts. This section also includes a discussion of the self (*nafs*), considered the representation of the human will that was thought to be driven by material desires under most circumstances.

The third section considers, first, the heart (Persian *dil*, Arabic *qalb*, used interchangeably), the highest organ within the body that enables human beings to sense and experience realities pertaining to the interior world. This is followed by Sufi understanding of the science of physiognomy that indicated that human beings are predetermined to behave in certain ways based on characteristics involving the shapes, sizes, and colors of their bodies' observable parts. But the Sufi view of physiognomy also affirms the idea that individuals can overcome the characteristics inherent in their bodies through expending effort under the guidance of those whose bodies are already endowed with higher and more praiseworthy capacities.

As seen in the cases I discuss, the Sufi imagination of the body portrays it as the primary conjoiner of physical and metaphysical aspects of existence. Similarly, even in theoretical discussions, the body also consistently engages social aspects, showing that Sufis' investment in the idea of the interior did not free them from paying careful attention to the construction of the material world in all its various dimensions. The Sufi social world was predicated on dividing both persons and the cosmos at large into exteriors and interiors, with all different components overlapping and interpenetrating in a plethora of ways.

BODY WITHIN A BODY: THE HUMAN EMBRYO

It is reported that the famous Sufi master and poet Shah Qasim-i Anvar (d. 1433), whom I will mention a number of times in this book, was once asked whether the source of humanity's nobility was the physical form of Adam, the first human being, or his internal nature. He replied that it was the combination of the two, "neither solely the form nor the [internal] meaning by itself. His composite being is the locus of manifestation of the whole cosmos and the place where all divine qualities can arise. Whoever can be described in such a way is noble. If we say that the nobility of the human species is because of its internal meaning, it is only because this meaning refers to his sacred spirit (*ruh*), which is the closest thing to God, the great, the most exalted. And whatever is closest to God is the most honorable and noble among all that God has created."[2] This statement specifies the significance of the body within the understanding of the composite human being that can be substantiated further by considering understandings of the human embryo.

Sufi discussions of the generation and maturation of the human embryo in the womb derive from hints found in the Quran as well as understandings of human life absorbed into Islamic thought from Hellenistic metaphysical and medical discourses that went into the formation of the medieval Islamic intellectual tradition. The Quran provides a rudimentary vocabulary for the generation of the human body by talking about phases in which male and female fluids intermix inside the womb to produce an object that passes through the stages of being sperm (*nutfa*), blood clot (*ʿalaqa*), and morsel (*mudgha*).[3] Most Muslim religious scholars and physicians in the medieval period adhered to the idea that human generation involved equal participation from the male and the female, a theory that was ratified also by the Galenic medical system inherited from late antiquity.[4] The fetus's development through the three stages was pegged at forty days each on the basis of both hadith and medical reports; a survey of Islamic works suggests that medieval Muslims were generally able to correlate prophetic statements with Galenic medical concepts remarkably successfully on the question of human generation.[5]

Persianate understandings of the embryo from the period that concerns me follow from earlier medical traditions, as exemplified in the popular work *Tashrih-i Mansuri*, composed around 1396. This work survives in numerous manuscripts that are notable for including four or five detailed diagrams of the body, one of which illustrates a pregnant woman. The work begins its presentation of the body by citing the Sufi maxim "whoever knows himself knows his lord" to justify its subject, indicating the wide circulation of Sufi ideas in this period.[6] Beyond these references, this work is a standard medical text not of direct interest for the present study. Sufi authors who discuss the embryo repeat the developmental program found in standard Islamic medical works but with added metaphysical elements related to Sufi cosmology. A detailed example for this is to be found in the *Mafatih al-iʿjaz fi sharh-i Gulshan-i raz* (*Miraculous Keys for Explaining The Secret Garden*) by Shams ad-Din Lahiji (d. 1506–1507) written circa 1477. This work—an extended commentary on Mahmud Shabistari's (d. 1317) narrative poem *The Secret Garden* (*Gulshan-i raz*)—was a widely popular text for teaching Sufi basics to new disciples.[7]

Lahiji writes that when the sperm settles in the womb it produces a spherical entity filled with a creamy liquid. The natural force that generates form acts within this liquid, first turning it foamy and then causing the appearance of three dots that are the places where the heart, the liver, and the brain will eventually come to be situated. Then appears the place for the navel, and the whole organism becomes enveloped in a thin membrane. Some of the liquid within the membrane turns to blood, the navel takes shape, and the whole organism turns

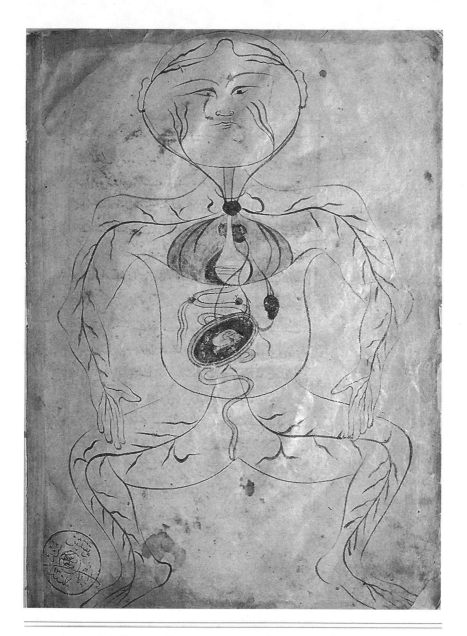

1.1 Anatomical diagram of a pregnant woman from a copy of Mansur b. Muhammad's *Tashrih-i badan-i insan*. Isfahan, Iran, 894 AH/1488 CE. National Library of Medicine, Bethesda, Maryland, MS. P 18, fol. 39b.

into a blood clot. This blood clot then turns into a morsel (*mudgha*), within which the major organs of the body acquire their specific shapes. This is followed by the appearance of bones, the separation of various organs from each other, and the establishment of powers particular to various parts of the body. Each of these processes spans a set number of days within the gestational period. The embryo is completed and ready for the spirit (*ruh*) at 120 days, which now enters and quickens the body. At this point, the fetus becomes fully human and is distinguishable from other animals. Fetal development then continues with the hardening of the bones, the accumulation of flesh on joints, and the formation of facial features and the organs that contain the senses.[8]

Sufis such as Lahiji utilized medical texts for their understanding of the formation of the physical body, but they also went beyond this to delineate the relationship between the formation of the fetus and the cosmos. Doing this underscored the point that the generation of each human being was not merely the coming into being of an animal but the production anew of all the possibilities of the cosmos. Lahiji writes that in each of the first seven months of fetal development the new being is under the influence of a different heavenly sphere. During conception and the first month, the fetus takes effect from Saturn, and so it continues every month with the successive ascendancy of Jupiter, Mars, the sun, Venus, Mercury, and the moon. The child has a good chance of survival if it is delivered in the seventh month because the moon is "hot" and "wet" in terms of the humors that govern the material cosmos. This is so because heat and wetness indicate life. The chance of survival goes down in the eighth month because the cycle starts again with Saturn, which is cold and dry and is antithetical to life. The fetus is under the influence of Jupiter in the ninth month and has the best chance of survival because this planet is also hot and wet and supports life.[9] The correlations Lahiji draws between the development of the fetus and the heavenly spheres reflect the significance of astrology in the medieval Islamic world. The spheres are constantly acting upon the world, most particularly by influencing human affairs on both the individual as well as the social levels. Their connection to the development of the embryo underscores the link between human life and the structure of the cosmos.

A sustained description of the development of the embryo as the replication of cosmogony is provided in the thought of the Sufi-inspired Hurufi sect founded on the ideas of Fazlallah Astarabadi (d. 1394). Hurufi views cannot be taken as the standard for all Persianate Sufis but they are instructive inasmuch as they represent the radicalization of common notions.[10] The author of a short anonymous Hurufi treatise states that the two ultimate created entities in the cosmos are the Quran and the human body, both of which have seven levels. For the textual Quran, this means that seven different internal meanings can be ascribed to each verse. And for the body, the seven levels can be seen in the way the embryo is generated and matures in seven steps.

The first step in the process is the transfer of the male sperm into the female womb, which this author portrays, on the basis of Arabic morphology, as a transaction between the exterior and interior worlds. The man's sperm is said to reside in his back (*zahr*) and its receptor is the woman's stomach (*batn*). The word *zahr* is from the same root as *zahir*, the exterior world, while *batn* is connected to *batin*, the interior world. Following inception, the fetus matures, hidden from direct observation, in the mother's womb by going through more stages: it becomes 2. a blood clot, then turns into 3. a lump of flesh, then successively acquires 4. bones and 5. flesh, and eventually becomes imprinted with the 6. seven facial lines that the Hurufis thought were the hallmark of the human species. The seven lines, which represent the presence of a sevenfold cycle within the overarching embryonic cycle, are the hairline on the forehead, the two eyebrows, and the set of four eyelashes. The seventh and last step in the completion of the human being occurs when God blows his spirit into the completed body. The overall cycle is directly comparable to the production of the cosmos when God created Adam on the seventh day after creating the rest of the world.[11]

The Hurufis were particularly invested in rationalizing all aspects of existence into systems that could be put adjacent to each other to show the mathematically consistent nature of the cosmos. Their understanding of human generation is a direct reflection of this approach, and one of its most interesting features is the idea that the generation of the human body is a transaction between the exterior and interior aspects of existence. In their view of the embryo, the possibility of crossing the interior-exterior boundary is inherent in the very process through which human bodies acquire their material shape. Accessing interior knowledge as a fully functioning human being in later life is a kind of recovery of the body's own preexistence and past. To do so requires "reading" the body from its skin inward, much the same way as one may begin with the literal sense of Quranic verses and then probe deeper to get to higher, interior meanings.[12]

The understandings of the embryo I have presented show human physiology to be a matter intertwined with the social realm as well as the cosmos as a whole. The birth of a new human being requires the relationship between a man and woman, and the product of their union reenacts the cosmogonic drama. It is no surprise, then, that the human body is not comparable to ordinary material objects or even the bodies of other animals. From its moment of inception to full maturation, the physical body is enmeshed in social and cosmological relations that stick to it like strings attached to a puppet. To understand Sufi views of the full body requires scrutinizing matters beyond mere flesh and bone.[13]

We have already been introduced to the "spirit" (*ruh*), the animating principle that becomes attached to the embryonic body at a particular point during its development. The spirit is an essential concomitant of the living human body, although the combining of the two raises a number of questions on which we can find varying views. These include: how do the two bond to each other? Do both have the capacity to influence each other and, if so, how? And what happens to the spirit when the relationship is severed? These issues find mention in Persianate Sufi theoretical speculation as well as in descriptions of religious experiences.

Khwaja Muhammad Parsa's work *Fasl al-khitab* (*The Decisive Speech*), whose title refers to a Quranic verse (38:20), is an extensive compendium of discussions on Sufi topics presented with copious citations from classical Sufi works. For many centuries this work was a staple of educational curricula, particularly in Central Asia. On the issue of the spirit, Parsa writes:

> The togetherness between the spirit (*ruh*) and the body (*jasad*) is akin to the togetherness between the Truth—may He be praised—and the whole created universe. . . . In the words of some people of knowledge ('*urafa*')—may God have mercy on them—the human body is composed of four opposing elements: earth, wind, water, and fire. These four exist in a truly combined state in the body. The place of the earth in the body is obvious and evident; water has a place within earth, subtle and appropriate for the subtlety of water; wind has a place within water, more subtle than the place of water; and fire has a place within wind that is more subtle than that of wind. The spirit is truly present in every atom of the body but without being contained in a particular place. Containment and transfer are accidentals related to bodies, none of which can be applied to the spirit.[14]

This description attributes distinctive properties to material and nonmaterial elements on the question of the formation of mixtures. The four material elements are nested into each other on the basis of a perceived hierarchy, while the nonmaterial spirit is capable of impregnating everything without being subordinated to anything else. Moreover, the spirit is shown to retain a separate identity despite being present in all atoms of the material entity. These ideas emphasize the spirit's quality as an "essence" not subject to any notion of confinement in space or accretion of accidental qualities. The spirit is, nevertheless, portrayed as an entity, which requires further consideration of the type of relationship it maintains with the body.[15]

Some Persianate Sufi authors portray the spirit as a being incarcerated in the prison of the body as a part of God's larger plan behind the creation of the human species. An illustration for such an understanding comes from the hagiography of Amin ad-Din Balyani (d. 1334), a Sufi master who spent most of his life in Shiraz in southern Iran. The hagiographer purports to convey the master's own words when describing the body as a prison necessary for the spirit's self-realization:

> The wisdom behind imprisoning the spirit (*ruh*) within existence (*wujud*) is this: When the spirit came forth in the original world ('*alam-i asli*), it had no veil. It had come forth within the blessing of union [with God] (*visal*) and did not know the value of this blessing. It flew around in the desert of nonexistence, free of pain and sorrow, peaceable and uninhibited. It was unacquainted with tasting and desire, affection and love, and all the stations and degrees. It had no sense for witnessing itself. It needed a mirror in which to witness its own beauty and a secluded place where it could do spiritual exercises and acquire perfection. The heart was made its mirror and the body was made its seclusionary chamber. Then it was turned from the world of union to that of separation so that pain and sorrow, and love and desire, come forth in it. . . . Then [the expectation was that] it would shun this world, have no regard for anyone, become a seeker after its point of return and true end, and enter the state of servanthood. Then whenever it would reach a new station among the stations of this path it would reach a fresh light and [eventually] attain perfection through this journey.[16]

This description emphasizes that the spirit must endeavor to overcome its bodily prison. However, Balyani's views are not so much a condemnation of the body as a plea for it to be seen in appropriate perspective. In a different place in the same work, Balyani is made to say that the reason human beings are fearful of death is that they think of themselves as bodies and nothing else. They see that, when bodies die, those who are still living find them detestable and worthy of avoidance, which is why they bury them in the earth. Such people fail to recognize that death actually pertains to the jail cell that is the body and not to their life's principle. The spirit, while it is attached to the body, should be seen as being half-dead; when the body dies, it is released and acquires a new life upon its return to God, as envisioned in God's plan from the beginning.[17] In ideas attributed to Balyani, the body has a kind of passive agency, rooted in its material nature, which the spirit has to overcome. Its qualities are like an impartial examination that the spirit has to sit for in order to reach salvation. It is not that the body is evil or incites to anything by itself, but that it is the essential obstruction that provides the spirit the opportunity to redeem itself through effort.

Another perspective on the spirit's existence together with the body uses food as a metaphor to differentiate between the two entities. In a treatise devoted to the Sufi path, the master 'Ali Hamadani writes:

> Know that the Truth—may He be praised and exalted—has created the human being from two different essences: a subtle, light-filled essence that is called the spirit, and a dense, dark essence that is called the body. Each one of these essences has a diet and its own types of health, illness, and medicine for the illness. The body's food are delicacies and water, and that of the spirit and heart are recollection, love, and knowledge of the Truth. The indication of illness in both essences is that, contrary to their natures, their diets become abhorrent to them.[18]

He then goes on to explain that, in the case of the body, the lack of appetite must be cured through medicines appropriate for particular cases that rebalance the elements within and expel corrupting materials. Similarly, diseased spirit are in such states that they have either stopped responding to their purpose of inclining toward God or are doing so only in name for the sake of externalities. Different spiritual illnesses have different causes and remedies in the form of "penances and various species of remembrances and worshipful acts whose realities are known only to religious doctors such as prophets, God's friends, masters of the path, and religious scholars."[19] This understanding takes us to the social realm so that the fate of both the body and the spirit appear connected to relationships between human beings along with those between humans and God.

The words of the Naqshbandi master Khwaja Ahrar as reported in a hagiography further crystallize how one might see the connection between the spirit and the body as a critical intermediary link connecting a chain of entities spread in the cosmos. Ahrar is shown to say: "The tongue is the mirror of the heart, the heart that of the spirit, the spirit that of the true reality of humanity (haqiqat-i insani), and this reality that of Truth, may he be praised. Hidden truths travel a long distance from the absolutely hidden essence [i.e., God] to arrive at the tongue. Here they acquire verbal forms and then reach the true ears of those who are prepared."[20] This description makes elements of the human body such as heart and tongue into critical filters for the conduction of divine truths into the material realm. The spirit is, then, the entity that both endows the body with life and makes it into a divine agent active in the material sphere. Although attached to a particular body, each spirit connects to God via the interior realm on one side and to other human beings through what it can induce into the heart and tongue in the exterior realm on the other. The possible connection between one person's tongue and another's ears constitutes the grounds on which multiple bodies and spirits can communicate across their own boundaries.

Spiritual Bodies

I have so far provided examples of how Persianate Sufis considered the question of the spirit's impact on the material body. The articulation of the relationship between the two entities provides evidence for my suggestion that Sufis saw the body as a critical doorway between the interior and exterior realms. In this context, one can ask if the spirit could be colored by the body as much as the other way around.

The answer to this question leads to the Sufi notion of a special realm termed the imaginal world (*'alam-i misal*) that is perceived to be situated in between the world of bodies and spirits. As we will see extensively in this book, much of Persianate Sufi literature that describes the inner states of Sufi adepts who follow the prescribed path to become subjects of extraordinary experiences does so in distinctively corporeal terms. Such descriptions are most often a function of alternative states of consciousness, like dreams and visions, in which the subject is presumed to travel inside this imaginal world that is distinguished by the fact that it has no material existence but contains forms in the images of material bodies. The imaginal world is, therefore, *corporeous* rather than *corporeal* since it can be described in the language of everyday experience, but without the kind of limitations that impinge on action in the material sphere.[21] In Persianate Sufi descriptions, experience in the imaginal world is predicated on the presumed existence of an imaginal or corporeous body that is formed in the image of the physical body. Such a body is necessitated by the fact that describing experience requires the implicit presence of an experiencing body, although the actual physical body cannot have any access to the imaginal sphere. This idea is best understood through examples.

Amin ad-Din Balyani's hagiographer relates that a man came to the master one day to ask the following:

"I have heard two different things from different elders. One says that the spirit has a form like that of the body, meaning that it has hands, feet, eyes, and ears, and that it has a food and a drink. The other says that the spirit has no form, and it is free from eating and drinking. What do you say about these two opinions?" The master—may God preserve his secret—said: "The first statement is believable in that the spirit has a form, but this is a spiritual one (*ruhani*) and its food and drink are also spiritual." When that man had left, he said, "Once I saw in a vision that I had reached the end of time and my spirit had become detached from my body, which was lying there dead, and I was standing on my feet in the same form that I have now. I observed this body to note that it had hands, feet, eyes, ears, and all the other organs. But these were all spiritual so that when I lifted a hand to grasp one of the other organs, it could grasp nothing and was itself made of spirit."[22]

The type of spiritual body Balyani is describing is presumed in Persianate Sufi literature without extended theorization. To see how it could be understood in theoretical terms, we can consider briefly the writings of Ibn al-ʿArabi, the prominent Sufi philosopher and theoretician whose ideas greatly influenced Persianate Sufi thought. Ibn al-ʿArabi presents the corporeous body as an exact nonmaterial counterpart tethered to the physical body. This body cannot be apprehended by the five physical human senses; however, it does have definite reality to it, which is felt during dreams and visions. These experiences are not mere mental projections but real encounters with other corporeous rather than corporeal bodies. The corporeous body is tethered to the physical body as long as the latter is alive, although it is liable to drift away when a person is unconscious as during sleep or in a trance. The tether is severed when the corporeal body dies, and all that is left is the corporeous body attached to the spirit. These two entities continue to exist together until the promised resurrection from death at the end of time. Then God provides another corporeal body for the spirit so that the afterlife is experienced physically. Human beings are resurrected in material bodies, though these are not the same as their original bodies. However, a kind of impression of the original physical body in the form of the corporeous body sticks with the spirit throughout its existence.[23]

Not all Persianate Sufis may have agreed with the details of the perspectives of Balyani and Ibn al-ʿArabi that I have cited, but the general principle at the base of these views appears to have been common coin in Sufi thought and practice. Dreams and visions were major venues for encountering heavenly beings as well as judging one's progress on the Sufi path, and the corporeous body (or an idea akin to it) allowed Sufis to express their experiences in concrete rather than abstract terms. The corporeous body had its own set of senses that enabled it to see, hear, touch, taste, and smell other corporeous bodies in the imaginal world. Just as the physical body and its senses made it possible to apprehend the material cosmos, the corporeous body and its senses made the imaginal world an existent reality that could be experienced and described in language.

In most descriptions of Sufi experiences, the material and imaginal worlds, and the respective bodies that can sense these, remain separate. This is exemplified in views of the author of a hagiographic narrative dedicated to ʿAli Hamadani who states that the transition between the two types of senses—corporeal and imaginal—is what causes one to have an odd bodily feeling upon waking up. In this liminal moment some impulses from the alternative corporeous senses coexist together with physical sensations generated by the ordinary senses, although the feeling passes when one is fully awake or asleep.[24] We have an instance that shows interaction between the two bodies of a single person in the hagiography of the rural Central Asian master Shaykh Sayyid Ahmad Bashiri (d. ca. 1461–62). The author of this work relates from the master himself that one day, when he was traveling in the early morning, he saw a bodily form that looked like himself standing at a distance. As he approached this being he felt that he was getting away from himself and, by the time he reached it, he had completely lost all sense of his physical body and had become one with this body, which felt as if it was made of light. This event was a memorable experience for Shaykh Bashiri, and every time he related it he pondered over it and was filled with the joy he had felt at the original occasion. The hagiographer states that the body Shaykh Bashiri experienced was what Sufis call the acquired body (*badan-i muktasab*) or a type of being that is a gift from God (*vujud-i mawhub-i haqqani*). The acquisition of this body was to be understood as a second birth, which provides one the ability to experience the higher, nonmaterial world that is hidden from the senses of the material body.[25]

This understanding of the second body is different than what is suggested in works by Ibn al-ʿArabi's and others since it comes into existence as a result of spiritual endeavor instead of being present with the corporeal body by definition. But the eventual import of the formulation is the same in both cases since the purpose of the second body is to make the imaginal world available to humans. What Farghanaʾi calls the acquisition of the second body amounts, in others' terms, to an acquisition of the *realization* that one has such a body attached to the physical body. However one understands its origin, the corporeous body helps one to escape the limitations of the material world and allows one to describe the nonmaterial world in ways that are understandable in the vocabulary of normal human existence. In the end, human beings' religious status is indexed to their ability to experience the unseen world through their corporeous bodies and to relate these experiences to others through exercising the powers of the organs of their corporeal bodies. In light of these views, at least those human beings who are capable of fulfilling humanity's ultimate potential possess corporeal as well corporeous bodies.

Bodies and Spirits Intermingled

Most Persianate Sufis would have agreed with the formulation that human bodies need to be harnessed to reach salvation and that spirits reach their destiny by becoming capable of experiencing the unseen world through the intermediacy of corporeous or acquired bodies. However, in a minority of cases, the privileging of the spirit over the earthly body could be inverted. That is, some

Sufis exalted direct action in the physical world above that which could be experienced in the imaginal world. As can be expected, this was the case with individuals invested in salvation through history that unfolded in front of one's eyes rather than through an escape from ordinary time and space. We find the most elaborate formulations of this view in arguments put forth by Sufi masters who led messianic movements in the fifteenth century.

The most cogent example for this view of the body is presented in the work of Muhammad Nurbakhsh (d. 1464) who proclaimed himself the messiah in 1423 and wrote a messianic confession explaining his views. He argued that the bodies of the elect among prophets and saints can contain multiple spirits simultaneously since the earthly activity that issues from them represents God's direct action upon the world. Nurbakhsh saw himself as humanity's savior at the end of time, whose actions were the fulfillment of Islamic messianic prophecies. This claim was difficult to justify in the face of the fact that most Muslims in Nurbakhsh's time believed that the messiah was an identifiable historical person named Muhammad al-Mahdi who had gone into heavenly hiding in the year 874 in Samarra and was expected to descend to the earth as an adult at the end of time. Nurbakhsh's solution to this problem was a concept that he called projection (buruz), according to which the messiah was not a long-lived heavenly figure but someone like himself whose body had came into the world through a normal birth. But, with spiritual maturation, his body had become host to the spirits of Jesus, Muhammad, the expected messiah, and many great Sufi masters of the past. The actions performed by the messiah's body were thus to be identified with the wishes of the spirits of all great religious leaders from the past. Since he saw himself as the messiah, Nurbakhsh thought that his physical work in the world was an exteriorization of all the spiritual work carried out in the imaginal sphere in previous times. In his view, God had decreed this transfer of salvation from the interior to the exterior world as the mark of the end of time. By this token, Nurbakhsh's body was the ultimate instrument through which God intended to fulfill the destiny of the cosmos.[26]

Nurbakhsh's views are echoed in a different form in the work of Muhammad b. Falah Musha'sha' (d. 1462) who also declared himself a messianic redeemer based on his claims of being the greatest Sufi master of his age. Instead of the idea of multiple spirits in a single body, Musha'sha' made a distinction between the essences of particular beings and the material "veils" that made these essences present in the world. He maintained that the earthly bodies of prophets and Shi'i imams—the last of whom was the hidden messiah living in the heavens—had been veils for the presence of God's essence. He saw his own body as a veil over the veil of the messiah and thought that this last great deliverer can be present in the material world only in the form of such a veil. All that Musha'sha' did using his own body was to be seen as the activity of the messiah that originated directly in God as the essence situated behind two corporeal veils.[27] As in Nurbakhsh's case, Musha'sha''s formulation subsumed the spirits of others, and even God's essence, into the activities of his corporeal body. This was the ultimate inversion of the normative pattern since divinity and spiritual entities of the higher spheres were seen to descend into the material sphere rather than spirits imprisoned in material bodies using corporeous bodies to ascend the cosmic hierarchy to reach higher levels.[28]

The Self (Nafs)

In addition to the spirit, Sufis and other Muslim authors also employ the term *nafs*, which I translate as "self," to designate a nonmaterial aspect of the human person. The self is sometimes used as a synonym of the spirit, although in the Sufi context it usually comes quite close to what is meant by the term *self* in modern psychological understandings.[29] While spirit is thought to be an uncorruptible and indivisible essence that attaches to the body, the self is not an entity but the sum total of a person's attitude toward the world. The self is, therefore, quite changeable and can even be reduced to nonexistence. Indeed, the major Sufi goal known under the term *fana'*, or annihilation, refers to the total decimation of egotistical and concupiscent aspects of a person's self in favor of an orientation toward God alone.[30]

The standard medieval Sufi understanding of the self's capabilities divides it into three parts as can be seen in the following description by 'Abd ar-Razzaq Kashani (d. 1330), author of major treatises on the definition of Sufi concepts:

The inciting self: This is the one that commands toward wrong acts; it deceives one into thinking that benefit lies in performing these acts rather than in shunning them.

The censuring self: This is the one that knows, when it nears a sin or an injustice, that benefit lies in shunning [such an act]. It censures itself with respect to such an act but finds arguments against itself rising from within.

Peaceful self: This is the one that finds itself peaceful because it perseveres in acts of obedience—finding no inclination within itself toward abandoning them—and has no desire for sinful acts. This is what is referred to in His saying: "Self at peace, return to your lord; well-pleasing and well-pleased; and enter among my servants and enter my garden (Quran, 89:27–30)." Its entry among the servants—those attached to the [divine] presence—is entry into the group of noble spirits who have been granted intimacy and who "do not disobey God in what he commands them and do what they are commanded" (66:6). This equips the peaceful self with the qualities of those who are cloistered in prayer in the sanctified presence. It [also] endows it with their behavior, which includes remaining untouched by earthly, corporeal enjoyments as well as deviant qualities that characterize the created, materialized world. It separates it from habits that bring to ruin and establishes it in many types of worship that lead to deliverance. With this, it enters the interior (*batin*) of the garden, meaning that it breaches the obstruction that obscures [God's] hidden essence behind the veils of the forms of [his] attributes—as you know. Doing this delivers it from the dress of createdness and affirms it in the quality of true singleness.[31]

Kashani's division of the self into three parts is in fact a categorization of three types of actions the human being is capable of undertaking in the light of religious injunctions. The self at peace in this description appears synonymous with what I have described regarding the Sufi understanding of the spirit. The extended description of the third self implies that the self in general inclines to these functions in inverse proportion to its subservience to the material body, within which it or the spirit are located during a human being's existence on earth. Here, as elsewhere in Sufi thought, discussion of the self and the spirit presumes a concomitant body whose propensities determine how the self measures up with respect to what it has been commanded to do in religious terms. The self's incitement to evil, censuring, or peacefulness are modulated fundamentally by its relationship with the body that is the actual interface between an individual being and the negatively marked material world. Peace in the presence of God's essence, the Sufi's ultimate aim, is achieved when the self draws aside the veil that separates the material world from hidden truths. From the perspective of human experience, the most significant manifestation of this veil is the human body itself since this entity instantiates a person as an aspect of the material world. In this understanding, which formed the basis of much of medieval Sufi thought, to become peaceful requires the self to firmly regulate its connection to the body. I will discuss the practical implications of this perspective in the course of analyzing Sufi religious actions in chapters 2 and 3.

THE BODY'S ORGANS, INSIDE AND OUT

The previous discussion indicates that, for Persianate Sufis, the relationship between the spirit and the body was not simply that between a privileged noble element and a troublesome dense object. During its living condition, the body's atoms were seen to be permeated with the noble spirit and, conversely, the spirit could be imagined to be corporeous, imprinted with the form of the body due to the association of the two elements. The mutual interpenetration of the spirit and body reflects the intermixing of the interior and exterior elements of reality in Sufi thought; when we scrutinize Sufi literature carefully, the purportedly clear distinction looks more like a scene of shifting sands than a dichotomy.

In this section of chapter 1 I focus on Persianate Sufi understandings of specific elements of the body that determine its relationships to the interior and exterior worlds. These include the heart, which sits inside the body and is regarded as the noble organ able to experience the interior world. The obverse of that is the external form that constitutes the object of the science of physiognomy. The outer form interfaces with the physical world and is understood as a signifying palette that can be read by others to evaluate the being who inhabits the body. The ensuing discussion further substantiates my suggestion that bodies in Persianate Sufism come across as doorways between the exterior and interior realms.[32]

The Perceiving Heart

In Sufi literature the heart is usually discussed not as a physical object but as the organ whose powers and attributes define humans as living, apprehending, and acting beings in the world. In the words of Qasim-i Anvar, the heart within the human being (microcosm) is like the human being within the universe (macrocosm). In both cases the entities inside reflect the most highly valued aspects of the larger beings in question. The human heart can then be said to be the most valued element in the cosmos as a whole.[33]

We can get a sense for the functions attributed to the heart from an extended taxonomy presented in a widely influential work by Najm ad-Din Razi Daya (d. 1257–58). This work is worth considering for understanding Sufi thought and practice in subsequent centuries since it was widely used as a manual for training and is cited often by later authors. Daya writes, reflecting associations found in prior works, that the "relation of the heart to the microcosm is the same as that of the throne [of God] to the macrocosm. The heart, however, has a property and a nobility that the throne does not possess, for the heart is aware of receiving the effusion of the grace of the spirit, while the throne has no such awareness."[34] A later author who likens the heart to the throne perceives the issue differently, stating that the sympathy between the two means that they are constantly emitting things toward each other. If one side is stronger, it absorbs the other, which is not desirable. But, if they possess the same intensity, this results in love's perfection between the two, the ultimate goal.[35] The heart therefore acts as the conduit between God and the human being and is the seat of human life and intellect.

One particularly interesting aspect of Daya's understanding of the heart (which is repeated verbatim in a significant fourteenth-century Naqshbandi work, among other places) is the idea that the heart is itself a shadow body within the body.[36] It has its own five senses, which mirror the body's senses, and its correct functioning depends on the health of these senses. Just as the physical senses make the material world available to human consciousness, the heart's senses bring sensations of the interior world into the heart's purview: its eyes see the sights of the unseen, its ears hear God's speech, its nose smells the perfumes of the heavenly realm, its tongue tastes divine love and interior knowledge, and the sense of touch, which is spread all over its exterior, gives a comprehensive experience of the unseen world. Just as the physical senses aggregate together to create a feeling for the body's presence in the physical realm, so do the heart's internal senses provide spiritual intelligence. And, just as the correct working of the physical senses makes a person physically capable, the heart's senses make it possible for the person to travel in the metaphysical realm.[37]

Daya's taxonomy of the heart divides it into seven parts: breast (*sadr*), heart (*qalb*), pericardium (*shaghaf*), inner heart (*fu'ad*), grain of the heart (*hubbat al-qalb*), the black dot (*suvayda'*), and the blood of the heart (*muhjat al-qalb*). The heart's sevenfold structure is to be seen as parallel to the seven spheres of heaven so that a descent to the core of the heart is the microcosmic equivalent of an ascent in the macrocosm, both journeys leading eventually to God.[38] Daya's description of the heart as a body with senses that parallel the senses of the physical body should be reminiscent of the notion of the corporeous or acquired body discussed earlier in this chapter. Both the heart and the corporeous body are shadow images of the physical body, one perceived to be buried inside the chest and the other shown tethered to the outside. The similarity between the two is not coincidental: the conceptualization of these entities reflects the imperative that human experience can be represented only through corporeal metaphors even when it is understood to take place in the metaphysical realm. These Sufi speculations on the heart and the corporeous body constitute fundamental presumptions that make it possible for Sufis to imagine crossing the exterior-interior boundary to experience nonmaterial realms.

Standing outside Sufi metaphysics, we can say that the heart and the corporeous body are nonmaterial images of the physical body that enabled Sufi theorists to expand the body beyond its limits. Getting to the heart did this by diving into the body, to discover that the whole cosmos was within it. This represented a case of exploring the macrocosm through the microcosm. And the corporeous body accomplished the same by equipping the person to fly away from the physical body and roam through the macrocosm. This, then, was a case of making available senses that allowed access to worlds and knowledge that were beyond perception under ordinary circumstances. The centrality of the heart and the corporeous body in Sufi thought underscores the point that for Sufis the imagination of the body far exceeds what can be seen, heard, smelled, tasted, and touched through the body's physical senses. To concentrate on the Sufi understanding of the body is not simply to explore a physical object but to see how human beings have imagined the cosmos as a reflection of their own beings.

The Readable Body

I have already mentioned the notion that the body can be read from the outside in the context of describing Hurufi views on the development of the human embryo. The principle involved in this instance finds wide application in Persianate Sufi literature, although full-fledged metaphorical interpretations of the body's various parts as could be observed externally are quite rare.[39] Hurufis are an exception here since they were particularly keen to show the correspondence between text in the Arabic script and the body. One instance of such mapping of the body is the argument that each bodily organ corresponds with a letter of the alphabet on the basis of its shape. Thus, the head is likened to the letter *hay*, the ear to *fay*, the eye to *zad*, the nose to *ta*, and the mouth to the *hay* again. The body as a whole resembles the combination of two letters *lam-alif*, which the Hurufis regarded as a single letter in the Arabic alphabet put there as a stand in for the four letters (*p-ch-zh-g*) that have to be added to this alphabet to write Persian.[40] The overall effect of this mapping between the alphabet and the body is, once again, to compel people to think of the form of the body as a kind of text that could be read.[41]

In medieval Islamic societies, a more mainstream and quite widespread form of "reading" the body than the Hurufi system was the science of physiognomy, known in Persian under the term *firasat*. Concerned with divining the moral and other qualities of particular human beings on the basis of physical properties of their external body parts, this science had precedents going back to both pre-Islamic Arabia and Hellenistic traditions of late antiquity. Authors concerned with the science in Persianate societies divide it into two branches based upon what were thought to be the sources of the knowledge. The first branch, which the prominent polymath Fakhr ad-Din Razi (d. 1209) likens to medicine, was predicated on the idea that the optimal human body holds all the elements and humors of nature in perfect equilibrium within itself. All the organs of such a body are exactly proportional to each other, conveying an overwhelmingly pleasant effect on anyone who senses it. Most bodies do not have this perfection and have organs disproportionately large, small, fat, thin, long, or short. The expert in physiognomy knows, on the basis of normal study, how to correlate particular complexions and shapes and sizes of body organs to a person's natural instincts and habits. For example, such an expert's knowledge of the literature on physiognomy would indicate the following about eyebrows: "(a) Overly bushy eyebrows indicate that the person is inclined toward sadness and brooding. This is so because hair is formed of a smoky matter, and the abundance of hair on the eyebrows indicates an excess of such matter in the cranium. This, in turn, points to the predominance of black bile from among the natural humors, which produces sorrow and anxiety. (b) If the eyebrows are long, extending toward the temples, then the person is arrogant and pompous. (c) Someone whose eyebrows incline downward on the nose side and upward near the temples is arrogant and foolish."[42]

In addition to this kind of straightforward observation of corporeal features that led to knowledge of a person, Razi mentions that great prophets and friends of God have the ability to read bodies and bodily behavior since they possess intuitive knowledge.[43] The basis for such intuitive physiognomy is described in a work by the prominent Naqshbandi shaykh and prolific author Khwaja Muhammad Parsa. He writes that perfected friends of God are able to see the light of the true, interior world, which is the underlying nature of all human beings but is, among ordinary humans, hidden from view because of the denseness of natural elements and human nature. Friends' complete access to this light means that they can, through physiognomic interpretation, know the "inner states, abilities, thoughts, intentions, and hidden acts and situations of all people. They apprehend these hidden matters through studying their physical states and bodily organs. With this same light of true life—which is the light of God—they enliven the hearts of disciples who are prepared."[44] This type of physiognomy could not be learned from books and resulted from the physiognomist's access to the interior world. As we will see in many discussions later in this book, visual inspection is represented as being a major tool in the hands of masters to decipher the spiritual states of their disciples and indicate the correct path they need to follow.

In literature produced during the fifteenth century, Muhammad Nurbakhsh's popular treatise on physiognomy repeats the arguments found in earlier works, but also ties the science directly to Sufi religious aims. Nurbakhsh represents physiognomy as a highly useful science, even though it ranks lower than the knowledge gained from revelation and mystical unveiling (mukashafa), which is limited to prophets and God's friends, and the sciences of astrology and numerology practiced by philosophers (hukama').[45] His justifications for its validity include statements from Muhammad as well as the observation that if the characteristics of various species of animals can be understood from observing them externally the same should be possible for humans who represent the aggregation of all possibilities of living beings into a single species.[46]

As in the case of Razi's treatise, Nurbakhsh provides specific interpretations of the sizes, colors, and shapes of different bodily organs, placing particular emphasis on the eyes. More interestingly, he then goes on to acknowledge that it is quite possible to have a composite body whose various organs signify opposite characteristics. In such cases the interpreter must follow the rules of basic mathematics. For example, if two organs suggest intelligence and one stupidity, the person ought to be considered intelligent.[47] Moreover, properties associated with bodily organs can be overcome through deliberate effort and the company of the religious elect. He exemplifies this principle through a story about Plato, who purportedly sent some students to India to visit a philosopher. The Indian philosopher asked the students to describe Plato to him, and, when they did, he proceeded to list all the negative attributes obvious from his appearance. When the students got back to Plato, they declared the Indian philosopher to have been an ignoramus. However, when they told Plato what he had said, the Greek philosopher said that he had been right in identifying those negative characteristics as part of his nature. However, Plato argued, the philosopher had failed to realize that he had overcome these physical attributes through hard work.[48]

The story about Plato shows that physiology need not be regarded as a prison for human beings, even though it acknowledges that all bodies are born with particular propensities inherent in their physical constitutions. Sufi intellectual and social programs covered in detail in later chapters take this view for granted. They recognize the body's agency as an actor by itself, but they also insist that Sufi prescriptions are aimed at maximizing its positive characteristics and suppressing the negatives on an individual basis.

Overlapping Bodies

A miniature painting dating to the early sixteenth century shows the figures of two Sufi men framed by a doorway with the inscription "O you who opens doors."[49] The doorway—pictorial as well as textual—can be read as referring to the point of access between the interior and the exterior realms. The verbal invocation seems to address two beings: God, who may allow one to access higher truths, and the Sufi master, whose teaching and training enables one to see and walk through the doorway. The two men's heads are drawn as separate, and are distinguished from each other on the basis of facial hair and headdress. Their postures suggest that one is entering the doorway while the other hesitates before following him or leaving the scene. The bodies overlap; whether they would continue to do so beyond the pictured instant depends on the moment of decision encapsulated in the scene.

This is an admittedly speculative reading of the image, one that reflects our lack of information about the painter's intentions. But it is useful to think of this image in conjunction with what I have argued regarding Sufi representations of the body in this chapter. If the human body can be regarded as a doorway between the interior and the exterior, the decorated portal looming over the human forms adds to the body's status as an object that encapsulates liminality

1.2   The entry into the grave. Persian, Safavid period, early sixteenth century, Iran.
Opaque watercolor and ink on paper, possibly a manuscript page, 7.4 × 3.6 cm.
Photograph copyright © 2010 Museum of Fine Arts, Boston. Francis Bartlett Dona-
tion of 1912 and Picture Fund 14.572.

and transition. Critically, the scene in the painting presents two overlapping bodies rather than a solitary figure negotiating the doorway.

The togetherness of the two bodies as depicted in this painting is a significant feature of the theoretical discourses I have presented in this chapter. Although each particular human being is thought to have a body and spirit, the pair never exists in strict isolation. The body and spirit of each person are connected to other bodies and spirits, across all boundaries that define the person as a discrete entity. Similarly, the multitiered heart requires the guidance of a master to realize its functions, and particular bodies' physiognomic handicaps can also be overcome through one's affiliation with a master. The bodies of such masters are open doorways to the interior world, a status they acquire through instruction under their own masters. For a Sufi novice, the aim is to transform one's body from a closed to an open doorway that connects the interior and exterior worlds. As indicated in the quotation from Khwaja Ahrar with which I began the chapter, masters can eat up disciples by allowing the bodies of seekers to enter their own. The theoretical perspectives on corporeality I have discussed in this chapter provide a map for the stage on which dramas of interactions between masters and disciples get played out in Sufi hagiographic works. The remainder of this book is dedicated to discussing the narratives of the dramas themselves.

2

BEFRIENDING GOD CORPOREALLY

The views on human embodiment I covered in the last chapter were concerned largely with the form of the generic human body as a component of the cosmos. The body's place vis-à-vis the interior-exterior dichotomy demarcates its functions with respect to Sufi understandings of the purpose of existence. In this chapter I take the discussion one step further, by concentrating on intentional corporeal action that may lead to the fulfillment of religious goals. My main concern here is to provide a general picture of the range of observances and activities that go into the construction of saintly personas in Persianate Sufi literature. The materials I cover indicate practices that Sufis thought enabled them to overcome perceived inherent weaknesses of their bodies and turn the higher potential invested in them into reality.

This chapter is divided into three sections that aim to convey an umbrella picture of actions associated with the bodies of those who came to be regarded as great Sufi masters. I begin with Persianate Sufi views on Islamic legal precepts that constitute the most universal Islamic injunctions concerning the body. The body figures extensively in medieval jurisprudential discourse (*fiqh*) in such contexts as rules for purity, mandatory rituals, and the delimitation of legal and illegal foods. A vast majority of Sufis who concern me regarded strict adherence to the regimen of the shari'a as a necessary first step on the Sufi path. The relevance of law is everywhere in evidence in Persianate Sufi literature, although many Sufi authors indicate dissatisfaction with the legal formalism associated with juridical discussions. Perceiving intricate arguments about minute details of all actions as casuistry, they sought to rationalize shari'a injunctions through symbolic interpretation or sustained philosophical inquiry into the nature of the connection between corporeal action and spiritual attainment. I present examples of such rationalizations, followed by Sufi interpretations of some aspects of rules regarding ritual purity, the daily prayers, fasting during the month of Ramadan, and the hajj pilgrimage.

Extended hagiographic descriptions show that Sufi practices in the Persianate world extended beyond shariʿa regulations through the belief that some bodies are born with special religious power that matures through deliberate and systematic suppression of corporeal desire. The second section of this chapter illustrates this idea of differentiated potential of human bodies and its actualization through examples that pertain to key moments in the lives of famous Sufi masters. This theme is addressed in numerous places throughout this book, and my brief discussion in the context of this chapter is meant to indicate some general patterns in the consideration of the way Sufi masters' bodily performances are implicated in the construction of their hagiographic images.

The last section of the chapter concentrates on *zikr* and *samaʿ*, rituals quintessentially associated with Sufi practice. *Zikr* means "remembrance" and involves repeating one of God's names or a religious formula in conjunction with maintaining or moving the body in particular ways. My treatment here attends to the controversy surrounding proponents of silent versus vocal zikr that exercised many a Sufi in the fourteenth and fifteenth centuries. The point of difference between the two sides on this score was the question of whether the body should be outwardly still while performing zikr or be allowed to speak and move in particular patterns. Both these ways of performing zikr implicated the body and held relationships with theories regarding the exterior-interior divide. The issue of how the body could represent internal states while acting in the exterior world is implicated in stories about great masters' *samaʿ* (literally, "audition") in which they reacted to music through dance. When performed with religious sanction, Sufi dance marked moving bodies as conduits between the interior world and the exterior cosmos filled with movement. Samaʿ was sometimes a controversial practice, and attending to arguments by practitioners and opponents illuminates a source of internal differentiation similar to the variance constituted by vocal and silent zikr.

LAW IN THE LIVES OF PERSIANATE SUFIS

Demarcating the rules of shariʿa law is one of the most elaborate and widespread discourses in the history of Islamic thought and is indeed one of the hallmarks of Islamic civilization. The extent to which shariʿa law can be shown to have mattered in the functioning of specific Muslim societies varies greatly in different geographical locations and time periods. However, there are very few instances one can point to in history where Muslims have not held up the shariʿa as a rhetorical ideal for the conduct of personal life and the management of societal affairs. In theory, the shariʿa provides principles to judge between right and wrong with regard to all actions undertaken by human beings. In history, however, the actual sphere of the shariʿa has been limited to issues Muslim have been interested in discussing on the basis of agreed upon sources and methodologies for argumentation. A historicizing view of shariʿa injunctions requires that we not only register scholarly discussions about the rules but also see how these were understood in the context of extrajuridical religious imperatives in particular sociohistorical settings.[1]

Rationalizing the Shariʿa

To explicate Persianate Sufi efforts at interpreting the shariʿa, I will concentrate on works by authors who belonged to Khwajagani-Naqshbandi lineages.[2] The prominent master Bahaʾ ad-Din Naqshband (d. 1389) is reported to have described the relationship between the shariʿa and true reality (*haqiqat*) as being comparable to that between the protecting skin of an almond and its meat: if the skin becomes corrupted, the same must be true of what is underneath.[3] Extending this understanding, Naqshband's disciple Khwaja Muhammad Parsa provides a lengthy abstract justification for the primacy of following the rules of the shariʿa.[4] He emphasizes the necessity of following the law in the context of a general discussion aimed at arguing that the Sufi path requires paying equal attention to corporeal and intellectual matters.

Parsa's point of departure is the relative merit of different types of perception through which human beings become cognizant of their surroundings. He begins by acknowledging some would argue that intellectual perception has a higher value than sensory perception since the purview of the latter "is limited to the body. Intellectual perception [in contrast] knows things by their essences and detail; it sees both the hidden and the apparent aspects of things through their realities, and its purview includes the [whole] earth as well as the seven heavenly spheres."[5] Parsa accepts that the intellect has greater value when it comes to the depth of knowledge it provides, but he argues that sense perception is a more primary aspect of human existence since it saturates every cell of the body, the very basis for existence, and is nullified only through either actual death or the kind of voluntary death prized by Sufis that involves giving up all concern for material things. For Parsa, the all-pervasive and ever-present nature of sensory perception under the circumstances of normal existence means that human beings' life trajectories are determined more by what they do with their bodies than by the disembodied knowledge that their intellects might make available to them during the course of their lives.

One of Parsa's main proofs for arguing for the significance of sense perception is his contention that the shari'a, God's law for humanity, is addressed one half to sensory aspects of existence and the other to the intellect. The two types of perception have to work in tandem under the guidance of the shari'a to reach the goals of human life. He illustrates the connection between the two through an analogy with the way a bird hatches out of the egg. Upon initial fertilization, the egg consists of a shell filled with liquid that has hidden potential to give rise to the bird's body. The application of heat to the shell from the outside gradually turns the liquid inside into the bird, which eventually breaks out of the shell and flies away. Parsa writes that the eggshell is like the senses, and the liquid inside the egg like the intellect. Shari'a rules that govern the body, and God's direct epiphanies (tajalliyat) that come about as a result of Sufi endeavor, are like the heat that has to be applied to the egg to lead to its hatching. While the process is going on, both the shell/senses and liquid/intellect have to be kept intact. In the end, it is the liquid of intellect that transforms itself into the bird of the knowledge of God that comes out of the egg and flies to the heavens to reach God. But the bird can come into being only if the shell remains intact until the end, and if its surface bears the heat of God's law and his self-manifestation in the form of epiphanies. Stringent attention to Islamic ritual practice is, therefore, an absolute necessity if one wishes to acquire intimate knowledge of God and, eventually, unite with him through mystical experience.

Parsa states that relatively few eggs laid by birds actually hatch into birds, and only a few hatchlings that come out of eggs live long enough to become fully grown birds. Similarly, only a small number of human beings make appropriate use of their senses and allow their intellects to acquire knowledge of God. Furthermore, among those who begin tasting this knowledge, relatively few actually put it into practice to reach the end of the path and become assimilated in God's reality.[6] According to this analogy, everyone must obey the shari'a, but its impact on performers varies based on the potential inherent in individuals with different intellects and bodies. With this understanding, those destined to become great Sufis must be especially attentive to the regulations of the shari'a in order to actualize their extraordinary potential.

Ritual and Metaphorical Purity

The idea that persons who have the potential to reach the highest stations in Sufi terms would also be the ones most committed to the shari'a can be observed throughout most of Persianate hagiographic literature. Parsa's point regarding the shari'a can be made more concrete by looking at metaphorical interpretations of a particular activity, the ablutions necessary before performing certain acts of worship. Virtually all Persianate Sufi descriptions of how one begins one's journey on the path start with the requirement that the candidate cultivate an absolute dedication to following legal rules regarding purification and the performance of required rituals. Authors of these works see the state of purity as emblematic of a body concentrated on God. In the legal context alone, purity is necessary only when performing rituals, but many Sufi authors recommend that one be in a state of purity as much as possible throughout one's day.

One prominent source describes the ablutions as a believer's ultimate weapon against the corruptions of the world, implying that those who want to protect themselves must be armed with the state of ritual purity at all times.[7] This author also cites his own master as having said that the shari'a is particularly necessary for the Sufi because it helps to starve the body's desires. When one has brought all the organs of the body under the control of the laws of shari'a, the body becomes filled with light and all its organs begin acting in a way fundamentally different from their prior behavior.[8] A body that is perpetually weeping (giryan) from the fear of God is described as being clothed with the possibility of meeting God, and the text implies that whatever causes one to weep, such as pain and suffering, is automatically of benefit to one's journey on the path to God.[9]

A work by Ya'qub Charkhi (d. 1447), a contemporary of Parsa and a disciple of Naqshband and his successor 'Ala' ad-Din 'Attar, provides an extensive interpretation of the question of legal purity in a work dedicated to masters of his lineage. Charkhi casts his work *Kitab-i maqamat va silsila-yi Khwaja Naqshband* (*Book of the Stations and Lineage of Khwaja Naqshband*) as a memoir of Naqshband's greatness, which he had seen personally on display as his disciple. His purpose in writing the work was to make Naqshband's teachings and personality available to later generations.[10] Charkhi writes that one of Naqshband's most emphatic recommendations was that a Sufi should attempt to retain the state of ritual purity at all times. This would, at a minimum, require very frequent ablutions, which he justifies through the hadith that God prefers those who clean themselves well. Charkhi's appeal to physical cleanliness takes him beyond the legal requirement of ablutions, which is aimed solely at ritual purity.[11] This tendency becomes even more emphatic when he cites a hadith stating that sins associated with each part of the body subject to ablutions wash away as water is poured over them. He recommends also that the Sufi should always go to sleep in a state of ritual purity since that compels an angel to entreat God to forgive one. He maintains that the Sufi should avoid remaining in the kind of impurity that requires the full bath (sexual emission, menstruation, parturition) because a hadith states that someone who is in such a condition cannot enter paradise.

Since one's death can occur at any time, it is critical to avoid this particular state of impurity for the sake of salvation after earthly life.[12]

After emphasizing ritual requirements regarding the physical body, Charkhi moves to what he calls ablutions that pertain to the Sufi's interior reality (*batin*). He equates these with establishing perfect sincerity of intention when one decides to become a Sufi. Such sincerity must precede all one's actions on the Sufi path, much as the ablutions precede the required rituals. For Charkhi, the effects of these internal "ablutions of the heart" are immediately obvious in that they compel angels to aid one in one's quest. Anyone who undertakes Sufi exercises without first establishing sincerity is subject to terrifying psychological experiences rather than any benefits.[13] All of Charkhi's comments on the significance of the state of ritual purity take the matter beyond a simple concern with formal legal requirements. His approach, which is quite typical of Persianate Sufis, is to interpret the laws by connecting them to other concerns such as actual physical cleanliness, the necessity of being ready for one's death, and Muslims' internal states, which are the true measure of their religious status. He takes for granted Muslims' constant concern with states of ritual purity and impurity in daily life and ties this kind of corporeal awareness to larger themes in Sufi thought and practice.

Charkhi, Parsa, and many other masters validate the rules of the shariʿa by pointing to the larger purpose behind regulations that pertain to physical actions. Their efforts to rationalize the shariʿa or give metaphorical meaning to ritual acts leave the precise rules behind and emphasize, instead, either their functional significance (such as cleanliness) or the overall necessity of disciplining the body as much as the intellect for religious purposes.

Performing Ritual Duties

Normative Islamic rituals constitute one major arena for shariʿa regulation, and over the centuries much jurisprudential ink has been spilt on discussing the exact ways in which to perform the so-called five pillars of Islam. According to a majority, these five pillars are profession of faith, ritual prayer (*salat*), fasting during the month of Ramadan (*sawm*), obligatory alms tax (*zakat*), and the pilgrimage to Mecca known as the hajj. Of these five pillars, ritual prayer, fasting, and the hajj are accomplished by following very specific rules involving the body, including, first of all, entering the state of ritual purity previously discussed.

Ritual prayers, performed multiple times during the day, form the backbone of daily corporeal submission from a legal standpoint. The kind of concentration in prayer Persianate Sufis sought in their practice is indicated in the story that states that the master Bahaʾ ad-Din ʿUmar (d. 1453) required one of his sons to stand next to him while he prayed in order to remind him of how many cycles he had gone through. Without this, he could go on performing the prayers endlessly because of the way they brought him close to God.[14] Similarly, during his illness before death, Shaykh Safi ad-Din Ardabili (d. 1334) insisted on performing his prayers through all the standing and sitting phases despite the fact that he was too incapacitated to do this himself and had to have attendants present on both sides to make the body transition from one posture to the next.[15]

Ritual prayers require bringing the body into specific positions accompanied by the recitation of parts of the Quran and various religious formulas. A story from the Naqshbandi hagiography *Rashahat-i ʿayn al-hayat* exemplifies the degree to which one's bodily comportment during prayer could index social acknowledgment of one's religious status. Precisely because they wielded power over other people, Sufi masters were subject to minute surveillance by disciples seeking assurance regarding their religious credentials. The author states that one day as he was praying behind Shams ad-Din Muhammad Ruji (d. 1499), he noticed that that master was putting all his weight on the right foot, leaving the left one free, while he was in the sitting posture that comes at the end of the prayer cycle. This was contrary to the rules of prayer, since one's weight is supposed to be distributed evenly across the feet. This seemingly minor observation was a serious enough issue that, after the prayer, the master divined the doubt occasioned in the author's mind and addressed him directly, without being asked. He said that when he was young his father once took him to visit Shaykh Bahaʾ ad-Din ʿUmar. During the trip, his left foot was exposed to extreme cold while he was unable to cover it for fear of appearing rude to the great master. Even though the foot appeared to be devoid of any fault, he had been unable to put any weight on it while praying since that time. The "disobedience" of the foot was thus excused because its condition had come about while maintaining proper etiquette in front of a great master.[16]

Turning to the actual bodily movements required during prayer, full symbolic decoding of the various positions and actions is relatively scarce in Sufi literature.[17] In the Persianate sphere, a rare example of such interpretation is found in the Hurufi sect mentioned in the previous chapter. The Hurufis held the radical view that they were living in the end times and the world was about to experience a cataclysmic apocalypse. They believed that they were the only righteous group to exist on the planet at this crucial cosmic moment and that, as a consequence of their status, God had revealed to them the precise meaning behind all ritual acts. Reflecting their general principle that all secrets of the cosmos could be deciphered by paying attention to the Arabo-Persian alphabet, they argued that the first three distinctive positions taken by the body during the ritual prayer corresponded with the shapes of the three letters *alif, lam,* and *ha* that combine to make the name of God (*allah*). These three letters were thought to represent the basis of all existence as well because their shapes— straight, bent, and rounded—encompass the shapes of all that exists in the world.

These two different associations of the three shapes taken by the body during prayer led to the idea that when humans pray they simultaneously articulate the name of God with their bodies and encompass the whole of the created world in their corporeal movements.[18] All Muslims who had been performing the prayer from the beginning of Islam to the times in which the Hurufis lived had been rehearsing this underlying truth regarding the human body's ability to unite God's name with the form of the cosmos through ritual. Hurufis' sense of their own special status derived from the fact that God had revealed this cosmic secret to Fazlallah Astarabadi, the prophetic figure after whose inspiration the Hurufi movement had been formed.

Just as daily life of observant Muslims revolves around the cycle of prayers, the ritual year is calibrated to two of the remaining five pillars: the month of Ramadan, when adult able-bodied individuals are supposed to fast from dawn to dusk, and the yearly hajj pilgrimage that takes place over the course of multiple days in the twelfth month of the Islamic lunar calendar. The relationship between fasting and managing the body is obvious, and I will provide more details on this subject in chapter 6, which focuses on miracles relating to food. In the context of the present discussion, it is significant to mention that Persianate Sufis usually saw the fast in a similar vein as ablutions and prayer, emphasizing full execution of one's ritual obligations during Ramadan and often recommending periodic fasts throughout the rest of the year. Great masters are shown to have had unlimited capacity for fasting according to legal rules, often subsisting on a bare minimum of nutrition even during the hours of the day in Ramadan when they were not expected to observe the fast.

Similarly, for those who had the opportunity to make the journey, the hajj was a significant moment in their lives. However, many great masters never performed the pilgrimage, and their hagiographers convey the sense that their disciples regarded the very abodes of these men as being equal to the shrine in Mecca. The author of an early Khwajagani work makes this explicit by stating that in the exterior world people follow the path of religion by going to Kaʿba, which is a beacon of God's presence in the cosmos. No such path to a center is available directly in the interior world, the realm of higher religious experiences. In that world, only a Sufi guide, with whom one must develop an intimate relationship, can lead one toward ultimate religious goals.[19]

A specific illustration of this attitude is illustrated in an episode in a work devoted to Sayyid Amir Kulal (d. 1370/71). One day, this master was telling some companions about various activities involved in the hajj when a doubting person asked him how he knew all this, given that he had never been to Mecca. The master asked him to look up toward the sky, and he saw there the Kaʿba itself circling around the master. This vision caused the doubter to repent and become a firm devotee. Amir Kulal then admonished him to say that the ability to "see" something depends on the capacities to be found in one's eyes and not on physical proximity.[20]

Many more illustrations for Persianate Sufi interpretations of normative Islamic rituals can be added to what I have described in this section. While Sufis' perspectives on law and ritual could vary considerably in their details, they had a common denominator in the idea that rules for purity and other ritual actions can be interpreted to divulge greater meanings. This shared characteristic had the effect of heightening the significance of the law beyond the formalistic concerns of the jurists. For Persianate Sufis, standard Islamic ritual actions were significant first steps in religious programs that went beyond what was mandated for all Muslims.

EXTRAORDINARY EXERTIONS

As I have remarked previously, Persianate Sufism was a heterogeneous milieu, and the evidence available to understand it presents interrelated but contrasting attitudes and practices. One particular arena that reflects this characteristic is the Sufi attitude toward practices involving asceticism or deliberate corporeal mortification. Great feats of sensory and nutritional deprivation are a regular feature of Persian hagiographic narratives, although, for a majority, asceticism seems to have been a prominent feature of their lives only in the years of early adulthood, when the body needed to be "tamed" most assiduously. Many great masters are depicted as living to old age in comfortable circumstances. However, a small but highly visible minority rejected all material comforts and cultivated a lifelong dedication to shunning ordinary life altogether. These masters wore their asceticism and rejection of society on their bodies through antinomian and socially radical practices. For the purposes of understanding asceticism as a general attitude in Sufi thought and practice, it is fruitful to focus on two questions that can enable us to differentiate between various types of Sufi ascetic acts and actors: 1. Why did medieval Sufis think that subjecting their bodies to ascetic practices aided in reaching religious goals? 2. Did acts deemed ascetic attempt to conform to or subvert the norms that dominated in the social context in which they were performed? Contrasting attitudes on these two questions allow us a textured view of the societies in question.

Important as it certainly was, living up to shariʿa regulations was only the beginning of the type of behavior that won Persianate Sufis the title of being a friend of God. As I will discuss in chapter 3, hagiographic narratives often portray saintly bodies as being special by nature. However, they also show masters exerting strenuous control over their bodies in their early years. The overall impression one gets is that the inherent sacral potential of certain bodies is evident to other masters who come in contact with them, but the individuals who actually are these bodies come to a realization of their natures in moments of grand revelations preceded by extensive corporeal work. The material basis of these bodies may be sacred from the beginning, but they have to ripen through corporeal effort to realize their full potential.

As we see them represented in hagiographic sources, a majority of prominent Persianate Sufi masters took poverty seriously as an ideal and undertook ascetic exercises in at least certain phases of their lives. Even when not actively seeking pain, most led and advocated a simple life in which the absence of material comforts was meant to act as a reminder of the idea that they were more concerned with their relationship to God and the interior realm than with worldly matters.

Asceticism is a common theme in the study of religions, although it is impossible to provide a universal definition for what it entails across traditions and time periods. What behavior can be deemed ascetic varies from context to context, depending on such factors as the intentions and self-understanding of the performer and the way particular actions contrast with the norms of a given society.[21] The contrastive nature of Sufi asceticism in particular is evident in pictorial representations such as the examples in figures 2.1 and 2.2. The first of the two is the sole image in a manuscript of a Turkic work by Haydar Khwarazmi, completed in Tabriz in 1478. In the scene, the legendary Sultan Mahmud of Ghazna pays a visit to an ascetic and beseeches him to take up residence in his court, where he would be protected from natural hardships like cold weather. The dervish rejects the offer and challenges the ruler that he should worry about his own well-being since he had not made adequate preparations for his death. When the sultan responds angrily, asking how prepared the ascetic was himself, the man dies with a smile on his face since he held no relationships with the material world whose severing would cause him any remorse. The painting signifies the opposition between the religious and worldly sides through the nakedness and bare heads of the ascetics versus the sumptuous clothing, headdress, and servants and horses that belong to the king. Moreover, the background to the Sufi master's image is left blank while the prince

2.1 Bodily contrast between a Sufi ascetic and a royal visitor. Haydar Khwarazmi's *Makhzan al-asrar*, Tabriz, Iran, 1478. Spencer collection, New York Public Library, Astor, Lenox and Tilden Foundations, Persian MS. No. 41, fol. 27b.

2.2   An ascetic in a winter landscape conversing with worldly man. Attributed
to Bihzad, Tabriz, ca. 1525. Opaque watercolor on paper, painting 19.6 × 13.5 cm.
Freer Gallery of Art, Smithsonian Institution, Washington, DC: Purchase, F1946.13.

is pictured in a verdant landscape.[22] In the second painting, dated to circa 1525 and attributed to the great master Kamal ad-Din Bihzad, the relative physical locations of the ascetic and the worldly man with respect to nature are inverted. The ascetic sits out in the open in a barren winter landscape, while the courtier stands behind a portal looking out. Nevertheless, the overall message of both paintings is the same at the level of drawing contrasts between Sufi and non-Sufi modes of life through variant contextualization of human forms. In both cases, architecturally elaborate doorways signify the separation between ascetic and worldly actors.[23]

It is clear from hagiographic narratives that the general import of Sufis' inclination to asceticism lay in causing a sense of deficiency or pain in the physical body by either denying essential corporeal urges, such as food, or actively seeking painful situations. Textual descriptions of such situations convey the sense of Sufis "struggling" with their bodies, where the tussle indexes their effort to disassociate from worldly desires and ambitions.[24] A story from the hagiography of ʿAli Hamadani illustrates this point well: we are told that when Hamadani first arrived in the company of the master Akhi ʿAli Dusti as a young man, the shaykh would make all his disciples move large stones from one part of his lodge to the other on a daily basis. Unable to see the point of this after a few days of hard labor, Hamadani questioned the master regarding the work's benefit. In response, the master took off his shoe, hit Hamadani with it on the nape of his neck, and said: "The benefit is this: it forces unbelievers to come under the category of people of Islam."[25] In the view of this master, then, becoming a Sufi equated to becoming a Muslim, and intense bodily effort was necessary to progress on the path irrespective of the actual product of such work.

In hagiographic accounts, the extent and severity of Sufis' struggle against their bodies varies not only in reports about different individuals and groups, but also within the lifetimes of particular individuals. The harshest ascetic acts are almost universally limited to the great masters' early adulthood, the period in which they had to prove their extraordinary religious potential. A particular emphasis on suppressing the body's natural urges during this period makes sense in that this is when the body was thought to be most vigorous in its powers and demands; controlling it through ascetic measures at this time was a greater imperative in comparison with childhood or middle or old age. A number of masters in hagiographies are depicted as saying that their comfortable circumstances in old age were a reward for the fact that they had undergone severe hardships in early life.[26]

After the decision to become a Sufi, Khwaja ʿUbaydallah Ahrar adopted a lifestyle of subsisting on the bare minimum of necessities and exerting himself in extraordinary ways for the sake of others. He is said to have worn the same fur robe and socks for a period of three years, to have taken care of patients with typhoid (including washing their soiled bed linen despite being feverish after having contracted the disease himself), and to have aided people bathing in heated public baths, without any remuneration and irrespective of their social and moral status. The experience of spending extended time in the heat during his early years affected him so much that he avoided baths as much as possible throughout the rest of his life.[27]

The master Amin ad-Din Balyani is said to have subjected himself to severe discipline throughout his life. His hagiographer writes that he grew up extremely poor but would say that the deprivations he experienced in his early years were necessary for his spiritual progress. The poverty meant that even ordinary obligations were sources of considerable pain for him: he could not afford to heat water and had to take baths with cold water in winter after having had wet dreams. He abstained from eating meat because it connoted luxury and would not even eat broth if it had been made with meat. He also shunned water, usually for ten days at a time and sometimes even a month. Once an attendant brought a cup of cold water to him during warm weather; he stared at it for a while and then asked that it be taken away, saying that he could not drink it because it would extinguish the fire of love for God within his chest.[28] Exhibiting a similar concern, a man known as Master Morsel (Pir-i Luqma) came from India to settle in Herat and made it a practice to beg people for scraps that he would mash together with salt and feed himself while telling his carnal self, "This is your livelihood; eat it or ignore it as you wish."[29]

While Balyani put restrictions on his daily rations, Shah Ni'matullah Vali (d. 1430) took it upon himself to live in the wilderness. Once, while he was in Samarqand, he resolved to go and spend the winter in snow-covered mountains outside the city. People tried to dissuade him, since that would mean certain death, but he insisted and departed alone. At the end of the winter people went to the mountains, thinking they would have to collect his dead body, but found that he had survived by just eating snow for many months.[30] He had such control over his body that he would do the ablutions and then pass a whole forty-day retreat without any flatulence or the use of the toilet that would make him exit the state of ritual purity. What made his feat particularly remarkable was the fact that he was able to do this despite eating and drinking heartily in the evening during the forty-day period.[31]

The master Hajji Nasir ad-Din 'Umar Murshidi (d. 1423) is shown choosing a particularly dramatic path in the beginning of his career. His experience, as described in his hagiography, equates to the idea of Sufis acquiring new bodies through ascetic practice before being able to provide guidance to others. His hagiographer states that once he had chosen to become a Sufi he was greatly bothered by the fact that people would come and disturb his religious exercises. He therefore asked his father's permission to go into the wild in order to be free from all social interactions. His father agreed, but asked what would happen if he fell sick or died. He replied that then it would be fine for his body to become food for wild animals and that his father could distribute the money for his funeral to charity. He was so intent on being alone that he even refused to let his father know the direction in which he was headed.[32]

Armed with this high determination but no food or other provisions, he set off from home on a Tuesday evening. On the very first part of the way, he was struck with severe diarrhea, which completely emptied his body of any food and made him feel very slow and tired. He then decided to make his home in a cave near a waterway; the first three days he felt very tired and even had to perform some of his prayers sitting rather than standing, but then his strength returned. He stayed in this cave for a month without eating or drinking anything and then first moved to another cave and, eventually, to a small niche in a mountainside. Here he once felt very thirsty, but, since he did not have the strength to get water from afar, God caused a stream to flow out of the rocks to satisfy him. After a total period of seventy days, during which nothing passed out of his body, so that he was not required to do ablutions, he decided to return and made his way to farmland owned by his father. He is reported to have said:

> I saw a man from afar and motioned him to come to me. When he got near, he hesitated to come all the way, given my condition. I had become so weak that it was impossible to lift even my eyebrows and I could not recognize anyone. That man said, "I am afraid because you do not seem even to be a human being." Then God gave me the capacity to tell him who I was and ask about the news of the area. He said, "How odd is this, that you know everyone but I do not recognize you." Then I told him that I was Hajji ʿUmar, the son of Daniyal, and that you are so and so. When he heard this he went and brought this news to my father.[33]

His family then took care of him and he began to eat and drink so that he eventually regained all his earlier strength. In later life he lived quite normally and even took up the family profession and farmed his share of his father's lands. The hagiographer who relates this story states that his own father, who was one of ʿUmar's brothers, told him that the miraculous stream that sprouted near the master's mountain hiding place continued to provide water for the fields at the time of the book's writing in the year 846 AH (1442–43 CE).[34]

Radical Shunning of Society

While described internally as a matter of personal religious motivation, ascetic practices always derive from existing social practices by offering contrast with established norms. No practice can be termed ascetic in the abstract since all things deemed extraordinary presume the existence of an ordinary. In the context of Sufi asceticism, this issue is reflected in the division of Sufis between those who abided the law and the antinomians. The asceticism of a majority of Sufis meant a radicalization of practices that were accepted as normative by the larger population, represented most often by hyperattention to legal strictures and sensory assault or deprivation. Such Sufis deviated from the norm solely by being immoderate, as a person obsessed with cleaning deviates from the norm although he or she is fulfilling a normative imperative. In contrast, antinomian ascetics wished to challenge social norms by carrying out "mortifications" deemed contrary to the law. Reflecting a Dionysian spirit, the practices of such ascetics were a direct challenge to Muslims generally and to other Sufis in particular. Antinomian Sufi groups remained a small minority through Islamic history, although the late medieval period saw a considerable expansion in their numbers so that they were a regular feature of the social scene in the Persianate world. As Ahmet Karamustafa has argued, the upsurge was no accident since this was precisely the period in which normative Sufis acquired their greatest social prestige, which often implied modification of their religious programs for the sake of accommodating material interests. Antinomian asceticism was therefore an aspect of the internal Sufi reaction to developments in Sufi practice and thought during the late medieval period.[35] Antinomian actors were a source of fascination for contemporary society and are depicted in miniature paintings from the late medieval period. The image in figure 2.3 presents a man with hair shaven from his face and head and scant clothing made of leather and animal fur indicating separation from ordinary society.[36]

Divided among groups known under the names of Qalandars, Haydaris, Abdals of Rum, etc., the antinomians actively cultivated a corporeal aspect meant to shock the sensibilities of the ordinary observer. Because they shunned society, the attitudes and practices of these Sufis were not recorded extensively in sympathetic written works. However, a versified Persian hagiography devoted to the antinomian master Jamal ad-Din Savi (d. ca. 1232) gives us a picture of such Sufis' attitude toward Islamic law, asceticism, and the conduct of ordinary social life. While this master's life falls earlier than the period that is my focus in this book, the text in question was composed around 1350 and reflects Sufi paradigms relevant to the present discussion.[37]

Khatib Farsi, Savi's hagiographer, writes that the master's peculiarities included spending most of his time sitting naked in graveyards, shaving all hair from the body (including eyebrows and eyelashes), eating only that which was minimally necessary to keep the body alive, and avoiding speech and social contact as much as possible.[38] Despite his clear lack of desire for social contact, throughout his life Savi attracted followers who would often leave their

2.3 A dervish. Safavid, about mid-sixteenth century, Iran. Ink and pale color on paper, 12.5 × 7–9 cm. Photograph copyright © 2010 Museum of Fine Arts, Boston. Francis Bartlett Donation of 1912 and Picture Fund 14.553.

ordinary existences to adopt his religious style. Such persons' attraction to Savi and his attitude to the world are captured in an incident that the hagiographer describes in some detail.

Farsi relates that, toward the end of his life, Savi arrived in the Egyptian city of Damietta while trying to escape the large numbers of devotees that had started to congregate around him in his previous abode in a graveyard near Damascus. His peculiar appearance caused many in the local population to denounce him as unholy and dangerous, and some people informed the city's judge that such a man had installed himself in the local graveyard. The judge went to visit him with the aim of asking him to either leave the environs or face punishment, but the sight of him made him realize that this was a genuinely exceptional religious man. The judge was able to tell this because he was himself inclined to Sufi pursuits and could, unlike the city's ordinary people, appreciate Savi's inner reality despite his reprehensible outward appearance. He approached Savi very respectfully and asked him why, despite his knowledge, he had chosen to take on this lifestyle. Savi replied that this was the most explicit way of affirming the Sufi maxim that one should die to the material world before one's death. He treated his own body like a corpse that had no need for the comforts of ordinary life, and he spent his time sitting silently in graveyards because that provided the kind of solitude ordinarily available only after death.

The judge then asked him why he also did not observe the strictures of Islamic law or follow the example of the prophet Muhammad as all Muslims were commanded to do. He replied that no religious deficiency accrued to him from the way he had chosen to live because one's outward form was a mere veil that was of no consequence according to his particular religious path. To prove that this was true, he told the judge that he could change to a normative appearance whenever he wanted in the blink of an eye. Following this, when the judge looked at him again he saw his face transformed, with regular eyebrows and other facial hair. But then he changed again in an instant, reverting to the antinomian form. The judge found the argument and Savi's ability to transform himself quite convincing and immediately asked to become his disciple. Savi replied that this was not worthwhile since he was good at what he did and the conduct of the world required the presence of honest judges like him. The judge then left him to go back to his own normal life, although by then he had acquired an appreciation for the type of religious vocation Savi represented.[39]

This story's resolution affirms both the normative and the antinomian forms of Sufi practice, suggesting that it should be regarded as a way in which proponents of the high Sufi literary tradition attempted to co-opt the attraction of figures such as Savi while maintaining their own mainstream perspectives. The fact that the narrative is sympathetic to Savi, however, means that it can be regarded as at least somewhat close to the antinomians' viewpoint.

The most crucial moment in this narrative is when Savi shows the judge how he can change forms without any trouble. The fact that he eventually changes once again to the antinomian affect underscores the point that he and other Sufis like him saw their bodies as canvases for proclaiming their religious choices. They quite literally wore their religions on their bodies, cultivating the image of an ascetic who had not only given up the cares of the world but who also actively manipulated the body to mock the convention-bound lives of ordinary people. Along with its internal justification, the antinomian mode of Sufi practice was meant to act as shock therapy; it was fairly well the opposite of the viewpoints of people like Khwaja Ahrar, Hajji ʿUmar, and others whose corporeal mortifications were only reminders to people to pay less attention to their material desires.[40] This function of antinomianism is acknowledged directly in normative Sufi works such as the hagiography of ʿAli Hamadani where the master criticizes groups such as the Qalandars by saying that the problem with them is that whatever they see in the interior world they want to show in the exterior.[41] In other words, their practices threatened to eliminate the fundamental interior/exterior dichotomy that I have discussed in chapter 1. By attempting to live religious injunctions in a literal and uncompromising way, the antinomians went against the grain of the overall basis of Sufi thought. In addition to such critique by normative Sufis, the antinomian position was also inherently ironic: it proved that to try to escape the body one must dedicate one's whole life to cultivating it in a particular form.

CONTROLLED MOVEMENT IN ZIKR

Zikr, or the effort to concentrate oneself on the remembrance of God, is traceable to the activities of the earliest Muslims who either called themselves Sufis or can, in hindsight, be recognized as the progenitors of Sufism as an Islamic perspective. In its origins zikr was a relatively straightforward meditation in which the practitioner's aim was to achieve an extraordinary awareness of God through excluding the thought of anything else while repeating divine names or liturgical formulae.[42] The practice underwent much evolution in later centuries as Sufis adopted various complex meditational techniques involving corporeal components such as breath control and moving the body repeatedly in set sequences with the aim of producing mental states. By the period with which I am concerned, the way a Sufi group performed zikr marked its communal identity and distinguished it from groups with variant practices. In the Persianate environment, zikr ran the entire gamut from a silent remembering of God to groups of individuals collectively doing elaborate dances to the accompaniment of music.

Amidst all this diversity about the ways of doing zikr, there were two points on which everyone seemed to have agreed: doing zikr regularly in some shape or form was essential to being a Sufi; and the way the body was used while performing zikr indicated one's affiliation with a chain of Sufi authority that was seen to have transmitted a distinctive religious practice through the centuries. I will illustrate the major perspectives on zikr here by concentrating on camps that advocated, respectively, a silent zikr marked by the body's stillness and a vocal zikr accompanied by vigorous bodily movement.

Silent Zikr

For a number of influential Sufi masters, the best way to perform zikr was to do it silently and without moving the body. Such a practice had the advantage that it could be done in the midst of other activities rather than being limited to the specific times when one was free from other chores of life. Moreover, the silent zikr avoided religious ostentation of any kind; it allowed one to practice the Sufi path without other people knowing about it and interpreting it in any way.

In the period that concerns me in this book, the silent zikr was advocated most strongly by Baha' ad-Din Naqshband and his followers. Naqshband's best-known hagiographer reports that the shaykh indicated that zikr was effective only when a master specifically instructed a disciple to perform it. This meant that the method of zikr had to be conveyed through a human chain down the generations and that it had no effect, or could even be harmful, if one took it up solely on personal initiative. Naqshband was affiliated with a chain of Sufi authority known as the Khwajagan, in which the prominent masters from the past had varied between preferring silent or vocal zikr. Naqshband himself had been instructed in the silent zikr by a master and had chosen it over the vocal method because he considered it "stronger and better."[43]

The silent Naqshbandi zikr did not involve moving the tongue or the body, but descriptions of how it was done nonetheless convey the sense of intense attention to one's corporeal demeanor. In versions attributed to Sa'd ad-Din Kashghari translated here, the zikr requires the practitioners to force internal energy into different parts within the body through concentrating the mind and regulating one's breath. It consisted of repeating the Islamic profession of faith "there is no god but God, and Muhammad is the messenger of God (*la ilaha illa'llah, Muhammad rasul allah*)" in the following way:

> The master says in his heart "There is no god but God and Muhammad is the Messenger of God." The disciple brings his heart to presence and places it in front of the master's heart. He opens his eyes, purses his mouth, presses his tongue against the roof of his mouth, and places his teeth together. He gathers himself and obediently, with all his power, begins the zikr together with the master. He says this in his heart, not by the tongue, being patient and doing three iterations per each breath.[44]

As the zikr formula gets repeated, the practitioner has to observe further specifics that correlate words to locations on the body: "The beginning of the word *la* is at the navel and its [eventual] seat is at the right breast; the letter *alif* [in the next word] begins from the seat in the right breast, going into the pineal heart [on the left] to form the word *allah*; and [the remaining formula] *illa'llah Muhammad rasul allah* is attached to the heart."[45] This description offers a contrast between the body's external stillness and the practitioner carrying something from one part of the body to the next in the inside.

The body's outward passivity as it is depicted here did not stop a master from being able to tell the situation inside. In one instance, after Kashghari had taught a disciple the zikr, he observed him doing it and said that that was wrong because the man had not managed to keep his heart absolutely still.[46] Similarly, Kashghari's disciple ʿAlaʾ ad-Din Abizi once instructed one of his disciples to inscribe the formula to be repeated during zikr on his heart and then stare at it. When the disciple failed to understand what this meant after being told twice, the master asked him to sit facing him. He then put his hands on his chest and, when he next looked down, he saw the formula imprinted on his heart. He was astonished to see this and became a firm devotee of the master.[47]

A hagiography dedicated to Bahaʾ ad-Din Naqshband states that he placed special significance on the moment when a master instructed the disciple on how many times the formula "there is no god but God" had to be repeated during zikr. This "knowledge of numbers" (*vuquf-i ʿadadi*) represented the first level of an intuitive knowledge (*ʿilm laduni*) that God bestowed upon Sufis in consequence of their religious endeavors. When conveying the knowledge of numbers to his own disciples, Naqshband made a point of reciting the names of the transmitters through whose mediation he had acquired this knowledge. In one instance of doing this, he affirmed the superiority of the silent practice by referring to a conversation between Khwaja ʿAbd al-Khaliq Ghijduvani and his master Imam Sadr ad-Din, two early members of the chain to which Naqshband belonged. One day as he was working on interpreting the Quran with the master, Ghijduvani stopped on the verse "Call on your Lord, humbly and secretly; He does not love those who transgress" (7:55). He understood this to mean that the zikr was to be performed silently but thought that this led to a conundrum: if one were to use the tongue or the body to do zikr, it could not be kept secret since others could observe one's actions. But if one did it solely inside oneself then it could be observed by the devil since Muhammad had said, "Satan flows in the veins of Adam's descendants like blood." Ghijduvani questioned Sadr ad-Din about this and was given the answer that he had to wait to come across a master who could impart to him the intuitive knowledge that would make this issue understandable. Ghijduvani did eventually learn the secret of the matter from a master, and it was this very understanding, denoted by the "knowledge of numbers," that was conveyed to Naqshband through a chain stretching from Ghijduvani to his own times.[48]

This story is, at one level, disappointing in that the text does not reveal the exact reason for Naqshband's preference for the silent zikr, and we are not told the actual number of times the formula had to be performed because that is a secret. Naqshband's choice thus appears largely an issue of adhering to a tradition that was transmitted through intimate personal contact. But Ghijduvani's alleged puzzlement reveals something quite significant about this Sufi group's view of the place of the body in Sufi practice. His formulation of the problem sets up an opposition between the body's exterior (that which others can see) and its interior (veins susceptible to the presence of Satan), and his question points out that practice confined entirely to either side of the body is of doubtful value. Exterior practice risks ostentation, while purely interior practice is easily corruptible since it cannot be judged or corrected by someone with greater knowledge or authority. The solution to the problem lies in the link with a master who must be seen as the only appropriate audience for a person's religious effort. The main point of Naqshband's teaching is that one can expose one's internal religious practice to the master without the fear that this will enmesh one in worldly concerns. And the master can preclude the presence of the devil in one's veins by teaching the right interior method and guarding against corruption by judging the disciple while being in a sustained interpersonal relationship. The correct way to perform the "silent zikr" involves eschewing public performance by not using the tongue or the body, and being intimately involved with a master who first teaches how to move internally through the zikr and then keeps an eye on the practitioner's progress with periodic face-to-face contact. The silent zikr is not marked by outward body movements, but it implicates movement within the mental image of the body as well as the crucial interface between the bodies of master and disciple.

The extensive Naqshbandi hagiography *Rashahat-i ʿayn al-hayat* puts particular stock in the performance of zikr according to the silent method advocated by the Naqshbandis as the marker of correct Sufi practice, showing those who do zikr vocally to have been subject to chastisement. Reports on this score provide useful windows onto the competition between different types of Sufi practitioners: in one case, someone who rejects the criticism of his vocal practice is told that his cow would die if he did not stop, and this is what comes to pass.[49] In another incident, the master Bahaʾ ad-Din ʿUmar ciriticizes the Naqshbandi practice of holding the breath during zikr, leading the Naqshbandi master Khwaja Yusuf ʿAttar to write to him that his criticism went against the practice established by Naqshband and his foremost disciples, which made ʿUmar retreat from his stance.[50] In a third case, the Naqshbandi master Shams ad-Din Ruji said that when he first decided to follow the Sufi path, a follower of Zayn ad-Din Khwafi in Herat was recommended to him as the master to whom he should attach himself. But, when he heard the din made by the master and his followers doing zikr, he was disinclined to join them. On the way back he came across an acquaintance who told him to visit a Naqshbandi shaykh instead, which he did, and was greatly impressed by the calm and stillness that reigned during silent zikr. He joined the Naqshbandi path based on this experience.[51]

Vocal Zikr

Unlike the Naqshbandis and some of their predecessors, most Sufi groups in Persianate societies did not consider it a problem to use the tongue and the body during zikr. For them, the benefits of using corporeal techniques to reach desired states outweighed the danger of affecting ostentation and becoming ensnared in worldly concerns. Major chains of authority such as the Kubraviyya, the Yasaviyya, the Ni'matullahiyya, and the Safaviyya had particular zikr practices involving bodily movements. As mentioned in a number of places in this book, performing zikr openly was a significant component of the hagiographic public personas of most masters belonging to these lineages.

A good case in point to show the use of bodily zikr is the practice of the Kubravi master 'Ali Hamadani (d. 1385), whose lifetime overlaps with that of Naqshband almost exactly. In a hagiography written by one of his disciples, the master traces his own initiation into Sufism to a pious man whom his maternal uncle had taken in for the sake of his young nephew's education. Hamadani started paying attention to this teacher's habits when he reached the age of twelve and noticed that he would go to a secluded place in the morning and the evening and would sit and move his head left to right continuously as a religious exercise. He asked him what this was and got the reply that this was zikr; he then asked if it was necessary to move the head in this way for zikr, and the old man responded yes, because this is what he had learned from his shaykh, the Kubravi master Mahmud Mazdaqani (d. 1364–65). He then asked the teacher to instruct him in the zikr, to which he agreed. Three days after starting the practice, Hamadani suddenly went into a trance (*ghaybat*) and saw Muhammad sitting high above on a rooftop. He expressed the desire to join the Prophet but got the reply that he could not come up there by himself and needed the aid of Mazdaqani. He then decided to travel to the place of this master and began practicing the zikr in his company.[52]

Like Ghijduvani's affirmation of the silent zikr, this story hinges on a question about the use of the body in zikr, asked by a man who is, in the long run, destined to be a great saint and a role model for other Sufis. In both cases the questioners adopt a recommended method of zikr as a tradition and have to wait to come into contact with masters to receive the full explanations of the practice. The actual modes of doing zikr are primary in both cases and establish the young disciples' affiliation with particular Sufi paths. However, the full benefit of performing zikr materializes only when it is done under the guidance of masters who convey its true meaning after accepting the young men as personal disciples.

The Kubravi zikr that ʿAli Hamadani adopted in this story and conveyed to his disciples actually resembles the Naqshbandi practice, except for the crucial differences that the words of the religious formula are said out aloud and the body is moved externally rather than internally. The practice is known as the "four-beat" (*chahar zarb*) zikr:

> [From the upright position, the Sufi] brings his head down to the level of the navel while saying the word *la*. Then he becomes upright while saying the word *ilaha*. Then he inclines the head toward the right breast and says *illa*, followed by inclining toward the heart, which is on the left side, while saying *allah*. The words have to be said connected to each other and in a single breath. Although some of God's friends do the zikr while holding their breath, the honorable Sayyid [ʿAli Hamadani] taught me to do each cycle of zikr accompanied by a single breath.[53]

This zikr could be performed alone or in the company of other Sufis. Citing statements from Muhammad, Hamadani's hagiographer states emphatically that the vocal zikr as it was practiced and taught by Hamadani was not an improper "innovation" (*bidʿat*), one of the usual ways to proclaim a practice as being religiously deviant in Islamic thought.[54] To the contrary, the verbal invocations contained in zikr were expected to settle in all parts of the practitioners' bodies and become like a natural sound within them.[55]

Whether silent or vocal, the ultimate purpose of all types of zikr was to bring Sufis closer to God. All descriptions of progress along Sufi paths can be related to the practice of zikr, although the following description by the prominent master Zayn ad-Din Khwafi (d. 1435) provides a sense for its immediate results:

> During the zikr, or after it has finished, a flash of lightning flickers from the cloud so that the veil is torn up and the light of the one who is recalled in zikr shines forth in the form of a special overseer and presence. It is necessary that, at this point, all parts of the individual person, both the inner and the outer, should be still as if dead, absent from the world as if annihilated. Observing this light relieves him from paying attention to the rest of his surroundings, although, eventually, these things crowd in to force the eye of his heart away from staring at the light.[56]

The contrast between the body's movements during zikr with its stillness afterward indexes the ritual's function as a mediator between ordinary earthly experience and the direct communion with God sought by Sufis. The fact that practitioners can maintain the sacred condition only as long as they are immobile reinforces the notion that embodiment is a kind of entrapment from which one needs to escape as much as possible through religious exercises.

Comparing the two ways of zikr, it is easy to see that the body was at the center of this quintessential Sufi ritual irrespective of the production of movement or sound. This is obvious in the case of vocal zikr, but the silent version is also keyed very strongly to the practitioners' consciousness of their bodies. Keeping still while holding the breath requires intense bodily work, and the way the zikr is described makes clear that practitioners projected their internal energies toward various parts of the image of their bodies that they held in their minds. Both types of zikr were also aimed at controlling the body and bringing its internal and external movements under the purview of one's conscious control as much as possible. The effort to restrain the body temporarily in this way during ritual could be seen as a practice on a continuum with more stringent ascetic practices.

ABANDONMENT IN DANCE

ʿAli Hamadani's hagiographer states that in the very beginning of his journey he was unable to derive any benefit from zikr until he was able to prepare himself internally for the journey. Once zikr started to take effect, he got to the point where he would lose himself completely upon hearing vocal zikr, and his master forbade other disciples from performing it in his hearing lest his spirit completely leave the body. His overall reaction to the outside world then changed so drastically that he lost all consciousness of his surroundings and was kept in chains for three months and force-fed in order to keep him alive. Once out of this condition, he began to practice sama ʿ or audition and would dance in the courtyard of the lodge twice a week. He later told his hagiographer that anyone who does not love audition in the beginning of the path is not going to produce great work later in life.[57] A work by Hamadani affirms this attitude through the remark that the ear is the bodily organ with the most sensitive connection to the heart. Unlike the eye and the mouth, which can be closed to stop seeing or talking, the ear can be precluded from sensing only if one removes oneself completely to a place where no sound is being made at all.[58]

As can be seen in ideas attributed to ʿAli Hamadani, zikr and samaʿ are related but slightly different concepts: both are meant to carry a Sufi practitioner forward on the religious path, although zikr requires cultivation of actions in a particular sequence while samaʿ is a matter of reacting to outside stimuli. Also, zikr performed by one person can lead to samaʿ for someone who is listening, which makes it difficult to differentiate the two. In the present context, I would like to focus on sama' as a matter of reception since descriptions of Sufi masters' reacting to music and poetry highlight a different aspect of their bodily practice than the orderly performance of zikr.[59]

A particularly lively case for sama' is to be found in the extensive hagiography devoted to Shaykh Safi ad-Din Ardabili. His practice of sama' is described as being extraordinary in that not only was he greatly moved by audition, but the whole surrounding world seems to have moved with him. Once when he decided to participate in a gathering, observers saw that the lamps of the mosque where the event was taking place had started spinning in the same rhythm as his and the walls had picked themselves up to keep time. On another occasion he danced so energetically, and for so long, on top of some debris that people performing the exercise with him had bloody feet by the end. However, his own feet were protected by angels and he was also seen to rise into the air above the crowd when in complete ecstasy.[60]

Once when Shaykh Safi himself had not participated in sama' for a whole year, he was sitting in a gathering where other Sufis suddenly began to dance. Since none of the regular singers (qavvalan) were around at the time, a certain Mawlana 'Abd ar-Rahman Hafiz began to recite a verse from the Quran to aid the practitioners. Hearing this, Shaykh Safi went into ecstasy (vajd) and began crying profusely. Once the dance had come to an end, he told those present that he had started because he had had the vision of a man arriving there in the company of his master Shaykh Zahid Gilani. This man had beseeched him to do sama' with intercession from Shaykh Zahid, and he had had no choice but to follow the master's wishes. On another occasion, Shaykh Safi had become very sick and lay on his bed completely weakened when he asked that a particular qavval named Farrukh be presented to him. The man came running when called, and the master asked him to recite something. As soon as he started, Shaykh Safi's illness evaporated, and he sat up and shouted loudly before starting sama'.[61]

While hagiographic narratives depict the great masters in the throes of sama', a short work by a certain Shams ad-Din Ibrahim Abarquhi written in the early fourteenth century provides an understanding for what could be seen to occur in sama' from a physiological perspective. Abarquhi first provides references from earlier authors to justify the practice, and then explains:

Know that sama' is an incoming element whose heat collides with the coldness of certainty (yaqin). If this gives birth to sadness (huzn), that warms the temperament (mizaj). And the same occurs if it gives birth to passionate yearning (shawq). But, if it gives birth to contrition (nadamat), it first warms the temperament and then cools it. When heat and cold meet each other in bodies' cavities, it may happen that they instantiate the removal of moisture that flows out in drops from the fountain of the eye, which is known as weeping. Or it may happen that, by chance, they meet in the inner space of the heart, the effect of which appears in the body in the form of cringing. This is what is meant in the Honorable Speech by the verse: "The skins of those who revere their Lord cringe from it [i.e., when the Quran is recited]" (Quran, 39:23). Or it may be that they meet at the surface of the ocean of the spirit so that it rises up in a wave from the intensity of their collision, giving rise to a cry and perturbation in the manner of what happens in the ocean when the wind and water move rapidly.[62]

This explanation presents the body like a prism for sounds capable of inducing sama⁣ᶜ. The three possible reactions inside the body are keyed to the hierarchy of its internal elements, showing a progression from the body cavity itself to the heart and, eventually, to the surface of the spirit that interfaces with the material body. The internal reaction then surfaces externally in the form of weeping, cringing, or crying aloud. After explaining the basic principle in this form, the author goes on to say that the profound corporeal agitation caused by samaᶜ further affects others who may be present around the person exhibiting the

2.4   Dervishes dancing. About 1500 CE, Iran. Ink and color on paper, 6.5 × 8.6 cm. Photograph copyright © 2010 Museum of Fine Arts, Boston. Francis Bartlett Donation of 1912 and Picture Fund 14.560.

intense states. This leads to the creation of a cycle so that the scene encompasses multiple bodies reverberating with each other through the reception and production of sounds. The overall result of this is a scene of abandonment of ordinary bodily comportment that depends on the presence of appropriate instigating stimulation, such as music and recitation, as well as a group able to come together in the context of the ritual. Sama' involving dance is a common element in the depiction of Sufis in Persianate painting. Figure 2.4 contains a painting dated to around 1500 CE showing three Sufis performing sama' to the accompaniment of a group of musicians.

The direct exhortations and stories concerning normative rituals, asceticism, zikr and sama' that I have cited in this chapter have individual as well as social sides to them. On one level, actions of great Sufi masters pertain to the potential vested in them as extraordinary beings. On another level, their bodily performances act as advertisement for lesser Sufis to become attached to them. In the words of one author purporting to cite the famous early Sufi master Junayd of Baghdad, "Stories and traditions regarding the masters of the path . . . are akin to what can be said of the Truth, may He be praised. Through them, the Truth provides power to the broken hearts of disciples and seekers, and aids them."[63] In hagiography's internal logic, masters' exemplary commitment to the shari'a, their cultivation of asceticism, their assiduous performance of zikr, and their shows of abandonment in sama' are all matters that exemplify their dedication to their own paths and their special functions as exemplars for those who have not yet reached stations equal to their own. In the next chapter I investigate the social functions of Sufi masters' religious performances in greater detail.

3

SAINTLY SOCIALITIES

Once Shaykh Abu l-Hasan 'Ishqi had come to a disciple's house that was in
Mawlana Nizam ad-Din's neighborhood, God have mercy on him. As soon he
entered the house, he began to sniff, turning his nose this way and that way, and
said: "No smell of [a true] man comes from these environs." When they delivered
these words to Mawlana Nizam ad-Din, his eminence said: "Faqir Abu l-Hasan
has contracted a cold. His brain is stuffed up with a concern for status."

— KARAKI, *MALFUZAT-I AHRAR*

Sufi actors' significance in Persianate societies derived from the fact
that the ideas and practices they espoused were treated as potent
means for understanding and managing human affairs. This makes descriptions
of communal life found within Sufi literature a major venue to observe the articulation of relations of power between individuals and social groups active
in the Persianate context. As a prominent and influential domain, the Sufi social world with its various modes of cooperation, competition, and argumentation can be seen as a microcosm for the larger surrounding society. Although
rhetorically invested in the superiority of the interior world, Persianate Sufis
were keen contestants in struggles involving ideas, practices, and individuals
that were played out in this-worldly terms. To get a relatively full sense of this
world, we need to complement prescriptive statements with an assessment of
how masters and disciples competed with each other while employing Sufi ways
of claiming and cultivating prestige.

This book as a whole constitutes an account of Sufi social interactions as they
come across in Persianate hagiographic literature. My specific purpose in the
present chapter is to lay out the major axes of social differentiation deployed
in these interactions that can act as a grid for discussions to come. As in the
previous two chapters, my aim is to give an overall sense of the matter rather
than providing a summary or an exhaustive account. I begin by highlighting the
place of rules of etiquette described in Sufi sources that represent the foundations on which the edifice of Sufi social interactions was constructed. Taken as a
whole, these rules amount to prescriptive programs operating in hierarchically

arranged social groups that require individuals to act based on their positions relative to others. The two defining points of reference in such programs in the Sufi context are the positions occupied by the master and the disciple.

Mastery and discipleship are roles that could be occupied by the same person, depending on who he or she was confronting: great masters remained disciples in front of their own masters no matter how many others saw them as masters. The behaviors expected of masters and disciples presume the other half of the dyad, each one being thoroughly interpenetrated by the other. The repercussions of this paradigm are evident by considering the behaviors ascribed to some of the great masters. The rules of etiquette defined Sufis as a general group in society who were attempting to live in a certain way. But etiquette also helped some Sufis to coalesce around particular masters, to whom they would pay special respect as their spiritual guides. Such smaller groups were designated *tariqas* or fellowships of disciples devoted to the charismatic presence and particular practice of specific masters.

The principle of status differentiation at the base of the master-disciple relationship had a more universalistic application in the notion of a hierarchy that Sufis perceived to be embedded in the world at all moments in time. The idea that living friends of God constitute a hierarchy has roots in the earliest period in which Sufi ideas began to cohere as a distinctive Islamic paradigm. Such a hierarchy depended on the idea of friendship with God that allowed for differentiated proximity with the divine in conjunction with one's spiritual achievements. In the Persianate sphere during the fourteenth and fifteenth centuries, Sufi authors understood this hierarchy as both a theoretical idea and something realized in the world in which they lived in the form of great masters.

The synchronic social world constituted of masters and disciples that comes into focus through considering Sufi etiquette and a worldwide hierarchy was cut through by diachronic lines of affiliation represented by genealogies and Sufi lineages going to earlier periods. The two most consequential principles in this regard were the status of being a sayyid—meaning claiming descent from Muhammad and ʿAli—and belonging to *silsilas* or chains of Sufis extending backward in time. The record indicates Sufis coming to place greater and greater emphasis on these lineages over the period 1300–1500. Valuations of lineage could sometimes stand in opposition to the interests of a charismatic master who claimed initiation via otherworldly experiences. In all, while the lineage never became an absolute paradigm for the assertion of Sufi legitimacy, its prestige certainly seems to have increased over the course of the fourteenth and fifteenth centuries. Lineages were venues for social cohesion as well as dispersion and competition since masters nearly always had genealogical descendants as well as many prominent students who competed with each other for their mantles after their deaths. This process produced an atmosphere of rivalry between lineages as well as among different masters in the same lineage that is a prominent aspect of the social world reflected in hagiographic narratives.

The overlap between representations of individual bodies and the social body is a recurrent motif in this book. In the remainder of the present chapter, I take up, one by one, the playing out of this theme in the sphere of etiquette, universal hierarchy, and the organization of Sufi communities around lineages. Perhaps the most salient issue to be observed in abundance in these discussions is the fact that all human bodies we see represented in hagiographic narratives acquire their significations through linkages to the bodies of others. A focus on corporeal themes therefore consistently leads to social matters, here exemplified in patterned interactions expected of Sufis active in the Persianate world.

ETIQUETTE: MASTERS AND DISCIPLES INTERTWINED

According to his hagiographer, Baha' ad-Din Naqshband is said to have recited the following verses in the context of defining an accomplished Sufi:

> A friend of God has three markers, the first being this:
>   When you see his face your heart is drawn to him.
> Second, when he speaks in gatherings,
>   He steals everyone from his being to what he is saying.
> And the third indicator of the friend, the elect of the world, is this:
>   No wrong deed ever comes from any organ of his body.[1]

Friends of God are to be seen as charismatic masters of their surroundings who have complete power over all the organs of their own bodies as well as the hearts and minds of their companions.

In referring to the master's bodily organs, Naqshband's primary allusion in these verses is to the fact that masters' bodies avoid all unlawful or unethical actions. Many hagiographic descriptions of masters' public comportment take the kind of corporeal control indicated here many steps further by showing them to be ultimate masters of social etiquette. Maintaining *adab* or proper etiquette while following the path was a major concern of Sufi authors from the earliest period and gave rise to a whole literary genre containing extensive prescriptions for how masters and disciples should behave in various situations.[2] One such popular manual of etiquette, written by the Suhravardi master 'Izz ad-Din Mahmud Kashani (d. 1335), prescribes that Sufi shaykhs should always be sincere, should live up to what they teach, should not abuse their disciples' trust in them, and should be humble in front of disciples despite their power over them.[3]

Handbooks prescribing Sufi behavior provide greater details for the behavior expected of disciples rather than masters since the latter are presumed to have already reached high stations. However, we can observe the etiquette expected of masters by looking at texts that describe them for the sake of attracting disciples. In this vein a hagiographic work dedicated to Niʿmatullah Vali states that, when sitting in company, the master never moved his hands to touch his limbs or facial hair. He never did uncouth things like spitting, and no one ever saw him sleeping. He ate and drank very little and wore simple clothes and headgear in the tradition of Muhammad and earlier Sufi masters. A belt around the waist was the only thing that indicated he was a Sufi, since he never wore robes and other paraphernalia used by some Sufis to flaunt their religious vocation in public. His room was often adorned with flowers, and he spoke with such eloquence that one thought one was reading a book rather than listening to a person.[4]

Similar qualities are attributed to the Naqshbandi master Khwaja Ahrar. Because he refused to participate in childish games with his companions, his seriousness of purpose was evident throughout his childhood. One of his cousins recalled that other children would insist on his joining their play, and sometimes he would agree and get ready but would then refuse at the last moment. This is interpreted as an indication of his protection from sin (ʿisma), since this way he could not cross the bounds of appropriate behavior even inadvertently.[5]

Ahrar maintained his impeccable manners when he became a renowned master in later life. One man who acted as his personal attendant for many months on two occasions said that he never saw him yawn, cough, or expel phlegm or any other liquid from his mouth. He also never sat cross-legged, whether alone or while in company. Another person who observed him for thirty-five years claimed that he never once saw him spit even a fruit skin or stone from his mouth. He never blew his nose in company even when he was suffering from a cold because his bodily organs were simply incapable of creating an unpleasant impression for onlookers. On one occasion, some visitors decided to participate in his regular vigils and were impressed that, despite his age, he could sit erect for hours at night without moving a muscle or giving the least bit of indication of slumber. On this occasion he performed the morning prayer with the same ablutions that he had done at the beginning of the night, indicating his complete power over not only his limbs but even his internal organs.[6] As seen in these descriptions of Niʿmatullah Vali and ʿUbaydullah Ahrar, the fully mature master is marked most strongly by a sense of total control over his body's functions and acts. Indeed, in considerable part, it is the very fact of such control, which ordinary human beings lack with respect to their bodies, that defines Sufi mastery as it is depicted in hagiographic literature.

As can be readily imagined, the imperative of proper etiquette pertained even more strongly to disciples than to masters, and prescriptions toward this end form the bulk of the contents of Sufi *adab* literature. A brief but usefully illustrative example is a work by the master Muhammad Khabushani (d. 1531–32) that gives specific details for the way disciples' bodies are supposed to position themselves in the presence of masters. Khabushani writes that when the disciple enters the master's quarters he opens and closes the door carefully, steps lightly on the floor, and does nothing that would upset the master and compel him to withhold the benefits of his company. He sits so that the points of his toes or his profile never face the master and he never walks in front of a source of light, such as the sun or a lamp, so that his body is never in a position to cast a shadow on the master. He does not get too close to the master, fearing him to the degree to think that if the master's shadow were to fall on him, he would burn. He never closes his eyes or goes into meditative contemplation in front of the master. He never touches the master's clothes, prayer rug, or cane without being in a state of ritual purity, and never puts his feet on the place where the master sits even when he is not present. Khabushani states that these are just a few rules that apply since the overall paradigm requires each and every minute action on the part of the disciple becoming attuned to the master's presence in the world. In his view: "When the dervish performs a bath in the sea of etiquette, thereby dissolving in the fire of the master's company and finding the elixir of the master's gaze, then he becomes deserving of being in the solitary retreat (*khalvat*)."[7]

The self-negating dedication the disciple is required to show to the master is in evidence throughout the numerous stories cited in this book. An extreme example of this is given in the *Rashahat-i 'ayn al-hayat* where Khwaja Ahrar praises a certain Rukn ad-Din Khwafi for his unreservedly humble attitude. This man is reported to have said that he attached no hopes to the actions he had performed in life save for one: "One day the master Zayn ad-Din 'Ali Kula, a shaykh in Shiraz, was busy purifying himself, and I rubbed the clod of dirt he was going to use to clean himself after the call of nature on my cheek before giving it to him."[8]

This very brief consideration of etiquette literature conveys the connectedness of the roles occupied by masters and disciples in Persianate societies. Of course, the very idea of a Sufi master presumes the presence of disciples, and vice versa, making the two roles mutually interdependent by definition. As a consequence, in hagiographic works, we see disciples observing and memorializing the masters in their attempt to preserve their words and their physical demeanor. Disciples, on the other hand, are shown fashioning their lives in the images of masters, molding each and every action of their bodies to the masters' physical presence. Abstract rules of etiquette articulate these two imperatives in theoretical terms while hagiographic texts exemplify them in both content and form: they provide images of masters for disciples to emulate, and their whole literary demeanor drips with unqualified devotion to masters, conveying the disciple's part in the theater of Sufi social performance. In a similar manner, paintings depict people placed around the master in carefully arranged scenes to display their relative positions based on age and religious status. For example, a painting attributed to the great master Kamal ad-Din Bihzad shows the poet Nizami instructing his son sitting in a group of older men (figure 3.1). The verses at the top right comment on the boy's transition into adulthood at the age of fourteen, comparing the moment to a cypress tree raising its top to display its height. The inscription above the door in the facade that occupies the left side of the building gives the painting's date. A verse within the frieze at the very top states:

> Company of dervishes is the eternal paradise.
> Servitude to dervishes is a tremendous treasure.

The painting depicts the incorporation of a young man into a Sufi collectivity, paying attention to the idea that this required the cultivation of devotion and servitude calibrated carefully with respect to the master and other members of the hierarchically arranged community.[9]

A look at some specific hagiographic stories can help us appreciate the fact that mastery and discipleship were functions performed according to societal scripts rather than reflecting personal predilections of particular individuals. Most revealingly, some masters are shown to react ambiguously to disciples' obeisance. A dervish reported that once when he was with Baha' ad-Din Naqshband in the public baths, disciples were arriving and would rub their faces against his feet. An attendant at the bath then came in and proceeded to kiss this dervish's feet before pouring water over the master's feet. Naqshband intuited that this made the dervish uncomfortable and reassured him by saying, "He is a supplicant coming through from the door of supplication. Since you are below me, he had to come through your door first."[10] In a slightly different attitude, Shaykh 'Umar Murshidi allowed disciples to kiss his hands and feet but insisted that he would first do the same to them.[11]

In a story that lays out the greater repercussions of proper etiquette, a man named Majd ad-Din Surkhi reported that he had a great desire to rub his face on the feet of Zayn ad-Din Taybadi (d. 1389). One day, as the master was showing special kindness to him, he mentioned this desire to him, but this caused the master to become enraged. When this caused Surkhi to become extremely regretful for having expressed the desire, Taybadi showered great kindness once again and said, happily:

> "Being a Sufi is all about etiquette. In the path of being a wretch (*faqiri*), etiquette is the root of all other works. All other acts must feed into etiquette

3.1   The poet Nizami instructing his son. Attributed to Bihzad, 1482. 26.5 × 16 cm.
Copyright © Musée d'art et d'histoire, Geneva. 1971-107/424.

since it is their great fruit and powerful result." After these instructions and gentleness, he said: "Just now the spiritual presence (*ruhaniyat*) of the Prophet, peace be upon him, appeared to me and I kissed his hand. The fortune of your hand that reached my hand, and the fortune of any hand that reaches yours, is that the fire of hell cannot touch it. Now take my hand and kiss it." I became extremely happy knowing this and went in front of him to kiss his hand and rub my face on it. I felt that I had been approved for, or rather had found, salvation.[12]

Connecting to the theme with which I began this book, this story displaces the meanings of the disciplinary and self-abnegating acts involved in following Sufi rules of etiquette from the physical acts to the necessity of acquiring religious merit and authority through connections to other persons. As such, the story is a stand-in for the overarching significance of etiquette as a social discourse that functioned to intertwine the lives of Sufis at many different levels of accomplishment.

HIERARCHIES OF DIVINE FRIENDSHIP

From the earliest extant Sufi discussions in Persian, we are told that friends of God were a form of divine mercy and that their presence in the world was necessary for it to continue existing.[13] Sufi theoretical discussions on friendship with God generally divide cosmic salvation history into two parts: the period from Adam to Muhammad is the era of prophecy, while after Muhammad begins the era of friendship. In the latter period, the teachings and companionship of friends constitute God's guidance for other human beings, and their miraculous powers represent God's beneficence in the world. These friends form a group of human beings that occupies a special religious rank, although its members live embedded in the general population and are quite often unaware of their chosen status. From an early period, Sufis also started to divide the saints into various classes, according to their achievements, perceived closeness to God, and the kind of miracles they could perform. Such classification is formalized in the notion of an elaborate hierarchy of God's friends spread over the earth.

In the Persianate historical setting, it was a commonplace Sufi idea that the continued existence of the world was contingent on the presence of this hierarchy of God's friends. The hierarchy culminated in a pole (*qutb*) who represented the consummation of all human qualities and abilities and was regarded as the perfect microcosmic mirror standing between the macrocosm on the one side and God on the other. All other friends were seen as weaker forms of this pole, and humans outside the category of friends were considered still weaker specimens of the species. For anyone who wanted to advance on the Sufi path, it was necessary to, first, recognize those who were already a part of the hierarchy and then become attached to them through discipleship. This imperative led Sufis to join one another in widespread social webs that emanated outward from the most famous masters, who were regarded as the poles of their times by their followers.[14]

Hierarchies in the Persianate Sphere

By the fourteenth and fifteenth centuries, most Sufis took the presence of some type of Sufi hierarchy in the world as a fact and used it to situate masters they themselves witnessed around them. This was particularly the case with hagiographers, whose attempts to establish the reputations of their subjects included frequent reference to them as the poles of their times. In addition, they also tended to give these masters' prominent companions epithets denoting the status of friends on the lower rungs of the hierarchy. Hagiographic appropriation of the idea thus turned the grand universal hierarchy into a local court assembled around masters who were the subjects of particular narratives.[15]

The exact details of the hierarchy of saints vary considerably between different accounts generated in the Persianate sphere. In fact, one gets the general impression that an exact plan for the hierarchy was not a matter of great concern for many. For instance, a work dedicated to ʿAli Hamadani provides many different schemes for the way the hierarchy can be constituted. In the first place in the text where the subject is mentioned, the author provides a long hadith report (used in earlier schemes as well) that states, "As long as the heavens and the earth subsist, God will maintain (on the earth) three hundred men whose hearts are like the heart of Adam, forty whose hearts are like that of Moses, seven whose hearts are like the heart of Abraham, five whose hearts are like the heart of Gabriel, three whose hearts are like the heart of Michael, and one whose heart is like the heart of Israfil."[16] Whenever a person in any of the levels dies, someone from the lower rung is promoted upward, and the whole hierarchy adjusts accordingly. The fact of death means that the structure is constantly in motion, with new individuals being inducted into friendship from ordinary people beginning at the lowest level.

A little later in the same text, however, the author provides various schemes consisting of 96, 4,000, 20,000, and 422 saints that also function on the same principle of substitution cited for the first case.[17] He seems to suggest that any and all of these schemes may be applied to the situation at a given time. These schemes appear as different but equally valid ways of taxonomizing friendship as a Sufi institution.

As mentioned previously, the hierarchy's most crucial figure is the pole, the position for which hagiographers usually nominate their protagonists. The pole's crucial cosmic function is stated succinctly in a work dedicated to Ni'matullah Vali that states: "All divine graces that reach the world and those who live in it do so through the mediation of the pole's being. These graces first descend upon his holy heart and then divide out from this ocean into brooks that are the hearts of other friends of God and close companions. From there, they branch out into rivulets to reach all that remains."[18] The pole is therefore the sole conduit for God's continuing interaction with the created world and all humans wishing to partake of divine emanation must relate to him either directly or through intermediaries close to him.

When hagiographic authors place their favorite saints at the center of the hierarchy with other companions strewn all around, the effect is that the world appears seeded with saints belonging to the various classes that are part of the hierarchy. In such a world the key issue for those who want to be Sufis is to identify those who are already in the hierarchy and become devoted to them or their associates. Ultimately, they themselves have to become friends of God to fully recognize others in the hierarchy, but the journey has to begin through attachment to masters identifiable as friends. Once such an identification has been made, the novices are required to submit to the masters in all their endeavors.

LINEAGES

So far in this chapter I have discussed matters that pertained to Sufis as a general social group in Persianate societies; etiquette and the hierarchy of God's friends are universal principles that mattered to Sufis across groups and subgroups. In the remainder of this chapter, I will consider the paradigm of membership in Sufi lineages that differentiated Sufis from each other on the basis of historical constructions connecting individuals to ancestors or forbears initiated into particular identities or modes of practice.

The two types of lineages that mattered most in the Persianate context, often invoked in tandem, are the status of being a *sayyid* (claiming descent from Muhammad and 'Ali), and belonging to a chain (*silsila*) of Sufis extending backward to the time of the Prophet. Famous masters such as 'Ali Hamadani, Ni'matullah Vali, Qasim-i Anvar, and Muhammad Nurbakhsh combined the honor of being sayyids with initiation into important Sufi chains. Their hagiographies make a point of asserting their genealogical distinction as a part of their claims. In a case reflecting respect for sayyids due from nonsayyids, a Naqshbandi hagiography relates the story of someone who saw Muhammad's daughter Fatima in a dream being very cross with him. When he inquired the reason for this, she replied that he had been rude to one of her descendants, who ought to be respected irrespective of any infractions of etiquette he may have committed.[19] In a similar vein, Muhammad is said to have appeared in a dream to Sayyid ʿAli Hamadani to say that whoever is descended from him has no reason to ask for aid from the ever-living prophets Khizr and Elias.[20]

In contrast to the more or less constant regard for sayyids, there is a general tendency over the course of the fourteenth and fifteenth centuries for the masters' personal charisma to become overshadowed by the legitimacy they derived from the chains to which they belonged. This is an understandable development given that this period saw a considerable expansion of Sufi communities that were subdivided into smaller groups centered on masters with varying ranges of influence. By extending backward in time, Sufi chains provided legitimacy for the new communities being formed by the various competing disciples of any major master.

Two different angles on interrelationships between Khwajagani-Naqshbandi masters can illustrate the opposing forces that coexist in the lineage principle (figure 3.2). Seen from the viewpoint of a particular practitioner such as Khwaja Ahrar, the chain is imagined as a straight line connecting him to Baba Sammasi and earlier masters via the intermediacy of Charkhi, Naqshband, and Amir Kulal. But when examined as a historical phenomenon, this chain contains multiple subdivisions extending outward from each linking point. Historiographically, then, the Khwajagan-Naqshbandiyya consists of multiple collateral chains that include masters with no direct connection to Ahrar, such as Amir Kulal and his descendants, Muhammad Parsa, ʿAlaʾ ad-Din ʿAttar, Saʿd ad-Din Kashghari, and ʿAlaʾ ad-Din Abizi. Precisely because the chain mattered deeply for claims of authority put forth by an individual master and his community, it was the primary arena in which various masters and their hagiographers constructed their own rights of spiritual inheritance and negated those of their rivals. The same principle applied to the status of sayyids as well since many different genealogical groups competed with each other for being regarded as heirs to the Prophet.[21]

While the status of being a sayyid was a matter of genealogical claim by a person or a family, to be seen as belonging to a chain required Sufis to experience events that would connect them to masters already in the lineage. Hagiographic narratives represent the establishment of such connections in a number of different ways. To provide a sampling of this theme, in the following pages I will discuss three different cases of Sufis becoming incorporated into chains. These include: individuals perceived as being born into lineages, ritual initiations involving oaths that induct someone into a chain, and initiations in dreams and visions. These three ways of forming links to lineages are deployed

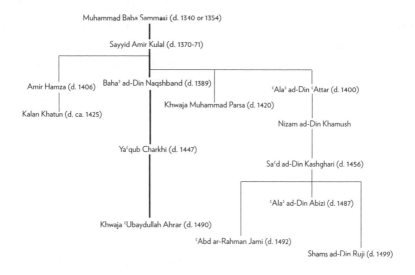

Muhammad Baba Sammasi (d. 1340 or 1354)

Sayyid Amir Kulal (d. 1370-71)

Amir Hamza (d. 1406)   Baha' ad-Din Naqshband (d. 1389)   'Ala' ad-Din 'Attar (d. 1400)

Kalan Khatun (d. ca. 1425)   Khwaja Muhammad Parsa (d. 1420)

Nizam ad-Din Khamush

Ya'qub Charkhi (d. 1447)

Sa'd ad-Din Kashghari (d. 1456)

'Ala' ad-Din Abizi (d. 1487)

Khwaja 'Ubaydullah Ahrar (d. 1490)

'Abd ar-Rahman Jami (d. 1492)

Shams ad-Din Ruji (d. 1499)

3.2   Chart 1: Cohesion and dispersion in Khwajagani-Naqshbandi lineages.

sometimes separately, and at other times together, in narratives aimed at legiti-mizing Sufi masters' claims.

Born to God's Friendship

Hagiographic narratives concerned with Baha' ad-Din Naqshband provide an example of someone being incorporated into a Sufi chain prior to his birth. The author writes that the great master was born in the village of Qasr-i Hinduvan (the "Abode of the Indians" that was later renamed Qasr-i 'Arifan, or "Abode of the Knowledgeable," in his honor) near the Central Asian city of Bukhara. Three days after his birth, the Khwajagani master Muhammad Sammasi passed through the village and Naqshband's grandfather, who was devoted to Sam-masi, presented the infant to him for a blessing. As soon as he saw the child he said, "He is our son and we have accepted him." After this instantaneous recognition, he turned to his companion Sayyid Amir Kulal and recalled that a number of times when he had passed through this village he had told Amir Kulal that the dust of this place emitted the smell of a special man. This time the smell had become intensified, and he had remarked that perhaps that man had been born. He then identified the child as the awaited one and expressed the hope that he would be a leader of his age.[22]

Naqshband's hagiographer writes that the master considered this incident his first incorporation into the Khwajagani chain of Sufi authority. The fact that Sammasi addressed his words to Amir Kulal was particularly significant since the latter eventually acted as Naqshband's immediate teacher and predecessor in the chain.[23] The most noteworthy aspect of this story is the close perceived connection between human bodies and the earth from which they are constituted. The body's origins in dust (*khak*) are universally acknowledged in Persian linguistic usage, but here this aspect gets accentuated through the notion that the saintly body is formed of special dust that gives off characteristics identifiable by other Sufis even before it is constituted into a human corporeal form. Also, this relationship between the earth of a particular place and the bodies that rise from it makes it possible to regard saints' birthplaces as sacred locations.

Stories similar to the ones told of Naqshband are found in the hagiography of the later master Khwaja Ahrar. One of his hagiographers states that for four months before the master's moment of conception his father felt like he was carrying a great burden. As a result of this he spent this time in seclusion and felt himself to be greatly relieved when the seed was transferred from him to the womb of the future master's mother.[24] Ahrar's body therefore had weight and potency before its formation in a recognizeable form. Later, a Naqshbandi master by the name of Khwaja Shihab ad-Din Shashi immediately recognized Ahrar's impending greatness when he saw him as a child. He rubbed his face all over Ahrar's body and lamented that he was too old to be alive at the time in the future when the promise he could see would become manifest in the world.[25]

Outside the Naqshbandi milieu, the idea that the elect among Sufis can recognize their successors even before their births is affirmed in an autobiographical narrative written by Muhammad Nurbakhsh, who claimed to be the messiah himself because he was the greatest Sufi adept of his age. Nurbakhsh's messianic confession is an isolated case that can be called an autohagiography: it is written exactly in the form of a hagiography except that, unlike other such texts, he eulogizes himself and his companions instead of earlier masters. Nurbakhsh claims that some time before he had been conceived his father (a sayyid) became seriously ill, and people thought that he was about to die. When he realized this, he assured them that that was impossible since he still had to father the future saint. When Nurbakhsh's mother was pregnant with him, his father would point to her stomach and say that this is my son Muhammad who is going to do such and such. The mother's companion teasingly told him it was a girl when the child was born. He flew into a rage and declared that he was not a sayyid if it was not a boy. She then told him that it was a boy with blue eyes. He rejected this as well, and when his eyes were proven not to be blue, it underscored the fact that he had substantial specific knowledge about Nurbakhsh's body before the child's birth.[26]

In claims put forth in these stories, lineages are seen as inherent in the materials that come to form Sufi bodies. This is, of course, the basis on which genealogical inheritance is privileged in every context in which it carries value. However, it is important to note that the hagiographers take care to show the claims being made and ratified in the social sphere, by being put in the mouths of those who are already in the lineages in question. Whether justified through parents or through Sufis acknowledged as masters, incorporation into lineages occurs through speech issued during public performances. In Nurbakhsh's case, this pertains to establishing his credentials as a sayyid from his father, whereas statements about Naqshband and Ahrar link the charisma perceived to be inherent in their bodies to the Khwajagani chain of Sufi authority. The process is bidirectional since in it masters' authority is domesticated to the abstract chains while the chains acquire local material hosts in the forms of masters' bodies.

Rituals of Initiation

Although Naqshband, Ahrar, and Nurbakhsh are presented as born friends of God in hagiographic representation, these men also underwent explicit initiations into the Sufi chains to which they belonged in later life. Such initiations were ritual processes whose symbolic elements marked particular moments in Sufis' lives as points of transformation and emphatic commitment. Here I would like to consider two examples of such initiations that are presented in the hagiographic record in appreciable detail.

The hagiography of the Iranian master Amin ad-Din Balyani provides a description of the method of initiation employed within his community in southern Iran.[27] The author of this work reports the shaykh to have said that the cutting of hair and wearing of a dervish's clothes that occurs during Sufi initiation are the equivalent of a master laying down the foundations of a fortress for someone who is under attack and needs to protect himself. The foundation alone does not carry out the whole work of protection, but no fortress can ever be built without first laying down the foundation. The initiation appears here as a foundation made out of words, upon which the disciple builds the fortress using the effort of his mind and body.

The hagiographer relates that, when carrying out the initiation, Balyani would sit the prospective disciple down in front of him and begin with Arabic prayers that consisted of greetings to Sufis of the past and present and a call for God's blessings upon the Prophet and those who have chosen to follow his commands. Then he would instruct the disciple to repeat after him that from here on he would abstain from acts against God's will and do only that which pleases Him. Then he would take scissors and, one by one, cut three hairs from the disciple's forelock, saying each time in Persian, "With the permission of God, the Prophet, Shaykh Abu Ishaq, and Shaykh 'Abdallah." Following this, he would slowly take hold of a quantity of hair from the right side, saying a long prayer in Arabic that recalled God as light and as the one who bestows light and guidance on human beings. The ritual would finish with the shaykh putting the cut strands of hair on his own head and saying more prayers in Arabic, calling on God's mercy, guidance, and aid, and asking for protection from the evils of sinning, pride, and doubt.[28]

This description provides a generalized initiation procedure to be followed in all cases, which would be adapted to the particular relationship between a master and a disciple in actual cases. The initiatory moment would then mark the crossing of a significant threshold within a longer history between the two individuals. To see the full impact of what the initiation accomplished requires considering the periods before and after it as well.

A good example for an initiation in context is Jaʿfar Badakhshi's description of his relationship with the Kubravi master ʿAli Hamadani, described in Bada-khshi's work *Khulasat al-manaqib (The Summary of Virtues)*. Badakhshi provides a number of details from Hamadani's early life, but his portrayal of the master as a shaykh is keyed mostly to the author's own interactions. He reports that as a young man in search of religious guidance he went to the village of ʿAlishah in Khuttalan in 1371–72 where one of his companions saw a dream informing him of the arrival of a friend of God in their midst in a year's time. Hamadani then appeared there exactly a year later and greatly impressed Badakhshi with his knowledge of Sufi literature and the ability to provide answers to religious questions.[29] Badakhshi tried to draw close to Hamadani, but the master rejected the overtures, which caused the latter to become sad and troubled. Eventually, however, he was accepted as a disciple when the friend who had originally seen the dream heralding Hamadani's arrival interceded on his behalf and the master promised to accept his oath after a forty-day Sufi retreat. This friend interceded on his behalf on two occasions: first, when he informed him of Hamadani's im-pending arrival through the dream and, second, when he asked the master to accept him. When he came to the master's presence on the appointed day, he felt confounded as he saw only a form of glittering light where Hamadani's body was supposed to be present. He came to his senses after a few moments, and the master asked him to sit down in front of him.[30]

Although Hamadani conveyed some of his opinions to Badakhshi on this oc-casion, he deferred the acceptance of his oath of discipleship, which eventually took place more than two months later, after Hamadani once again tried to dissuade Badakhshi from it. At the eventual moment of success, Hamadani took one of Badakhshi's hands between his own, and the disciple saw it enveloped by a light that filled the whole room. He then felt his turban taken away from his head without his knowledge. He presented it to the master as an offering, saying that the cloth could be made into the straps of his sandals. Hamadani replied that a handkerchief would be more appropriate. Hamadani then used a pair of scissors that had appeared miraculously out of nowhere to cut some strands of hair from Badakhshi's forelock as a part of the initiation (202–3.).

Hamadani led the life of an itinerant dervish, and, in the years after the initiatory oath, Badakhshi was physically present in his company only sporadically. However, Hamadani never reneged on his responsibility to guide him, sending him instructions in dreams or in messages conveyed by people who met him in various places and then traveled to where Badakhshi lived. Hamadani could be a severe master, once telling Badakhshi to leave his company or he would break open his head with his cane because he had failed to comprehend some instructions. He later called him back and said that the master's anger is a kind of mercy during the early stages of a Sufi's path (206–8).

Badakhshi's work carries the tone of a lover who finds pleasure in all aspects of the beloved's attention toward him, a type of relationship whose details are discussed in chapter 4. After reporting that Hamadani berated and mocked him in one instance, he immediately states that all this was for his own good and that he deserved to be treated in this way (293). He describes the pleasure of having experienced physical proximity to the master when he narrates the moment of seeing Hamadani's sweet-smelling body arrive in Khuttalan after the master's death on the way back from Kashmir: "This poor man, who is the collector of that noble man's effects, has trained other dervishes in seclusion for three months after having heard the sound of zikr from every part of his abode and every part of his body. He has smelled his perfume and tasted the honey of the path on every one of his teeth. These experiences are all branches that have stemmed out from that noble person to reach these beggars, the collectors of his fruit" (284). Badakhshi indicates his closeness to Hamadani as well by telling the reader that the master had entrusted him with his leather shirt and water vessel once when he had gone away on a trip and installed Badakhshi as the caretaker of other disciples. He felt a very strange, overpowering sensation whenever he put on the shirt, the like of which he had never experienced before. The closeness between the bodies of the master and the disciple in this instance is also marked by Badakhshi's report that he later had a dream in which the Prophet Muhammad gave him three things. After the dream, ʿAli Hamadani gave him three things in real life: a toothpick, a silver earwax remover, and iron tweezers for pulling nose hair (296).[31] These instruments are connected to three primary senses—taste, hearing, and smell—so that the master's gift was meant for the intimate grooming and training of the disciple's body in order to make it progress properly on the Sufi path. Additionally, the tools could be taken as gifts indicating Hamadani's confidence in Badakhshi's ability to take care of other, less advanced disciples.

Somersaulting Over Living Masters: Initiation in Dreams and Visions

Although lineage was the dominant form of legitimation among Persianate Sufis, belonging to one of the major chains through explicit connection to a living master was not a completely hegemonic principle. In cases that subvert the lineage principle, the imperative of having a Sufi pedigree is fulfilled through interactions with past figures that occur in the realm of dreams and visions. Such interactions are used to solidify masters' credentials even in cases where they are shown to have undergone initiation or apprenticeship with living masters. For example, although Baha' ad-Din Naqshband was ratified as a member of the Khwajagani chain through Baba Sammasi and Amir Kulal, his foremost claim of belonging to this group came from a vision in which Khwaja 'Abd al-Khaliq Ghijduvani initiated him as his follower in the presence of all the masters who formed the intervening links in the chain.[32] Similar stories can be seen in works devoted to 'Ali Hamadani, Muhammad Nurbakhsh, and others, who are shown to interact with figures such as Muhammad and earlier Sufi masters in their visions and dreams as a matter of course.

I would like to exemplify the presence of charisma outside the main charismatic chains by discussing the local shaykh Ahmad Bashiri whose life is memorialized in a single work. According to his hagiographer, Bashiri related to his companions that, in the beginning of his travels on the Sufi path, he grew completely tired of the sights and smell of normal life and would often retire to the wild, away from home. One day, as he was sitting under a tree by a stream, he went into a trance and saw himself go through seven levels of increasingly torturous hells where he experienced intense burning of his body and felt that all his negative qualities were incinerated one by one.

The journey eventually brought him to the source of the fire, where he realized that, by now, his whole body had come to be composed of nothing but fire. Here he saw many others with similar bodies and made his way to someone who appeared to be the leader. Upon being questioned, this person identified himself as the leader of hell and refused to help Shaykh Bashiri escape the place. The shaykh was downcast over this, but then he saw an immensely beautiful person appear in the same place and was drawn to him. This turned out to be Muhammad, and when the shaykh met him he got the sensation of a drop falling into the ocean. The prophet took charge of him and led him on an ascent to God's throne, which they circumambulated together. Shaykh Bashiri then came out of his trance and realized that the experience had lasted sixteen days, during which his actual body had become covered with dust, having been exposed to the elements. He then made his way home where his mother told him that the family had been worried about him and unable to find him despite extensive searching. She had trouble believing his account of where he had been because they had searched the area near the stream multiple times and had seen no one there. He explained this to his companions by referring to the accounts of prior Sufis who said that the body becomes invisible to ordinary humans when it is undergoing an extensive experience in the interior world, as had been the case with Bashiri's sixteen-day trance.[33]

As with initiations that occur in the material sphere, Shaykh Bashiri's experience in this story was a major transformational point in his life. The most traditional aspect of the narrative is the encounter with Muhammad and the ascension to God's throne in his company, through which the shaykh joined countless other Sufis before him who had gone on similar journeys that emulated Muhammad's celebrated night journey (mi'raj).[34] This part of Bashiri's experience marked him as an Uvaysi Sufi, a term that refers to the relationship between Muhammad and a man named Uvays Qarani who converted to Islam without ever meeting the Prophet.[35] More significantly, the story shows the shaykh undergoing a kind of rebirth into a new body that is ratified through both internal experience and external observation. On the interior side of things, he sees his original body completely consumed by fire and then, through his contact with Muhammad, he acquires a new body that receives the distinction of journeying to the proximity of God's throne. And, on the exterior side, first his normal body disappears from the sight of ordinary people for the whole period he is in a trance. When he reappears to his companions after his extraordinary experiences, he is in effect a new physical being, devoid of corporeal weaknesses and infused with the effects of his trance.

Shaykh Bashiri's experiences in this story exemplify the central Sufi concepts annihilation (fana') and subsistence (baqa'), the ultimate two goals sought by a person on the Sufi path. As discussed in chapter 1, the first refers to the ideal of annihilating one's self or ego so that the ordinary world becomes extinct to one's being, and the second indicates the further step of coming to subsist solely in and through divine reality. These concepts received extensive elaboration in Sufi theory early in history and were taken for granted by the period that concerns me in this book.[36] As we see them played out in Shaykh Bashiri's story, annihilation and subsistence have psychological as well as physiological aspects. Although much of the experience he recounts takes place within a trancelike state in the interior realm, it affects his body by first making it disappear and then transforming it into a new being upon his return to normalcy.

Experiences similar to these are attributed to saintly bodies in other narratives as well. For example, we are told that Baha' ad-Din Naqshband said that once, when he experienced a total annihilation, his body lost all qualities of life for a period of six hours. Then, when he came back to himself, all his organs started to function one by one, and it took some time before his body became fully normal.[37] In these cases as well as in numerous other examples in Persian-

ate Sufi literature, annihilation denotes a literal fulfillment of the Sufi imperative to die before one's death, and the body's coming back to life is presumed
to be a new corporeal presence marked by subsistence in God. In all the many
forms in which initiations could happen, they represented beginnings of the
paths that could lead Sufis to claim having undergone highly desirable religious
experiences.

COMPETITION IN A SHARED WORLD

The three forms of Persianate Sufi social practices I have discussed in this
chapter—emphasis on etiquette, hierarchies embedded in the world, and lineage as marker of authority—were significant for promoting cohesion among
Sufis on one side and causing dissension on the other. In a given community
formed around a particular master or family, the three practices acted as the
foundations for a collective identity. But, between such communities, charges
of lack of etiquette, rejection of charismatic status, and disputes over the values
of various lineages and sublineages formed the grounds on which to carry out
rivalries and ideological battles. The social world depicted in hagiographic narratives runs the gamut of all the possibilities of relationships between individuals and groups in this regard and presents all that one can imagine to be the
case in any large-scale social discourse operating in a complex stratified society.

In historical terms, the hagiographic record indicates a gradual increase in
mutual hostility between Sufi groups over the course of the fourteenth and fifteenth centuries. As Devin DeWeese has suggested in his many studies of Sufis
in the Mongol and Timurid periods, this rise in intergroup tension is concomitant with the hardening of communal boundaries, with a particular emphasis
on lineage rather than the perceived charisma of individual masters.[38] For the
purposes of my discussion in this chapter, it is worthwhile to consider briefly
some narratives produced toward the end of the period that concerns me in
order to see Persianate Sufism as contested domain in fullest bloom.

Over the course of the fifteenth century, various collateral lines emanating
from Baha' ad-Din Naqshband constituted the most widespread and powerful group of Sufis active in Central Asia. From a sociopolitical viewpoint, the
most important Naqshbandi figure of the period was undoubtedly Khwaja
'Ubaydullah Ahrar, who is the subject of numerous hagiographic narratives.[39]
The most famous such work, 'Ali b. Husayn Kashifi Safi's *Rashahat-i 'ayn al-
hayat* (*Dewdrops from the Source of Life*), is a composite text that relies on earlier
hagiographies to give a rationalized account of the whole history of Khwajagani-
Naqshbandi chains. Safi's account is quite tendentious, since he is compelled to
present the history as a planned unfolding of the chain leading to the life and

work of Khwaja Ahrar, which he presents based on his own observations as well as relaying from other disciples. Safi's narrative of his own incorporation into the chain mirrors some of the themes I have already discussed. He reports that his father said that when he was born in Sabzavar in 867 AH (1463 CE) he was blessed by a member of Khwaja Muhammad Parsa's family on the very first day of his existence. He then became subject to the illness of colic (*umm as-sibyan*), but the visiting master intervened again to cure him and reassured the parents by saying that this boy is destined to do great things and the disease would not be fatal.[40]

Safi's great work, to be accomplished as an adult, was, of course, the writing of the *Rashahat*. His representation of Khwaja Ahrar's life immediately before the master took an oath with a Naqshbandi preceptor is instructive for observing the atmosphere of competition between masters and disciples in Herat. Although Safi's reports claim to represent events that occurred in the first three decades of the fifteenth century, his interpretive gloss more likely reflects the situation of competition that prevailed toward the end of the fifteenth century when his narrative was written.[41]

Safi represents Ahrar as a gifted young man who went around to the various masters in Herat while attempting to define the path he wanted to follow. Before tying himself definitively to the Naqshbandi chain through Ya'qub Charkhi, he spent time with the triumvirate of Shah Qasim-i Anvar, Baha' ad-Din 'Umar, and Zayn ad-Din Khwafi, the most influential masters in the city at the time. In later life he described Qasim-i Anvar as an exceedingly charismatic and perceptive man who had met Naqshband in his early life. Marking a somewhat ambiguous incorporation into the appropriate lineage, Safi reports that Ahrar said that, "sometimes in his [Qasim's] company it seemed that his eminence, the Sayyid, considered himself to be on the path of the Khwajagan, may God sanctify their spirits."[42] Qasim's effect on his disciples is exemplified in the story of one Pir Kil, who, although otherwise quite loquacious, would become tongue-tied in front of the master. As soon as he saw him, his face would change color, and then keep changing to a different color in each passing moment. He was so overwhelmed by respect and deference for the master in his interior that he would do a prostration after every step when walking toward or away from him. Although not fully approving of this behavior, Qasim said that this was all the man was capable of, and he saw it as his job to bring people to the fruition of their innate qualities.[43]

Compared to this show of great awe in the presence of the master directed toward Qasim, in Safi's representation, Khwafi's followers seemed to have been lacking in proper conduct. On one occasion, when Ahrar was at Khwafi's place, the shaykh went into a trancelike state (*istighraq*). Then a certain Mawlana Mahmud Hisari, who considered himself a vicegerent of Khwafi, appeared there with some followers, desiring to study one of Khwafi's works with him. To have their way, this group proceeded to do rude things like stamping their feet and coughing so that the master would come out of his trance. When this proved unsuccessful, they decided to intervene upon him through the interior and sat down and concentrated their thoughts on the master until he awakened and gave them the lesson they sought. Ahrar found this episode to be a case of terribly uncouth behavior and reprehensible etiquette and avoided Khwafi's gathering from then on.[44]

Safi's description of Ahrar's opposing attitudes to Qasim and Khwafi are represented in a dream he saw in which he was standing in the middle of a great highway that had smaller roads leading away on the sides. Suddenly, Khwafi appeared and asked that he come along with him to his village, to which Ahrar felt disinclined. Then Qasim appeared on the highway, riding a white horse, and asked him to come with him on the highway itself, which led to the city. Ahrar climbed onto the horse and went along.[45] The relative sizes of the two roads and the habitations to which they led reflected Ahrar's estimation of these masters' stations next to each other.

Controversy Over the Ideas of Ibn al-ʿArabi

Khwaja Ahrar's experiences in Herat reflect his involvement in a general controversy that pitted Sufis against each other depending on their appraisals of the ideas of the great theoretician Ibn al-ʿArabi. In the history of Sufi thought, Ibn al-ʿArabi's work forms a watershed for the discussion of numerous topics, including the idea of a hierarchy of God's friends and the concentration of authority in a "pole" of the times. His ideas became major venues for Sufi discussion in later centuries when various authors tried to give cogent accounts of his system, often with modifications and further elaborations.[46] In the Persianate arena, nearly unconditional support for his ideas is exemplified in Khwaja Muhammad Parsa's statement regarding his two most influential works: "The *Fusus* (*Bezels*) is life (*jan*) and the *Futuhat* (*Openings*) the heart (*dil*)."[47] Prominent Sufi figures such as ʿAli Hamadani, Niʿmatullah Vali, Shah Qasim-i Anvar, Muhammad Nurbakhsh, ʿAbd ar-Rahman Jami, and Khwaja Ahrar can be shown to have held his works in high regard by writing commentaries on them or citing them in discussions reported in hagiographic narratives.[48]

Ibn al-ʿArabi's ideas were capable of generating tremendous hostility as well as admiration. Stories concerned with Zayn ad-Taybadi and Zayn ad-Din Khwafi show them as being particularly unsympathetic to his views. Taybadi's hagiographer reports that, after the master's death, his grandson Saʿd ad-Din once ran across the *Fusus al-hikam* (*Bezels of Wisdom*) and found it to be beneficial. Being aware of his grandfather's great dislike for this work, he then endeavored to connect with his spirit during the night to see what he would say about the discovery. Halfway through the night, when he was in between the states of waking and sleeping, Taybadi appeared and looked at him with such great anger that he began to tremble. He then proceeded to hand over his walking stick to the grandson, telling him, "Whoever reads the *Fusus* or makes a study of it, hit him with this stick until he quits. This is neither the knowledge of religion (*din*) nor the path toward certitude (*yaqin*). Instead, this is the road of darkness and error."[49]

Zayn ad-Din Khwafi is shown to have held a similarly harsh view of Ibn al-ʿArabi, as evident from the story of his falling out with a man named Ahmad Samarqandi whom he initially regarded as his foremost disciple. The fact that the feeling of respect had been mutual initially is reflected in one report that Samarqandi had proclaimed openly during the Friday sermon in Herat that, just as Muhammad had been the seal of prophecy, Khwafi was the seal of God's friendship.[50] Jami reports that Samarqandi used to teach the *Fusus*, basing his practice on the claim that the Prophet had asked him to do so directly during mystical encounters.[51] Zayn ad-Din Khwafi, who had been his main sponsor among the religious classes in Herat, became upset with him when he would not desist from reciting the verses of Shah Qasim-i Anvar, a well-known proponent of Ibn al-ʿArabi, during his sermons at the congregational mosque in Herat. He then proceeded to declare him a nonbeliever and persecuted him as well as anyone who would aid him in any way. Khwafi's intense antipathy toward Ibn al-ʿArabi was based on considering the notion of "unity of being" (*vahdat-i vujud*), a doctrine associated with Ibn al-ʿArabi and his followers, among the most reprehensible intellectual movements in Islamic history.[52]

In the narrative of the *Rashahat*, Ahrar's views on Qasim and Khwafi are brought to a conclusion through the intermediacy of Bahaʾ ad-Din ʿUmar's opinion regarding Ibn al-ʿArabi. One day, when ʿUmar asked his companions about news from the city, they replied that two things are going around: Shaykh Zayn ad-Din and his companions say that "everything is from him" (*hamah az u ast*), while Sayyid Qasim and his followers say that "everything is he" (*hamah u ast*).[53] When asked to provide his opinion on this, ʿUmar said that Khwafi's followers are correct, although when Ahrar paid close attention to the details of his justification, he seemed to be supporting Qasim's viewpoint. When he pointed this out, ʿUmar began providing even more elaborate explanations, all of which seemed to support Qasim and his followers once again despite the fact that he claimed to be in favor of the views held by Khwafi. From this Ahrar understood that ʿUmar's viewpoint was that outwardly he supported the perspective of Khwafi's followers while, in the interior, he believed in the truth of those who espoused the cause of Qasim.[54] The upshot of this was that ʿUmar was indicating that the doctrine of "oneness of being" ought not to be discussed in public since it was a preserve of the elect, who could comprehend references to it because of their advanced understanding. Among common people, it could lead to misunderstanding because of the lack of proper preparation.

These stories about Ahrar's experiences and attitudes can be related to all the major themes I have touched upon in this chapter. As represented in the opposing actions of Pir Kil and Mahmud Hisari, proper and improper etiquette in front of masters was a primary reason for Ahrar's attraction to Qasim and his lack of enthusiasm for Khwafi. Although preferring Qasim and ʿUmar, he is shown to have given due respect to a well-regarded master such as Khwafi. There is, nevertheless, a clear sense in these narratives that, when in the position of being a disciple, Ahrar placed masters in differing positions in the hierarchy of living Sufis. Although Safi makes no mention here of formalized hierarchies of the type I have discussed, his judgments reflect the same general principle. The conflict between Khwafi and Qasim's followers adjudicated by ʿUmar references the debate on "unity of being": Khwafi was opposed to this idea, seeing God as the *source* of created being but not consubstantial with it in any way whatsoever, while Qasim espoused Ibn al-ʿArabi's belief system, according to which nothing other than God could be said to be truly existent.

It is noteworthy that the solution to the conflict between Qasim and Khwafi as seen in Ahrar's perplexity over ʿUmar's views sidesteps the problem. Instead of giving unequivocal opinions, ʿUmar and Ahrar defer the problem to an issue of perspective, deploying the familiar Sufi differentiation between the interior and the exterior to affirm and negate both sides in equal measure. I believe that the fluidity of meanings exemplified in this story provides a critical clue to understanding the social world of Persianate Sufism. While ideas regarding etiquette, hierarchies, and lineages mattered deeply in this milieu, their actual deployment within specific situations was a matter of perspective and finesse of interpretation rather than an imposition of hard and fast categories. Persianate Sufis holding many different opinions and affiliations worked within a shared world of ideas and practices. Their interpretations of these elements were necessarily quite diverse and varied based on the exigencies of particular situations. The resulting sociointellectual scene was intensely contested and quite malleable at the same time.

In Safi's narrative, Ahrar's interactions with Qasim-i Anvar, Zayn ad-Din Khwafi, and Bahaʾ ad-Din ʿUmar prepare the ground for his eventual acceptance of the Naqshbandi path as his true vocation. A hint of this is provided in the report on Qasim, whom Ahrar clearly liked the best of the three: he is said to have met Naqshband himself and to have conveyed at least the occasional impression that he belonged to the Naqshbandi path. Ahrar's full incorporation into this affiliation occurred through his meeting with Yaʿqub Charkhi, which followed immediately after the narratives regarding the other masters discussed in this chapter. The details of that story belong in the consideration of love as the ultimate cohesive force that bound masters and disciples to each other in the Persianate context.

BODIES INDIVIDUAL AND SOCIAL

To end this chapter, I would like to focus on a vivid painting whose main features should be recognizable on the basis of what I have presented in the first three chapters of this book (figure 3.3). Attributed to Bihzad and dated to around 1490, the painting depicts the scene of a Sufi gathering in a garden. The painting is rich in details despite being quite small (16 x 10.8 cm), containing twenty-three human figures distinguishable from each other on the basis of functions, postures, and attire. Balanced sensitively along both vertical and horizontal axes, the image conveys symmetry as well as careful and precise construction.[55]

Moving from top to bottom, we see bodies depicted as self-consciously still, in vigorous motion, and carried limply in the hands of others. These conditions reflect the various states a person undergoes while pursuing the Sufi path, as described in theoretical works. If the body is to be regarded as a doorway between the interior and exterior realms, as I have suggested in chapter 1, the less agitation it shows during and after crossing over the threshold, the more the embodied person can be said to have mastered the transition. The two masters at the top, their bodies motionless and their heads inclining to each other, preside over the gathering. Their outer garments are in different shades of blue, matching the color of the sky above in a way that increases the association with realms beyond the earth. Their stillness is a reflection of their total control over the passage between interior and exterior realms. In comparison with the masters, the dancers placed in the middle of the painting represent Sufis progressing along the path. Their disheveled bodies show the transformative as well as disruptive effects of the process of crossing the boundary. Finally, the limp figures at the bottom, who have to be helped by others, show the aftereffects of having crossed the boundary earlier like the dancers.

The painting is also the representation of a ritual event, the Sufi samaʿ aimed at cultivating friendship with God discussed in chapter 2. Although they appear to represent states of abandon, the four dancers in the middle are part of an orchestrated performance with specific preparation and predictable outcomes. External inducements, represented by the small party of musicians on the right and the young man reciting poetry on the left, constitute well-acknowledged aides to achieve the corporeal states depicted in the painting and their purported spiritual concomitants. Taken together, the twenty-three human figures mark the occasion as a social scene in which the different bodies convey their

3.3 Sufi samaʿ in a garden. From a copy of Hafiz's *Divan*. Bihzad in Herat, circa 1490. Painting: 16 × 10.8 cm. Image copyright © Metropolitan Museum of Art, New York. Rogers Fund, 1917 (17.81.4).

characteristics not in isolation but through comparison with those that surround them. The postures of the human figures, and their relative positions on the vertical axis, reflect the implementation of principles of Sufi etiquette, the cornerstone of Sufi social life that I have discussed in the present chapter. The scene joins those present into a community participating in an event that marks their interdependence and solidarity.

What I have said so far amounts to noting the painting's formalistic features, corresponding to frameworks for approaching Persianate Sufism from the perspective of embodiment. But the painting also represents matters beyond structures and can be read more deeply than this. The scene of overlapping bodies at the bottom indicates the crossing of bodily boundaries within the represented community. In hagiographical materials, such interpenetration of bodies is tied closely to the effects of love and desire on the senses and body parts. It is noteworthy that the painting contains only male bodies, including beardless boys, young men with dark facial hair, and older men with grey or white beards. These figures' interrelated presence in a single scene indicates intergenerational mimesis between male bodies, a significant theme in Persian hagiographic narratives in the later medieval period. The absence of female bodies indexes the fact that, in this milieu, girls and women could not be represented intermingling publicly with unrelated men in the way shown in the painting. While female bodies do appear in hagiographic narratives, they are burdened with significant ambivalence in terms of socioreligious valuation. Their exclusion from the painting is, therefore, a marker of their marginality to the idealized world that forms the scene.

In addition to religious affect, the painting can be read to reflect the place of Sufism in the politics of Persianate societies. The figure on the top left leaning on a staff may represent the vizier ʿAlishir Navaʾi (d. 1501), an accomplished poet who was the chief sponsor of the cultural efflorescence associated with the reign of the Timurid king Husayn Bayqara in Herat between 1469 and 1506. This identification is possible on the basis of the figure's similarity to a portrait of the vizier dated to circa 1500.[56] Irrespective of a positive identification, the very fact that this precious painting ever came into existence marks the currency of Sufi ideas and practices in the highest echelons of society. Miniature painting was a private art, kept in books and albums, accessible to the very few able to afford such luxuries, and representing their ideals and aspirations as a class. Bihzad was first and foremost a court painter, paid to deploy his art in the interests of the Timurid and Safavid dynasties. The pervasive presence of Sufi themes in this art reflects the prestige held by Sufi men and lineages in this sociohistorical context. The likeness of Navaʾi in a painting depicting a Sufi community is symptomatic of the way Persianate Sufi actors were enmeshed in structures of power and authority in the society in which this painting was produced.

Bringing matters like love, desire, gender, intergenerational transitions, and political power into the reading of texts and paintings allows us to put Sufi bodies in motion. Such considerations enable us to lift still images from two-dimensional pages and make them multidimensional in space and time. In attempting to do so in the remainder of this book, my overall aim will be to reconstruct the socioreligious imagination that I see reflected in sources left behind by Sufis active in the Persianate world.

II. SUFI BODIES IN MOTION

4

BONDS OF LOVE

Love came and began flowing like blood, under my skin, in my veins;
    pushing my self out of me, it filled me up with the friend.
Now the friend has so gripped all parts of my being,
    all that is left to me of myself is my name, the rest is all him.
— POPULAR SUFI QUATRAIN

In Persianate societies during the centuries that concern me, being a Sufi implied that one had come under the spell of love. This is readily evident in the period's linguistic usage where words meaning lover and beloved are used ubiquitously to designate Sufis in prose and poetry alike. The ultimate object for Sufis' love was God, after whose beauty poets such as the famous Jalal ad-Din Rumi pined away while lamenting their own shortcomings revealed as a consequence of their passion. By this period the accumulated corpus of Sufi writings in Arabic and Persian contained extensive discussions on the necessity of loving God, who was himself characterized as a being who loved his creation.[1]

While Sufi understandings of love for God have been the subject of a number of studies, much less attention has been paid to the fact that medieval Sufis also considered love to be the primary force underlying human beings' intimate relationships with each other. Hagiographic narratives resound with the rhetoric of love as it pertains to human relationships, providing ample evidence that bonds based on love constituted the bedrock of Sufi communal life in these societies. My discussion in chapter 4 addresses this lacuna in our understanding by treating the general patterns as well as the social effects of the Sufi discourse on love as witnessed in literature produced during the fourteenth and fifteenth centuries. The material I cover here is complemented by discussions to come in chapter 5 that complicate the idealized Sufi notion of love by paying attention to gender and the problem of seduction that may lead to non-Sufi ends.

The focus on love feeds into this book's overall aim of using body-related themes to understand the functioning of Persianate Sufi communities in two ways. First, the question of love is front and center in the original sources, and highlighting stories that invoke the rhetoric of love conveys the overall social atmosphere that comes across when one reads hagiographic literature. Since love is intimately tied to corporeality in this context, uncovering the mechanics of love relationships provides a window into the imagination of the body. The second significance of love connects to the fact that human relationships described in terms of love produce obligations and expectations that are open to manipulation by those involved. The modulation of love relationships is intimately tied not only to affection but also to domination, submission, and control; concentrating on the way such relationships are represented in the sources provides a sense of the way power operated in a social milieu conditioned by Sufi ideas and practices.

The chapter is divided into sections that treat, successively, the bases, distinctive patterns, and social consequences of the medieval Sufi view of love. I begin by mapping out the general properties associated with love as a force and with lovers and beloveds as stock characters in Islamic discourses. This discussion centers on Persian poetic paradigms that acted as models for Sufi social relationships in the period. I argue that although medieval Sufi hagiographers relied heavily on the poetic rhetoric of love, their overall perspective on love saw it as something more than a fictional abstraction manipulated by poets to showcase their ingenuity. While poets' ultimate aim was to highlight the nuances of characteristics associated with lovers and beloveds, Sufis used the poetic love tale to underscore forces that acted upon Sufis as they were striving to live up to their religious ideals. For Sufis the fiction of love as elaborated upon in Persian poetry acted as a kind of flexible script they utilized to articulate their mutual relationships.[2]

Hagiographies narrating the full life stories of major Sufis work through a cycle of love that I have divided into three phases. Persianate Sufis destined to achieve great spiritual and social status are most often shown to begin their paths in earnest when they fall in love with masters. Descriptions of these events rely heavily on the language of "love at first sight," and, in a number of cases, the development of a relationship with a master goes hand in hand with coming of age and leaving the natal home. The middle periods of Sufis' lives, when they are on the path but have not reached perfection, show them tormented by their passion for masters. Sufis in this phase of the love cycle actively seek to transcend their bodies and minds in order to unite with masters and, through them, God. Stories concerned with this phase show masters and disciples acting upon each others' bodies in dramatic ways to exemplify uncontrollable passion and unexplained domination. The hagiographic love cycle ends when students become masters in their own right, attaining the aim of the most promising disciples. Fulfillment of this destiny is indicated in stories where the bodies of masters and disciples become indistinguishable from each other. This transmutation of bodies is the ultimate symbolic representation of the social mechanism through which groups of Sufis linked to each other through love might be understood as a single "social" body. Echoing themes discussed in chapter 3, this social body was both spread across space in the form of a community devoted to a specific religious path (*tariqa*) and continued beyond individual lifetimes through a Sufi intergenerational chain (*silsila*). The end of the chapter presents a work that argues that corporeal attraction is a necessity for falling in love and progressing along the Sufi path.

Stories of love that I retell in this chapter underscore the intensity of personal bonds between Sufis that ultimately guaranteed the cohesiveness of Sufi communities in the Persianate context. The primacy of corporeal exchanges in these stories indicates that the authors who produced them perceived the body as the primary locus of a person's self, which had to be deployed strategically before other bodies for the sake of spiritual as well as social goals. To excel in the Sufi milieu in this period, a person had to be able to become the subject as well as the object of love. That is, Sufis who climbed all the way up the ladder of spiritual hierarchy to be regarded as friends of God did so by forming relationships with other Sufis in which they sometimes acted as lovers and at other times as beloveds. This interchangeability of Sufi masters' functions within the context of love constituted one of the primary means through which they acted as powerful social mediators in the Persianate context.

THE PARAMETERS OF LOVE

Love in medieval Islamic literatures is considered a force known through its causes and effects. It is provoked by beauty, the hallmark of the beloved, which has a radically transformative effect on the lover. In lyric poetry the discussion of love takes place through the poet's play on a number of stock characters, metaphors, and scenarios with which the reader is presumed to be familiar. Chief among the characters are love personified as an active agent, the lover, and the beloved, each of them invoked through well-known properties. Poets usually write in the voice of lovers, who ruminate on their own state and its cause, the force of love unleashed by the beloved's beauty. Poets' ingenuity lies in their ability to manipulate the established vocabulary of love with the aim of saying something familiar in a new way or highlighting a nuance hidden away within hackneyed metaphors.[3] The essential framework of this poetic vocabulary of love can be summarized through a couple of representative examples from the Persianate context.[4]

In his narrative poem *Sifat al-ʿashiqin* (*The Qualities of Lovers*), Hilali Jaghataʾi (d. 1529) uses direct exhortation as well as aphoristic stories to highlight love's status as the preeminent human emotion. After customary praises of God, Muhammad, and the art of poetry, he begins his discussion of love in earnest with the following eulogy:

> The world is but a drop in the ocean of love,
>> heaven is but a plant in the desert of love.
> There is no station higher than that of love,
>> its foundations are devoid of any flaw.
> No vocation is better than the work of love,
>> no preoccupation greater than the madness of love.
> One who is captive to love does not want release,
>> even when dying from sorrow, happiness is not what he seeks.
> Worldly losses and gains are equally meaningless,
>> all that is there in the world is love, nothing else.
> Although love would throw up everything in turmoil,
>> all liveliness in the world stems from its sorrow and pain.
> No wilting ever comes to mar the spring of love,
>> passion's wine never relinquishes its headiness.
> Heart, throw yourself on the candle like a moth!
>> Become branded with its love mark, and burn!
> Be the beggar of love, who nonetheless is the assembly's king!
>> Go, be the sultan of your own times!
> When love comes, do not be sad, sit happy;
>> feel yourself liberated from the world's sorrows.[5]

Given the significance of love as described here, to be in love is a highly desirable state. The fact that love brings turmoil and pain to one's life is deemed inevitable, but those who fall in love are urged to take the long view of the situation since they have, by virtue of being smitten, entered the most worthwhile arena of human experience. What is most significant about love is that it stirs up human beings in a way more potent than any other force that can act upon their bodies and minds.[6]

As already mentioned, poets usually write in the lover's voice and portray themselves as victims of the beloved's beauty. Their descriptions of the state of being in love decry the fact that they have fallen in love involuntarily, though, if the love is true, nothing in the world is able to pry them off from the beloved.

While most words and actions described in poetry belong to lovers, beloveds are shown as the powerful party in the affair because their sheer presence grips the lovers' mental states at all times. The following ghazal by Shah Qasim-i Anvar captures the contrast between the lover and the beloved as seen in this paradigm:

Of your beauty and comeliness, what can be said?
A cypress tree, an idol, tuliplike cheeks—what can be said?
You have etched sorrows and happiness on my heart's page.
For what reason you have done so, my heart and life, what can be said?
We count ourselves among the dogs of your alley.
If you refuse to deem us one of them, what can be said?
Your sorrows we carry in our heart, day and night.
If none of ours finds a place in your heart, what can be said?
What is to be done with me: a heart-giver, a madman, a profligate!
Of your being a beautiful, heart-ravishing trickster, what can be said?
Upon remembering you my heart blooms like a fresh rose.
Of the qualities of such a spring wind, what can be said?
Friend, see, his work is to melt the heart of poor Qasim.
As to what may be the purpose of all this, what can be said?[7]

This ghazal contains common poetic themes, like the comparison between the beloved's form and the cypress tree, the company of dogs, the beloved's dismissive demeanor. These are also reflected directly in paintings, such as figure 4.1, which accompanies an anthology of poetry produced in Shirvan in 1468. The refrain "what can be said" (*cheh tavan guft*) in this poem is emblematic of the position of the poets/lovers, who feel unable to convey the full impact of the presence of the beloved upon themselves but are nevertheless compelled to speak of it endlessly. Beloveds are described in the form of entrancing pictures whose vision tethers lovers to them forever upon first sight. The greater a lover's attraction to the beloved, the less he becomes bound by the mores of ordinary society. Although caught helplessly in this way, lovers are also marked by bewilderment as exemplified in the last verse of this poem: the initial attraction and the relationship's eventual destiny are ultimately beyond rationality, so that there is no way for lovers to extract themselves from the situation by reasoning through it.[8]

The contrast of opposites between the lover and the beloved can be extended much further than what is given in this ghazal. Typically, lovers are active seekers while beloveds attempt to evade lovers' attentions, lovers give voice to their longing in poetry while beloveds are usually silent, lovers' bodies whither away due to self-neglect while beloveds are pictures of beauty and rude health, lovers

4.1 An ardent lover and a dismissive beloved from an anthology of poems by various authors. Shirvan, 1468. Opaque watercolor. Copyright © British Library Board. MS. Add. 16561 fol. 85b.

are marked by frustration while beloveds are shown to be self-satisfied, and lovers are always in earnest while beloveds are playful and trivialize the attention directed at them. These differences between the two parties produce a constant tension that lies at the heart of the premodern Islamic rhetoric of love. The love relationship continues as long as this tension is unresolved; without it, love either dies or is consummated in a full union that leaves little to talk about. Classical Persian poets, masters of the rhetoric of love, play upon this tension to bring out the nuances of love relationships.

As in poetry, hagiographic narratives depict most connections between Sufis in the form of dyadic relationships between masters and disciples who have different roles and expectations assigned to them. In parallel with the discourse on etiquette discussed in chapter 3, these relationships mimic the kind of differentiation between the lover and the beloved described in poetry, which the hagiographers cite very frequently to make the point. However, poetry in its own context is different from Sufis' use of poetry: in hagiography the overarching framework for Sufis' interrelationships derives from Sufi socioreligious imperatives rather than poetic conventions. In poetry read without reference to a particular poet's intentions within his context, the beloved is eternally beautiful, the true lover always hopelessly infatuated. Sufis progressing through their lives in hagiography are shown to occupy the positions of both lovers and beloveds at various points depending on periods of life and specific situations.

The mutability of Sufis' position in the discourse of love is most clearly visible in extended hagiographies that narrate the whole life spans of particular masters. As young disciples, gifted Sufis find themselves in the position of lovers whose Sufi journeys begin when they become infatuated with older masters. As they become more mature, however, they increasingly come to occupy the position of their masters' and others' beloveds because of their future function as subsequent links in intergenerational chains of Sufi authority. This transformation has corporeal markers, as evident in the following anecdote about Qasim-i Anvar:

> They say that in the end of his days, Amir Sayyid Qasim lived a life of comfort and had become fat, ruddy, and fair. An elder [once] asked him: "what is the mark of a true lover?" The sayyid replied, "decrepitude and sallow skin." The man said, "but you look much different than this!" He replied, "Brother, there was a time when I was a lover, but now I am a beloved." Then he recited the following verse from the Masnavi:

> > While a beggar, I lived in that pit of a house.
> > Then I became a king, and every king has to have a palace.[9]

4.2   Shaykh ʿIraqi bidding farewell to a beloved friend. From a copy of Mir ʿAli Shir Navaʾi's *Hayrat al-abrar*. 1495. 14 × 10 cm. Bodleian Library, University of Oxford. MS. Elliott 287, fol. 34a.

The contrast between bodies represented in this report is also depicted in miniature paintings of the period, such as the scene showing an older and disheveled Shaykh Fakhr ad-Din 'Iraqi (d. 1289) consumed by grief upon taking leave of a young beloved companion who looks upon the scene with considerable equanimity.[10]

In hagiographic narratives great Sufi shaykhs come across as masters of love because they know when to be beloveds and when to be lovers. While a great poet manipulates the vocabulary of love to make new meanings out of familiar tropes, Sufi masters use the same rhetoric to modulate social relationships between human beings in which love acts as a catalyst for change and development. Sufi masters' efficacy as spiritual guides derives from their ability to manipulate the tension induced by love for the sake of the larger purpose of leading the disciple on the Sufi path. Interhuman love in the Sufi context does not pigeonhole particular individuals into defined characters with consistent expectations. Instead, the discourse of love helps steer the course of close relationships that shift continually depending on situations and the passage of time. The full significance of this social use of the rhetoric of love will become clear through the hagiographic cycle of love traversed in the following pages.

FIRST MEETINGS

As in poetry, the starting points of Sufi love are first meetings between two individuals who become tied to each other in a hierarchical relationship. A number of hagiographic narratives depict these meetings in considerable detail, employing many tropes of love familiar from poetry. Unlike the usual situation in poetry, however, the identities of the lover and the beloved are reversible in these stories. On the surface of the texts, disciples are identified as lovers who fall in love with masters after being told of them or upon meeting them. In the larger contexts of the stories, however, masters are shown to transform themselves for the sake of becoming objects of love for worthy disciples. Since it is the masters' desire that drives the narratives, the subtext of the stories marks them as lovers who utilize their powers to attract young beloveds. This cross-cutting dynamic is reminiscent of Sufi discussions of human beings' love for God: while developing unconditional love for the divine is an imperative for Sufi novices, God is himself acknowledged as a lover of his creation.

Safi ad-Din Ardabili and Zahid Gilani

One of the most elaborate accounts of the first meeting between a Sufi master and a disciple occurs in the hagiography of Safi ad-Din Ardabili. Although a widely influential Sufi master in his own times, Safi ad-Din is best known in history as the progenitor of a line of genealogical successors who turned the Sufi lineage into the Safavid dynasty of Iran in the early sixteenth century.[11] He is the subject of one of the longest surviving medieval Persianate hagiographies dedicated to a single master, *Safvat as-safa'* (*The Essence of Purity*) by Tavakkul b. Isma'il Ibn Bazzaz Ardabili (d. 1371). This work has a complicated history in that portions of it were modified on the orders of the Safavid king Shah Tahmasp (d. 1576) to make Shaykh Safi's genealogy fit better with Safavid dynastic claims. Changes to the text are, however, not difficult to identify based on both variation in manuscripts and the blatant political intent of the later additions. Moreover, stories from Shaykh Safi's early years that concern us here were of little interest in the political realm and can be presumed to go back to the narrative completed approximately in 1358.[12]

Ibn Bazzaz Ardabili relates that Shaykh Safi was born in a village near Ardabil, Azerbaijan, the fifth child in a family with seven children. His father passed away when he was six so that his mother was his main caretaker as a child.[13] He was naturally inclined to religious pursuits from the beginning and had a number of experiences as a child that made him aware of future events. When his special qualities became apparent to his mother, to benefit from his charisma, she began to break her fasts by drinking the used water left over from his ablutions before prayers. He was uncomfortable with this and tried to dissuade her, but she was able to persist for twelve years, sometimes acquiring the water stealthily when he thought that it had been poured on the ground.[14] As Safi ad-Din grew mature, he realized that he needed a Sufi master to guide his instincts, but his mother was unable to part with him, and he could not begin his search. He eventually persuaded her to let him go through a ruse. Two of his older brothers, traders, had gone toward Shiraz; the eldest died there while the second married a woman there and had settled down. He asked his mother's permission to seek this brother, and she finally agreed because of her continuing sorrow over the death of her oldest child and her desire to see the second son, from whom not much had been heard for a while.[15]

Unknown to him at this stage, Safi ad-Din's separation from his mother through this journey was the beginning of his attachment to his eventual mentor, Shaykh Ibrahim Zahid Gilani (d. 1301). While staying with his brother in Shiraz, Safi became well known to local Sufis who were impressed by his innate religious aptitude and told him that only one person, a certain Amir 'Abdallah, was capable of guiding him. When he went to this man and told him his condition, he said that Safi was already more advanced than him and that the only person in the world who could guide him was Shaykh Zahid Gilani. Upon further questioning, Amir 'Abdallah described the exact location and physical setup of Shaykh Zahid's hospice in Gilan along with the following detailed physical profile: "He is a short man with a bright complexion, a black mark near his mouth, black eyes, flat brow with receding hairline, and a sparse but wide beard."[16] Shaykh Safi returned from Shiraz to Azerbaijan some time after this encounter and spent four years thinking about and visualizing Shaykh Zahid. No one mentioned the shaykh to him during this period, but his great ardor was known to Zahid himself in Gilan who would tell his disciples that "a young man in Ardabil who wears felt is confounded with desire for us; if he were to come here, his affair would be taken care of in a single day."[17]

Safi had given up normal life after his return from Shiraz and his four years of waiting to meet the guide were spent mostly in religious pursuits. The matter eventually came to a head through the intermediacy of a native of Safi's village named Muhammad Ibrahiman who went to Gilan on a trip to buy rice. After his business transaction, he visited one of Shaykh Zahid's two homes, which was nearby, and was so impressed by him and his followers that he took an oath of repentance on his hands and donned clothes marking his affiliation with this community. He then started on the road home but ran into trouble because of a snowstorm that left him and his entourage stranded near his village. A group from the village, which included Safi, set out to help him, and, when they met, the future master noticed immediately that Ibrahiman had changed his clothes and outer form. When questioned, he told Safi that he had become Zahid's disciple and then described the shaykh's outer form minutely in words that matched exactly what Amir 'Abdallah had told Safi earlier in Shiraz. Upon hearing this, Safi was completely beside himself and immediately got on the road to Shaykh Zahid despite his companions' warnings about the weather.

Ibn Bazzaz Ardabili writes that Shaykh Safi had a wet dream every night during the journey to Gilan, which caused significant hardship in the winter because he was then required to perform a full bath in the morning in order to pray. Every night after the event, Shaykh Zahid appeared to him wearing a green woolen coat and asked an accompanying servant to give Safi warm water to perform the bath. He used the water but was uncertain in the morning whether a "visionary" bath truly satisfied the legal requirement. To be safe, every morning he also took a real bath, although he had to use cold water because he was reticent to trouble people to warm it for him. But bathing in extreme cold with freezing water caused him to develop severe fatigue in all his outward senses. This led to a gradual diminishing of his hearing, sight, and sense of smell, so that "he trod on the path of love while trampling the world of sense objects under his feet."[18] The minimizing of the senses represents Safi ad-Din's gradual dying to the material world that becomes available to consciousness through sensory contacts.

Safi ad-Din eventually reached Shaykh Zahid's place during the month of Ramadan when it was the shaykh's habit to remain in seclusion, neither listening to disciples' experiences nor interpreting their stations or providing guidance. Safi entered the hospice and went to one corner to pray. Shaykh Zahid, who had been aware of his travels through mystical intuition, then asked the hospice's attendant to light a fire, even though the building was already warm. The heat of the fire slowly penetrated Safi's body as he stood praying so that, eventually, sweat began to pour from his nose, ears, and the pupils of his eyes. The three senses associated with these organs were then fully restored, and Shaykh Zahid asked an attendant to bring Safi to him. He kissed Zahid's hands and feet when he saw him, finding him exactly as the image he had carried in his mind for over four years. Shaykh Zahid then asked him why he had come, and he replied, "to repent," referring to the first step on the Sufi path, undertaken when someone becomes attached to a master. He then asked him if he had parents, and when he replied that he had only a mother, Zahid told him, simply, "welcome." Then, contrary to his custom during Ramadan, he called all his disciples to come together and told them that this was the man from Ardabil who had been seeking him for four years and that "there was only one veil left between him and God, and even that has now lifted."[19] Zahid then gave Safi his own clothes to wear and installed him in a special place of seclusion where normally only he himself performed Sufi exercises. From that point on, Safi became a permanent fixture at Shaykh Zahid's side, gaining from his guidance and, eventually, becoming his most prized disciple and successor.

Ibn Bazzaz's rendering of the young Safi ad-Din Ardabili's journey toward Shaykh Zahid is peppered with citations of Persian and Arabic verses that correlate the different phases of his progress to themes in the idealized love tale elaborated upon by poets. The story begins with Safi's desire for an attachment, which leads to his hearing about the remarkable master who lives far away and is the sole person in the world deserving of his love and devotion. The first informant takes care to describe Zahid's face and body in detail, and the image becomes imprinted on Safi's mind to act as the unceasing reminder of the beloved for a long period. His desire spills over the boundaries of rationality when the second informant confirms the correspondence between the real person and his mental image, and he begins the actual journey to the master heedless of practical difficulties. The path to the beloved is arduous and painful, but here too the beloved appears in visions that provide relief and keep him on the path. The deprivations of the journey are designed to empty his body of its existing content: he loses lust, as in the image of recurring wet dreams, and his other senses are reduced to a minimum because of the cold.

This is all reversed when he reaches the master and, in effect, acquires a new body. His senses come back to life from the heat of the beloved's home, and he acquires a new outward skin in the form of Shaykh Zahid's own clothes, which he puts on. While there is much left to happen in the relationship between the two in subsequent years, a sense of what is to come can be had from Zahid's statement that now there is no veil left between Safi and God. The implication here is that Safi fused with Zahid's body, which already had unrestricted access to God because of his spiritual attainments. The union of the earthly lover and beloved, the Sufi disciple and master, thus presages the fulfillment of ultimate love that lies at the end of the Sufi path.

As we see it enacted in this narrative, Shaykh Safi's extraordinary potential as a Sufi is fulfilled when he seeks and finds a master worthy of his desire. It is noteworthy that his attachment to Shaykh Zahid matures as he becomes increasingly distant from his mother, his initial caretaker in the hagiography. First, he hears of the master when he is away from the mother, after having concocted a ruse; second, his mother disappears from the narrative when he returns to Ardabil and remains obsessed with the master's image for four years; third, at the moment of union with the master, the latter pointedly asks him about his parents. Shaykh Zahid's saying "welcome" to him after hearing that his mother is alive marks a kind of change of guards in the text where the master takes on the mother's caring and loving functions. The transition is in fact not just of caretakers but of modes of love altogether. Shaykh Safi's connection to his mother is based on filial love, since he is a product of her body and has been nurtured by her. His affiliation with Shaykh Zahid, in contrast, is established through the kind of sensual love celebrated in poetry. The connection between Safi and Zahid is, in the long run, a link in the chain of Sufi spiritual authority that mimics an actual genealogy. Many of the functions of the two types of love are shared, but their material basis with respect to the body is different.

Khwaja Ahrar and Ya'qub Charkhi

Khwaja Ahrar is a towering personality in the history of Sufism during the fifteenth century, and I have already discussed his early years in search of a master in the previous chapter while commenting on competition between major masters in Herat in the early decades of the fifteenth century. To pick up the story from there, after spending quite a bit of time in Herat, Ahrar came to the Naqshbandi path through his encounter with Naqshband's student Ya'qub Charkhi. The story of his first meeting with Charkhi depicts, once again, a lover coming to the doorstep of a beloved in a stylized narrative reflecting poetic paradigms.

The meeting is described quite similarly in three lengthy hagiographies dedicated to Khwaja Ahrar's life.[20] The narratives from Ahrar relate that he initially came across Ya'qub's name in the village of Chihildukhtaran just outside Herat on his very first visit to the city. He saw a man sitting in the doorway of a Sufi hospice in the village and thought that he was doing the Khwajagani silent zikr.

He asked him where he had learned this and was told, from Mawlana Ya'qub in Halghatu who was a direct disciple of Naqshband. Ahrar was impressed by what this man said of Ya'qub's qualities but decided to proceed on his way to Herat where he spent four years in the company of various Sufi masters. After this delay he finally made his way toward Halghatu, to meet the shaykh as part of his quest for Sufi guidance in this early period of his life.[21] Just before reaching his destination, he developed a fever from the winter weather and had to spend twenty days in a village where some residents spoke ill of the shaykh. His enthusiasm for meeting the shaykh waned somewhat when he heard this, but he eventually decided to go ahead with the plan since he had already come all this way. The shaykh greeted him warmly the first day, but the next day he was angry and behaved harshly. Ahrar realized that he had become aware of the hesitation that had affected him just before his arrival and had been displeased by this. However, the next day Ya'qub was again very kind and related the story of his own first meeting with Naqshband in which the master had accepted him as a disciple only after he had received an indication from the unseen world.

After recalling this crucial moment, which established his own place in the Naqshbandi chain, Ya'qub extended his hand toward Ahrar and invited him to take an oath of affiliation. But, at that very moment, Ahrar saw a white mark on Ya'qub's forehead, which seemed to be a disease and produced in Ahrar a feeling of repulsion. Ya'qub sensed Ahrar's disinclination and quickly took away his hand, but he then transformed his appearance immediately, almost as if he were changing his clothes. He appeared in such a form that Ahrar felt drawn to him compulsively and, just when he was about to uncontrollably fling himself on the shaykh, Ya'qub again extended his hand and said that Naqshband had grasped his hand and had said that whoever grasps it in the future grasps my hand. Ahrar then took the hand with all willingness and became a part of the Naqshbandi chain.[22]

It is striking that, in this story, Ahrar's initial revulsion and eventual attraction to Ya'qub occur on a corporeal basis. As with Shaykh Safi, Ahrar also discovers the prospect of discipleship with the master by hearing of him from someone, although, in this case, he is first drawn to the possibility by seeing someone do zikr instead of receiving an image to carry in his mind. Just prior to reaching the master, he suffers from an illness that partially incapacitates the body, a theme that is reflected in stories about Shaykh Safi as well. In the end Ya'qub's body in its actual physical presence is the ultimate mediator of Ahrar's incorporation into the Sufi community. Ya'qub's competence as a master lies in his ability to sense Ahrar's hesitation and then change his form to make himself compulsively attractive. His statement at the end of the story signifies the idea that his body is a channel for the presence of Naqshband so that by taking the hand Ahrar was coming into bodily contact with his eminent predecessor. The oath incorporating Ahrar into the Sufi chain is then undertaken based on unbroken bodily contact between masters and disciples spanning generations. Ahrar's life's work from this point onward was to propagate the path so that, like Ya'qub before him, his body becomes a vehicle for the manifestation of the teachings and powers of the illustrious ancestors.

Ahrar's first meeting with the master presents a complicated picture regarding who among the two is the seeking lover and who the sought after beloved. In the straightforward reading of the story, Ahrar is the one who makes the journey to the master's hospice after nursing the possibility of the meeting in his mind for four years. But, in the end, it is the master who changes his form to make sure that he falls in love with him. The consummation of the story is thus driven by the master's desire to attract Ahrar. Ahrar seems to have taken this aspect of the master's role for granted in later life; a work devoted to him relates in his own words that, whenever he wanted to establish a relationship with another Sufi, he would put on the "dress of external form" (*kisvat-i vujud*) of a beloved so that the other party was forced to fall in love with him.[23] Once this occurred, the disciple would become beholden to him in the way a lover is helplessly attached to a beloved, which allowed him to direct the disciple on the Sufi path. In Ahrar's words, the disciple must fall in love with the master corporeally because "the master's form (*surat*) contains his reality (*haqiqat*), which, in turn, includes the totality [of existence] (*jam'iyyat*). The path to God is preceded by the disciple becoming affected by the totality through his concentration on the master's form."[24]

The principle at work here is reflected in a work dedicated to Ahrar's antecedent Baha' ad-Din Naqshband as well. One day he asked his disciples whether it was they who had found him or vice versa. When they responded that they had been the seekers, he suddenly disappeared from view and later reappeared to prove that their capacity to find him depended, in the first place, on his power to make himself available and apparent.[25] Similarly, Ni'matullah Vali is credited with the verse "To every friend that I see worthy of love / I show my beauty and seize his heart."[26] In the underlying ideological bases of hagiographic narratives, the interchangeability of masters and disciples as lovers and beloveds was a crucial prerequisite for the production of Sufi chains of religious authority whose significance goes beyond the depictions of first meetings.

THE CONSEQUENCES OF FALLING IN LOVE

Hagiographies written in the fourteenth and fifteenth centuries consist largely of vignettes in which great masters interact with disciples on a one-to-one basis. Since the narratives mostly show two individuals in action, it is easy to read the characteristics associated with poetic lovers and beloveds in almost all interactions among Sufis described in these texts. The power of the poetic love paradigm for the fashioning of social relationships and their literary representation is evident from the near total presence of this pattern throughout Persianate hagiography. In this section of the chapter, I concentrate on dramatic instances of corporeal interactions between Sufis who are already in master-disciple relationships. The general tenor of relationships considered here follows from what I have described already, although the kind of imagery employed in these instances provides greater texture to representations of the maintenance of love in Sufi dyads that aggregated to form powerful Sufi communities.

Love's Grip on the Heart

Some of the most dramatic stories I have encountered that show masters' control over disciples' bodies following the establishment of their relationship of love are found in 'Ali b. Mahmud Abivardi Kurani's *Rawzat as-salikin* (*The Garden of Travelers*), written around 1505.[27] This work repeats some material from earlier sources, but most of the detailed stories are told in the words of Sufis whom the author met personally during the second half of the fifteenth century. The descriptions are particularly striking for their ability to convey the fact that being in love is simultaneously an exhilarating and an imprisoning emotion.

Although the *Rawzat as-salikin* purports in the beginning to be a history of the Naqshbandi chain, the vast majority of its stories are concerned with the life of the author's own master, the Naqshbandi shaykh 'Ala' ad-Din Muhammad b. Muhammad b. Mu'min Abizi (d. 1487).[28] Kurani reports that when Abizi became a disciple of Sa'd ad-Din Kashghari (d. 1456) in Herat after traveling to the city from his native Quhistan, the master's first instruction to him was to discontinue all his studies to concentrate solely on duties assigned by him. Abizi stopped all his quests except his study of hadith, which he was pursuing at the time under another teacher who lived outside a gate to the city. When it came time for the lesson, he went on his way to the teacher but was faced with an extraordinary circumstance when he reached the gate. As soon as he put one foot outside the city wall, iron shackles appeared on his feet out of nowhere, impeding his speed and rattling as he took further steps. Then with each new step, parts of his attire began flying off his body. He first lost his turban, then his outer clothes and his undershirt, then even his shoes. Just when all that was left was his underwear, he decided to stop in order to save himself from the disgrace of being completely naked in public. He then turned back and each piece of his attire returned to his body at the exact same step at which it had been removed. Finally, the shackles disappeared as soon as he put his feet inside the city gate. Perceiving this experience to have been related to his new religious affiliation, he decided to go and see the master. When he went to the mosque where Kashghari usually stayed, he found the master sitting alone in meditation. As he entered, the master raised his head to gaze at him briefly and then dropped it again to concentrate on his meditation. Abizi understood this momentary acknowledgment to be a warning that made clear the meaning of his earlier experience: he was to obey the master completely after having begun his relationship with him or he would face severe consequences.[29]

While in this story Abizi found himself in the position of being a lover imprisoned by the beloved's desires, most tales in this hagiography portray the later years of his life when he was himself a master and a beloved. In one evocative account the author reports from a "lover" (*muhibb*) that one day as he sat at home he was suddenly overcome with the desire to see Abizi and immediately got on the road. On the way he felt as if he were simultaneously being pulled by a rope around his neck and prodded by a stick at his back to get to the master as soon as possible. Walking very quickly, and even running at certain points, he arrived at his destination to see the master sitting in the middle of a room. Confused and surprised, he sat down in front of him and, imitating him, put his head down on his chest. He then thought that it would be better to raise his head and perform a few rounds of zikr before sitting like this. But, however much he tried, he could not lift his head and became frightened that perhaps it had become stuck in this position.

Immersed in his panic, he then saw that the shaykh's chest opened up and a wrist and fist appeared from it that had strings attached to it. The fist began traveling toward him while he could observe that folds of the strings attached to it were sitting within the shaykh's chest. At this moment, he reminded himself that this was not a vision; rather, he was observing what was happening with his normal eyesight. The fist appeared in front of his own chest, which had also opened up in the meantime, and went inside to expand into a palm that grabbed his heart. He then felt a tremendous pain in his chest and when he looked down, he saw that the fist was squeezing his heart tightly so that parts of it were protruding from between the fingers in the way dough squelches out of the hand in the process of kneading. The fist then returned to the shaykh's heart, leaving him bewildered and impressed with the powers of this master. He looked toward the shaykh and saw him staring at him with great intensity and heard him recite the following quatrain:

When the command of my gaze falls in your direction,
    do not think that I have chosen myself for this job.
In my face is to be seen God's beauty,
    I reckon God's perfection in the copy that is my being.[30]

As reflected in these verses, Abizi's divinely ascribed beauty and perfection compel the disciple to be present in front of him. The organ reaching out from his chest that captures the disciple's heart represents the beloved's power over the lover in a most literal and graphic manner.[31]

The master's total control over disciples is reflected in stories from the life of Baha> ad-Din Naqshband as well. At one point he told one of his disciples that he had such power that, if he wanted, a slight movement of his sleeve could compel all the people of Bukhara to leave their preoccupations and follow him. Just as he said this, he pulled his hand inside his sleeve and the disciple noticed the movement. He immediately lost consciousness and, upon returning to his senses, felt that love for the master had completely overpowered his heart forever.[32]

The stories I have highlighted so far show the painful or restrictive side of love as it pertains to the position of the Sufi disciple as a lover. Even here it is possible to see that disciples put up with the pain of love for the ultimate pleasure of the master's company and, through them, proximity to God. Their situation is seen as being preordained for the human condition as stated in the following verse reported in a work dedicated to ʿAli Hamadani:

> Celestial beings have love, but not pain;
>   in creation, the human is the only being joined to pain.[33]

In hagiographic narratives, disciples are caught in the web of love and pain, but their persistence in continuing with the existing scheme of things is essentially voluntary and stems from both the actual pleasure of the company of the charismatic masters and the ultimate religious award. Kurani reports that Abizi related from one of his own masters that a true lover is like a person standing on a high mountain, who dives when called to do so by the beloved even when he knows that the valley below is like a forest of sharp nails pointed upward. It is only when a lover shows this much devotion and selflessness that the beloved catches him before he reaches the ground and saves him.[34] The same message is reflected in Naqshband's advice to his disciple Shaykh Amir Husayn: as long as his desire was that he was with him as the beloved, he would find him in his company as a protector no matter where he went.[35]

Masters as Lovers and Beloveds

Stories from the saintly lives of the great masters that I have related in this section underscore the restrictions impinging on a disciple who becomes the lover to a master and is bound by the master's desires. But, as I remarked earlier, the subtexts of hagiographic narratives indicate that Sufi masters deliberately made themselves "beautiful" in order to attract disciples who would fall in love with them. By this token, the masters ultimately occupy the positions of lovers in search of young Sufis who would become attached to them and, in time, continue their chain of initiation.

'Ali Hamadani's views as they are reported in the *Khulasat al-manaqib* give this aspect of the master's self-understanding concrete form. He is supposed to have said that Sufis who reach the stage of being the pole (*qutb*) of the Sufi hierarchy embedded in the world are simultaneously lovers and beloveds. If they appear to be beloveds, they are so externally, while their interior aspects have the properties of lovers; and if they show themselves to be lovers outwardly then they are beloveds on the inside.[36] The form they take in the exterior world (*zahir*) is significant in that it corresponds to how they relate to other human beings. Those who are outwardly beloveds attract others and become responsible for teaching the path. They are given total power over their followers and will not face any questions on the day of judgment even if they kill a thousand persons every day. In contrast, those who are outwardly lovers are interested solely in their own salvation; they must observe all rules of conduct and will have to answer for any infractions they might commit in the accounting of good and bad deeds after death.[37]

Although Hamadani's distinction here mentions two types of Sufis, being a lover or beloved on the outside could also be seen to refer to phases in the life of a given Sufi. At the beginning of the path, the Sufi is a lover of a master on the outside, although in the interior it is the master who has chosen him as the beloved. Later, for those who climb the spiritual hierarchy and become teachers in their own right, the situation reverses. They then become beloveds on the outside while being the lovers of their disciples on the inside. The interchangeability of roles is reflected in miniature paintings' depictions of Sufis from the period as well, where we find examples of compositions showing masters as beloveds and disciples as lovers and vice versa (figs. 4.3 and 4.4). The first image, dated circa 1470, shows a king bowing in front of a dervish after realizing that he represented a higher station despite living in the wild and being unsure of his subsistence on a daily basis.[38] Conversely, the second image, dated to 1485, shows a young man being pursued by an old Sufi in a scene of dazzling natural beauty.[39] Poetic rhetoric, hagiographic stories, and representations in paintings combine to present extensive evidence for the salience of this pattern in the Persianate environment.

Whether acting as beloveds or as lovers, the great Sufi masters come across in hagiographic narratives as controllers of the power of love. Their efficacy as religious adepts lies in the ability to change their form to keep alive the tension of love in order to drive disciples along the Sufi path. When a disciple is flagging, they appear as awesome beloveds who compel the disciple as lover

4.3 A king bowing to an ascetic in a scene of nature. From a copy of *Khamsa* of Nizami. Iran, ca. 1470. Opaque watercolor, ink, and gold on paper. Text and illustration: 25.1 × 16.4 cm. Arthur M. Sackler Gallery, Smithsonian Institution, Washington, DC: Purchase—Smithsonian Unrestricted Trust Funds, Smithsonian Collections Acquisition Program, and Dr. Arthur M. Sackler, S1986.61 fol. 101b.

4.4   An old Sufi man pursuing a young man. From a copy of the *Matla' al-anvar* of Amir Khusraw Dihlavi, 1485. 20 × 15 cm. Copyright © Trustees of the Chester Beatty Library, Dublin. MS. 163, fol. 38a.

to become more steadfast. And when the disciple is wrongly infatuated, they distance themselves as a kind of lesson until the correct balance is reached. During both processes they act as beloveds outwardly while inwardly seeking the disciple's allegiance and betterment as lovers.[40] The Sufi master's persona as it pertains to the discourse of love contrasts interestingly with the poetic paradigm of love. There the beloved is corporeally powerful because her or his beauty entrances and enslaves the lover. However, the power of words in poetry belongs to lovers. In the Sufi context, as I have shown, the mutability of lovers and beloveds places both power in the hands and tongues of the masters within narrative representations. However, it should be recalled that it was the disciples, and not the masters who are shown speaking, who produced these texts. Mutability of roles is, therefore, an inherent part of this whole discourse. The masters' excellence in this role is measured by what the disciples attribute to them in terms of their dexterity in managing the power of love for the sake of Sufi religious and social goals.[41]

LOVE'S END: MELDED BODIES

As I have mentioned previously, the two ultimate aims of the Sufi path from the earliest systematic expositions of Sufism as a prescriptive system were annihilation in God (*fana' fillah*) followed by subsistence in divine reality (*baqa' billah*). The Sufi's road to God represented a lover's progress toward the beloved, and the achievement of the ultimate states meant the elimination of all distinctions so that the lover, the beloved, and love itself all became one. As I have shown in this chapter, Sufi love pertained not just to the relationship between the human and the divine but also to the interconnections between Sufis themselves. In this vein the ultimate step for the consummation of the relationship between Sufis in the positions of lovers and beloveds was their subsumption into each other.

A number of hagiographic narratives I have cited in this chapter present the fulfillment of the relationship of love between masters and disciples through stories in which their bodies become mutually indistinguishable. Ibn Bazzaz Ardabili reports that as Safi ad-Din Ardabili became closer to his master Zahid Gilani, following their initial meeting, his body began to acquire the properties of the master. Their eventual merging into each other is reflected in the verse:

Between the same veins, brain, and skin,
  one friend became colored with the same qualities as the other.[42]

To prove this point, he relates a story in which Safi ad-Din experienced the same thing as his master even when they were a long distance apart. He states that Zahid suffered from ailments of the eyes by the end of his life, and one day in Gilan his eyes began to burn painfully when he put in some medicine. At this very moment Safi ad-Din left the companions he was sitting with and, much to their surprise, jumped into a pool of water for no apparent reason. They recorded the time of this event and realized later that this had occurred exactly when Zahid had felt his eyes burning from medicine. The burning sensation that originated in the experience of one body was thus felt in the other because of their identity.[43]

The interchangeability of Sufis' bodies is eventually predicated on the idea that individuals who either have natural religious aptitude or have reached high stations can act as mirrors for others. From the early years of Shaykh Safi's life, Ardabili reports that one day, as he sat in a mosque, a man appeared and told him that he should put his affairs in order because he was scheduled to die in exactly three days. Safi believed him and came to sit in the same place after three days with a heavy heart, awaiting his end. Then another man appeared and told him that the man who had initially told him about his impending death had himself just died at the appointed moment. The explanation for this lay in the idea, derived from a hadith report, that a true believer is like a mirror for another believer. The man who had informed Safi of his death had in fact seen his own death in a vision, but the bodies had been interchanged because Safi's body could act as a mirror for that of others.[44]

A similar phenomenon is described in Jaʿfar Badakhshi's memoir of ʿAli Hamadani, who reports that once when the master had just left Badakhshan for Khuttalan, one of his disciples went into his room and saw him sitting there. But when he was about to ask why, and when he had canceled the trip, the image of his body disappeared. He then figured out that the image of Hamadani's body had become so firmly lodged in his vision that he was liable to see it even when the master was gone. Badakhshi states that the ultimate example of this kind of vision of the master was when he himself would first see Hamadani's face upon looking into a mirror, the image then changing to his own face after a few moments.[45]

The ultimate effect of this kind of identity between the bodies of masters and disciples was to ratify the transmission of Sufi authority through an unbroken intergenerational chain. In effect, showing that the body of the disciple was interchangeable with that of the master was the most emphatic means of legitimating succession. Works on Niʿmatullah Vali report that, in his youth, he was greatly puzzled why the famous Uvays al-Qarani, who became devoted to Muhammad despite never having met him, proceeded to break all his own teeth upon hearing that Muhammad had lost some teeth in a battle. Uvays then appeared in a dream to him and said that breaking the teeth was the equivalent of digging a treasure, since by acting thus upon his own body he had created a connection to the body of the Prophet.[46] Similarly, a disciple reported that sometimes when he looked at Khwaja Ahrar he would see the face of Muhammad that he had earlier seen in a dream.[47]

In addition to the interchangeability of bodies, a number of sources reflect this imperative of the Sufi social milieu in reports that, toward the end of their lives, masters would start referring to their chosen successors with the name of their own earlier masters. In a case where the Sufi genealogy parallels actual descent, the Khwajagani master Sayyid Amir Kulal is said to have referred to his son and successor Amir Hamza as "father" (*pidar*).[48] Such a presumption of continuation over generations was especially potent in cases where the masters were, like Amir Kulal and Hamza, sayyids claiming descent from Muhammad and ʿAli. This is reflected also in the prominence of genealogy in hagiographies devoted to Shah Niʿmatullah Vali and ʿAli Hamadani, two other shaykhs with sayyid ancestry.[49]

Reflecting a situation where masters and disciples were not related, a number of links in the Kubravi chain are shown exhibiting this phenomenon in different hagiographic narratives. Badakhshi provides stories in which the master ʿAlaʾ ad-Dawla Simnani (d. 1336) treated his student Akhi ʿAli Dusti as his master.[50] ʿAli Hamadani inherited his Kubravi affiliation from Dusti and Mahmud Mazdaqani (d. 1365), another disciple of Simnani. Badakhshi's own claims with respect to Hamadani are couched in the incident of his looking into a mirror, and the pattern continued in later Kubravi links. Muhammad Nurbakhsh claimed that his master Ishaq Khuttalani (d. 1424) would often confuse him with his own master, Sayyid ʿAli Hamadani. The very same claim is made in a hagiography deriving from the lineage of Sayyid ʿAbdallah Barzishabadi (d. 1468), who was a rival to Nurbakhsh for the claim of being Khuttalani's successor.[51] And Nurbakhsh's praise for his own son and successor Qasim Fayzbakhsh includes the comment that there was no difference between the two of them save the fact that he was older than the son.[52]

The melding together of Sufis' bodies as represented in these reports worked to substantiate and solidify Sufi communities both synchronically and diachronically. When invoked for a master-disciple dyad, the process ratified the significance of the idea of the Sufi path (*tariqa*) shared by all who were part of the living Sufi community surrounding a master. And when appealed to for the connection across multiple generations, the process sanctioned the chain (*silsila*) that lay at the base of the Sufi construction of religious authority. As I have emphasized before, the path and the chain together constituted the two crucial factors in the formation of powerful and widespread Sufi communities in the Persianate world.

LOVE AND EMBODIMENT

The stories I have discussed in this chapter can help us understand the salience of the rhetoric of love in hagiographic narratives. Persianate Sufis in the fourteenth and fifteenth centuries articulated their strongest bonds with each other using the language of love, and this love was produced, sustained, and consummated corporeally. In Sufism's doctrinal logic, the ultimate purpose of these relationships was to lead disciples to God, though Persianate hagiographic narratives convey a clear sense that for most, if not all, this ultimate goal could be achieved only through the intermediary of love directed at a human guide. As I have shown in previous chapters, pursuing the Sufi path required Sufis to negotiate the physical world whose availability was contingent on the bodily senses. The emphasis on love, which connected human hearts to each other through the intermediacy of bodies, represented a continuation of this significance of the body beyond personal experience to the social sphere.

To end this chapter, I introduce a work that stridently exemplifies the patterns relating to love I have discussed in the preceding pages. The necessity of human love as a prelude to divine love is advocated most emphatically in Kamal ad-Din Gazurgahi's compendium of brief biographies entitled *Majalis al-ʿushshaq* (*The Assemblies of Lovers*) completed in the first decade of the sixteenth century.[53] This work presents heavily reworked versions of the biographies of Sufis and others whom the author describes as extraordinary lovers. The cast of characters consists of Sufis from the past as well as the author's own times, prophets, lovers of poetic legends (such as Majnun and Farhad), and famous poets, rulers, and viziers. Although most of the information presented in the work is not seen in other sources, it is distinguished by the author's single-mindedness in infusing history with the spirit of human love mediated by corporeal contact. Its significance lies not in being a source of information but in containing the most categorical presentation of a cultural topos prominent during the time it was composed.

All of Gazurgahi's biographies work according to the formula that a protagonist is identified for having a special capacity for love, which leads him to become infatuated with another person as a prelude to realizing his love for God. The most cogent explanation of this theme occurs in his entry on the great Sufi author Ibn al-ʿArabi whose significance for Persianate Sufism I have discussed in earlier chapters. Unlike other Sufi authors, Gazurgahi's interest in Ibn al-ʿArabi is not based on appreciating his writings and ideas. His entry on the master portrays him as a lover of his young and beautiful disciple Sadr ad-Din Qunavi (d. 1273–74). His obsession with the young man is depicted in numerous illustrated manuscripts of the *Majalis al-ʿushshaq* that were produced during the sixteenth century (figure 4.5).[54] The narrative surrounding the image states that one day, when Ibn al-ʿArabi was astride an animal, he ran into Qunavi, and the latter showed obedience to him. Ibn al-ʿArabi in turn got off the steed and fell on the ground in front of the young man, begging him to ride the animal. Qunavi refused, which led other people to praise Qunavi and condemn Ibn al-ʿArabi, calling him an unbeliever and a heretic. This embarrassed Qunavi, but

4.5   Ibn al-ʿArabi encountering Sadr ad-Din Qunavi. From a copy of Gazurgahi's *Majalis al-ʿushshaq*. Bibliothèque nationale de France. MS. Suppl. Persan 1559, fol. 103b.

Ibn al-ʿArabi told him, "Do not be ashamed; instead, expend effort so that you cut your relationship to created beings and become attached to the Truth."

Gazurgahi writes that Qunavi's shame over this incident led him to ensconce himself in his home for a few days, which caused Ibn al-ʿArabi to grow beside himself from desire. A companion then tried to distract him by suggesting that he visit the beautiful sights of Damascus. When Ibn al-ʿArabi indicated that nothing in the world was beautiful when the beloved was not around, the companion suggested that he should seek God directly rather than through an earthly intermediary. Ibn al-ʿArabi's purported reply to this criticism is worth citing in detail since it captures the main point of the general attitude I see reflected in much of Persianate hagiographic literature:

> The beauty of traces connected to metaphorical love is the shadow and extremity of essential beauty that is linked to true love. As in the proverb "metaphor is the bridge to reality," one is the means for acquiring the other and the road toward reaching it. The fact is, that a given person has limited innate ability for the love that is occasioned by the beauty of the Essence in itself . . . and much of it remains hidden behind dark veils. If a shadow from the light of that beauty makes itself apparent when it takes shape in the tapestry of clay that is the heart-ravishing, well-proportioned beloved, then:

> > Gentle manners, being well-spoken, and nimbleness
> >   are wound-dressers on every heart's mark of sorrow.
> > [From them, the heart] acquires the pure hem of a new blown rose,
> >   which is boldly free of all contamination.

> [Once this has occurred], the bird of the lover's heart promises itself to the beloved and spreads feathers and wings in the desire for requiting love. It becomes captive to the beloved's food and prey to his snare, and it renounces all purposes and indeed knows no purpose other than him:

> > From the mosque and the hospice (*khanqah*) he moves to the tavern,
> >   he drinks wine and arrives drunk at the beloved's door.
> > Whatever is not love for the beloved despairs him,
> >   he comes shopping for it with a thousand lives.

> Love's fire and desire's flames become lit within him and result in the burning away of the curtains of secrecy. [Love and desire] lift the veil of ignorance from his spiritual sight and clear the mist of multiplicity from the mirror of truth [within him]. Then his sight sharpens and his heart comes to discern the truth. Everything he passes, he recognizes and everything he lays his eyes on,

he sees. Every moment he turns his face to the attester within him (*mashhud-i khud*) and says:

> You were hidden in the breast, and I was oblivious.
> You were apparent to sight, and I was oblivious.
> My whole life I was seeking a sign of you from the world,
> you yourself were the entire world, and I was oblivious.

When [the lover] reaches this place, he knows that metaphorical love had been the equivalent of a smell from the tavern of true love, and the love of traces had been like a shadow from the sun of the Essence. However, if he had not smelled that smell he never would have reached that tavern and if he had not found that shadow he would never have had a share from that sun.[55]

As reflected in Gazurgahi's work as well as the rest of the material I have presented in this chapter, Persianate Sufis were in search of beloveds who could help them progress further on the Sufi path. For Sufis beginning their religious conditioning, beloveds were those acknowledged as the great living masters of the day, whose bodies acted as sites of beauty that invited love and desire, forming the ineluctable intermediaries between the human and the divine. But, hidden from ordinary perception, the great masters were also lovers in search of beloved disciples whom they wanted to compel into falling in love with themselves. The pursuit of disciples was as much of an imperative for the masters as the desire for a master was for novices, and everyone's fulfillment was predicated on being caught somewhere in the net of love. Love encompassed the circle of youth and old age, of life and death, which is why it thoroughly permeated the world of customary interactions depicted in most stories recorded by Sufi hagiographers.

5

ENGENDERED DESIRES

It is likely that the account I have given in chapter 4 makes Persianate Sufism appear as a world in which ideology and social patterns combine effortlessly to enable Sufi masters and disciples to pursue each other as lovers and beloveds. This impression flows in part from the idealizing tone characteristic of hagiographic narratives that are my main sources. Persianate hagiography and miniature painting are cognate genres in this regard. Both present human figures and interactions in abstracted forms that convey established conventions. Understanding the conventions provides us access to the authors' idealizations, which can, in turn, be regarded as symptoms of social ideologies. As I have argued in the introduction in the context of discussing embodiment as an analytical tool, conventional images regarding love or other matters cannot be taken as descriptions on face value. Instead, these images reflect patterns that we can interpret using phenomenological, sociological, and hermeneutical methods to arrive at judgments about the workings of society.

Stylized though they certainly are, hagiographic texts also provide substantial details that exceed the genre's didactic and prescriptive intent. On this score, texts are different from paintings since, first, the fund of material available to us is much larger, and second, verbal narratives have a higher capacity for accommodating incidental or peripheral details in comparison with highly condensed images that have to fit on pages of manuscripts. In this chapter I aim to exploit materials that occur at the margins of hagiographic narratives and allow us to complicate the story beyond understanding the authors' own investments. I see chapter 5 as a necessary companion to chapter 4; the two should be read in conjunction to see the overall picture I wish to convey in this book.

My rubric for discussion is the question of desire and its connection to the construction of gender in the milieu depicted in Persianate Sufi literature. Desire is a matter deeply interwoven through Sufi ideas from the earliest periods. In Sufi theoretical discourse, praiseworthy desire that has God or a master as its object is referenced under the term *irada*. The centrality of such desire to Sufi social practice is evident from the fact that the standard term for a disciple is *murid*, the one who desires, and the master is designated as *murad*, the one who is desired.[1] As stories discussed in the previous chapter can attest, *irada* as desire is the driving force behind love relationships between masters and disciples. However, along with providing the details of desire that leads to idealized love between masters and disciples, hagiographic narratives register the functioning of other types of desires in the context of human relationships that stand in tension with "proper" behavior. Represented as blameworthy, or at least of ambiguous value, such desires are nevertheless critical in defining normative or recommended behavior.

Desire is a multifaceted topic, and I should clarify that I am concerned here with it only in the narrow sense in which it finds representation in Persianate hagiographic literature. A treatment of desire as a general subject pertaining to these societies would require bringing in other materials as well as a consideration of methodological questions regarding gender, sexuality, and social history as a whole that are beyond my present scope. Such explorations are virtually nonexistent for the sociohistorical context I am discussing and would be welcome additions to the literature.[2]

I treat the operation of desire in Persianate Sufi discourse in four sections. I begin by considering an extended narrative poem composed in the fifteenth century that allegorizes desire and love through the entanglement of characters named Beauty and Heart. Comprehending the allegory's intent and internal details provides us a framework for understanding Persianate Sufis' view of the way sense perception of beauty in the form of the human body could lead to the production of desire and love among human subjects. In addition to being an anchor for the present chapter, this treatment of desire should help provide further depth to the stories I have discussed in chapter 4.

In the second section of chapter 5 I concentrate on Sufi representations of inappropriate desires, which play out differently when the parties involved are solely men or men and women. The available sources were all written by men and do not provide any information about women's homosocial contexts. Situations involving reprehensible love between men arise largely when one party is perceived to be religiously corrupt and responsible for leading a Sufi on a path away from a master. In hagiographic narratives there are occasional hints at proscription of male homosexual desire, but love as an emotional attachment, whether proper or improper, comes across as being a far more significant concern than sexual contact. My observation in this regard matches what has been said on this topic in other recent evaluations of various types of materials produced in pre-modern Islamic contexts. In particular, it is significant to note that what we find in these sources is not affirmation or condemnation of "homosexuality" as a mode of behavior but judgments based on the relative positions occupied by the parties. Any proscription of male-to-male desire proceeds not from a condemnation of homosexual acts but from the way the acts may signify the presence of a socially improper relationship between the men in question.[3]

While sexuality among men is a matter of hints, indirect reference, and the question of power, it appears front and center in the representation of relationships between men and women. The ubiquity of the dyadic construction of desire and love in which the lover and the beloved have different characteristics has significant repercussions for women's participation in the authority structures that governed life in Persianate Sufi communities. Almost all medieval Sufi thought takes men as its standard and, by implication, excludes women as significant Sufi actors. This exclusion pertains to the arena of love as much as it does to other spheres since males can occupy all the different positions available in the paradigm of love vis-à-vis other men. In addition, Persianate poetic paradigms that provide the overall framework for the articulation of Sufi love relationships largely presume both the lover and the beloved to be male.

When it comes to the question of representing male-female relationships in formalized literature, the critical concern that defines hagiographic authors' limitations is the possibility, or lack thereof, of marriage between the two parties. A woman married to a man could be shown interacting with him since their interactions provoke no legal censure. Similarly, there is no problem showing women interacting with their fathers, brothers, sons, and married uncles since such men are categorically prohibited from marrying them. Beyond these two possibilities lies the status of being *na-mahram*, which applies to men and women standing in such positions with each other that they could be married but are not.[4] Any interaction between such persons that involves desire has strict legal limits that work to exclude men and women from each others' social spheres. Since hagiographic and other Sufi literature is largely about men, its representation of women not tethered to the identities of men portrays the women in a particularly disadvantageous light. In this situation the question of power between the two parties parses differently than between men alone since it is presumed within the gender difference rather than being negotiated in the context of the mutual relationship between lover and beloved. Hagiographic narratives provide evocative stories that criticize acts involving contact across the gender line committed by male disciples in the beginning stages of the path.

In the third section of the chapter I concentrate on women and men in relationships that allow unrestricted social contact between them. This includes representations of Sufis' mothers, who are shown to compete with masters for the affection and allegiance of their sons who become Sufi disciples. In contrast with mothers, wives of celebrated masters sometimes appear as accomplished Sufi disciples and at other times as concupiscent and disrespectful persons who constitute trials for the masters and remind them of the low value of the material realm. The chapter's last section treats the exceptional but important case of a woman who appears as an accomplished Sufi master able to guide another highly regarded male master. The contrast here concerns social intercourse, and the representation of this woman's interactions with Sufi men is valuable for assessing the Sufi view of gender in the Persianate context.

The vast majority of Persianate hagiographic stories and representations concern men alone, with women making marginal appearances, usually in supporting roles. Nevertheless, my argument in this chapter is that gender is a critical place to look within this material to understand the social world reflected in the texts. One overarching reason for this is the pervasive tendency among Sufi authors to map the interior-exterior divide onto the presumed inherent difference between male and female. The following statement attributed to the Kubravi master 'Ali Hamadani summarizes this tendency: "Only women are interested in the physical world because this is the place of colors and smells."[5] Although this is a common enough sentiment in the literature, the details of hagiographic stories provide an abundance of evidence for great Sufi *men*'s seduction by the colors and smells of the physical world. The actual narrative material available to us thus dissembles from the stated ideology, indicating a more complex view on both gender and the material world than what first meets the eye when we read Sufi texts. Here again we see the thorough entanglement of what are portrayed as interior and exterior aspects of existence rather than the enforcement of a clear dichotomy. Desire and gender, my two foci in this chapter, therefore act as wedges that allow us to pry open some hidden recesses of the social and textual worlds being examined in this book.

SIGHT AND SEDUCTION

Citing an unnamed earlier source, the hagiography of Shaykh Ahmad Bashiri provides the following description of how love affects the human body:

> The heart is like a fire whose flames denote love. Arising conditions and premonitions (*ahval va ilham*) are like the wind that makes the fire blaze. When the wind stokes the fire, if the flames reach the eyes, it cries; if they reach the

mouth, it moans; if they reach the hand, it moves; and if they reach the foot, it dances. These conditions are called "finding" (*vajd*), because although love is in the heart, it is not really known until it is exteriorized. When the wind flares the fire, the traveler finds the way he had lost.[6]

To get a fuller sense of the complexities involved in Persianate Sufi notions regarding relationships between love, the senses, and aesthetic value hinted at in this pithy description, we can turn to the allegorical masnavi *Husn-o-dil* (*Beauty and Heart*) composed by Muhammad Yahya b. Sibak Fattahi (d. ca. 1448) in 1436. This work is a grand summation of the paradigm in question and underscores the centrality of desire and love in the Sufi religious quest. The narrative poem is around five thousand verses long and is so complicated and full of nuances that the author himself was compelled to write a prose explanation for it under the title *Dastur al-ʿushshaq* (*The Confidant of Lovers*). Between the two versions we get a useful window for understanding desire, love, and human sensory faculties.[7]

I have laid out the details of the allegory in chart 2 in order to provide a sense for the multilayered nature of the narrative. However, it would be a considerable distraction to go into all the details in my main narrative of this chapter. The story—in brief and excluding the minor characters—goes like this: a king of Greece named Intellect has a son called Heart, whom he keeps imprisoned in the castle of Body. Heart's companions tell him of the Elixir of Life, which bestows eternal life, and he becomes obsessed with obtaining it in order to live forever. His servant Sight volunteers to go look for the elixir and discovers, on the way, that it is to be found in a fountain called Mouth, which is within a garden called Face, which lies within the city of Vision. This city is the abode of a princess named Beauty, daughter of a king named Love. Sight undertakes the arduous journey to reach this garden, and when it arrives there after overcoming numerous opponents, it is greeted by Seduction, a protector of Beauty who turns out to be his own long-lost brother. Seduction takes Sight to Beauty, who welcomes it and tells of a stone statue in her treasury whose identity is a mystery to her. Upon seeing it, Sight informs her that this is a likeness of Heart. At this point in the story, Sight and Seduction have become united and have discovered a filial relationship, and Heart and Beauty turn out to have been seeking each other without knowing it themselves.

The discovery of the statue's identity makes Beauty want to meet Heart and she sends Sight back to him with her message and a confidant named Imagination. When the two get back to Body, Imagination creates a likeness of Beauty, and Heart falls in love with her immediately. At the same time, one of Intellect's soldiers named Doubt informs his master that Heart may escape Body because of his ardor for Beauty, leading Intellect to imprison Heart, Sight, and

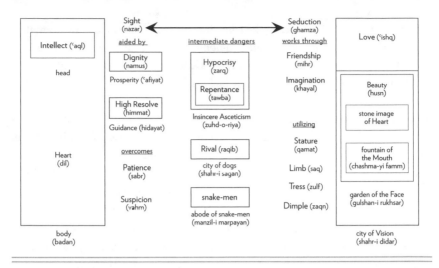

	Sight (nazar)		Seduction (ghamza)	
Intellect ('aql)	aided by	intermediate dangers	works through	Love ('ishq)
head	Dignity (namus)	Hypocrisy (zarq)	Friendship (mihr)	
	Prosperity ('afiyat)	Repentance (tawba)	Imagination (khayal)	Beauty (husn)
	High Resolve (himmat)			stone image of Heart
	Guidance (hidayat)	Insincere Asceticism (zuhd-o-riya)	utilizing	
Heart (dil)	overcomes	Rival (raqib)	Stature (qamat)	fountain of the Mouth (chashma-yi famm)
	Patience (sabr)	city of dogs (shahr-i sagan)	Limb (saq)	
			Tress (zulf)	
	Suspicion (vahm)	snake-men	Dimple (zaqn)	garden of the Face (gulshan-i rukhsar)
		abode of snake-men (manzil-i marpayan)		
body (badan)				city of Vision (shahr-i didar)

5.1   Chart 2: Schematic diagram showing the narrative of the allegory *Husn-o-dil.*

Imagination. Sight manages to escape using a ring given to it by Beauty that can make it invisible to humans and arrives back at the city of Vision after another difficult journey, which involves overcoming various opponents. Beauty is incensed by this state of affairs and calls upon her aides to overcome Intellect. Her helpers in this endeavor are her father Love and their combined forces, which include Friendship, Seduction, Stature, Limb, Tress, and Dimple. This she eventually accomplishes, following the scene depicted in a manuscript painting in which Heart and Sight capitulate to Friendship and a sword-wielding Seduction (figure 5.2). In the process, however, Intellect is able to turn Heart against Beauty. The victorious Love then decides to imprison Heart in the castle of Separation for a while after his defeat by Love's forces. This situation is corrected through the intervention of High Resolve, who convinces Love to bring Intellect back into the fold as the vizier of Body and to accept Heart as Beauty's husband.[8]

In the conclusion of the allegory, Heart comes to live in the garden of the Face and is permanently united with Beauty. He finally acquires the Elixir of Life from the well of Mouth, desire for which put the whole narrative into motion. Near the vegetation of the soft Down that surrounds Mouth, he meets Khizr, the prophet famous for eternal life based on a Quranic story. Khizr tells Heart that eternal life was his destiny because his status was always beyond being imprisoned in a body made of elements. Heart's drinking the Elixir of Life is therefore a fulfillment of his fate. Beauty and Heart have many children, one of whom is the narrator of this tale.

The four main characters in this allegory—Heart, Beauty, Sight, and Seduction—are particularly relevant for my discussion since they pertain to the

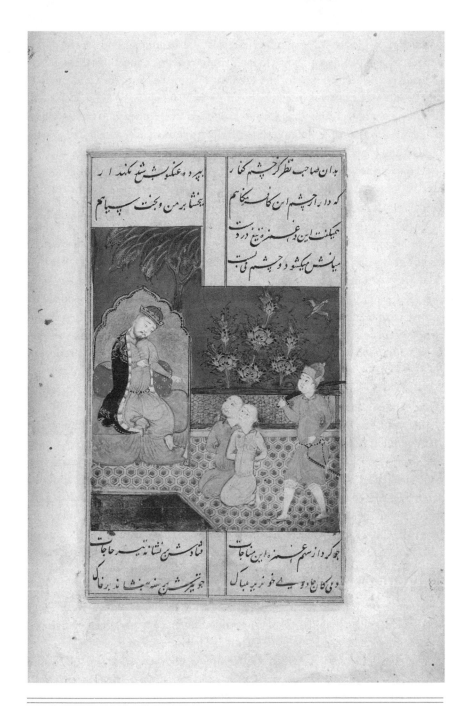

5.2   Heart and Sight in front of Friendship, with Seduction holding a sword. From a copy of Muhammad Yahya Fattahi's *Husn-o-dil*. Copyright © British Library Board. MS. Or. 11349, fol. 45b.

production of desire. Although separated in the beginning and joined at the end, Heart and Beauty are shown to have subterranean connections throughout, as evident in Heart's desire for the Elixir of Life in the first place and the idea that Beauty has a likeness of him in her treasury. The union between Heart and Beauty comes about through Sight and Seduction, their aides who go forth from the abodes of their masters to do their bidding. Importantly, Sight and Seduction are long-lost brothers who overcome their alienation to work together toward the narrative's overall fulfillment. Sight is an agent endowed with bravery, loyalty, and perseverance while Seduction deploys Beauty's warriors Stature, Limb, Tress, and Dimple to accomplish its job.

The story's allegorical message presents heart as an organ in search of beauty, where beauty carries the possibility of acknowledgment from the heart within itself. Heart's desire for beauty can be quenched only through sight, a sense that issues outward from the body to search in the external world. In its turn, sight can get to beauty and carry its news back to the heart only by being seduced by external forms such as face, stature, limbs, tresses, and dimple. Beauty is an abstraction encompassed by these physical elements, which sight must apprehend before approaching it. In the final analysis, then, heart and beauty are meant for each other, but they can be joined together only through the intermediacy of sight and seduction—a sense extending outward and a force pulling inward—that operate in the material world.

The aesthetic theory summarized in this allegory pertains to both material and nonmaterial forms. Although heart and beauty occupy pride of place, they are clearly dependent on apprehensions in the material sphere to come into contact. Sight is an agent of the heart's desire that finds certain material forms seductive and compelling. The beauty of external forms is a kind of natural force that arrests and seduces sight and the other senses and, through them, the heart. The interdependency of heart and beauty, on the one hand, and sight and seduction, on the other, should be reminiscent of the circle of love I described in the previous chapter. In this allegory, and in stories about great masters and disciples, heart's conjunction with beauty is a wholly desirable end. However, the inherent connection between sight and seduction as elaborated in the allegory also provides the possibility of their improper functioning: sight can be seduced by deceptive objects, leading the heart to fall for improper beauty.

The gender dynamic between the four main characters is particularly significant since it hints at different roles for male and female. The prince Heart is entombed in a negatively valued body, which his foremost servant Sight overcomes through its escape to Beauty. The primary aide to the princess Beauty, on the other hand, is Seduction, who works in conjunction with body parts. Male and female bodies get mapped to lover and beloved with opposite connotations: one is to be escaped from, while the other is to be displayed. This gender dynamic does not map directly to Sufi hagiographic representations of men and women. There, beauty is equally likely to be found in men and women, and those who possess beauty adopt the characteristics associated with it in this allegory irrespective of their gender identity.[9]

In the overall theory, beauty is both the ultimate objective on heart's true path and a disruptive force that can lead into error. Similarly, heart must rely on sight to get to true beauty, but it can get entranced by improper beauty as well. In considering this allegory as a guide for understanding Sufi hagiographic stories, it is important to keep in mind not just the beginning and the end of the narrative but also the various processes that unfold in the middle. Sufi narratives about the lives of masters and disciples provide ample examples for the many possibilities registered in the allegory regarding the creation, management, fulfillment, and denial of desire mediated through material senses and bodies. While the allegory works toward ideal ends, hagiographic stories convey desire's ability to induce proper love as well as to lead astray.

BODIES DESIRING AND DESIRABLE

Echoing a theme central to *Beauty and Heart*, the Naqshbandi master ʿAlaʾ ad-Din Abizi is reported to have told his disciples that God has endowed human beings with three preeminent organs: eyes for seeing, ears for hearing, and the heart for loving. These three organs operate without reference to volition: the eye sees whatever comes in front of it, the ear hears whatever sound enters it, and the heart falls in love when impulses from the external senses alert it to the presence of a beautiful being. Just as Sufis have to guard their eyes and ears from being in situations where they may be subject to reprehensible sights and sounds, they have to guard their hearts from beauty that can lead astray. The surest way to do this is to enter the orbit of a Sufi master so that one's capacity for love becomes occupied in the religious pursuit.[10]

This formulation of the role of senses is helpful for seeing the way the connection between sensations and emotions works in the Persianate Sufi context. Although Abizi puts the heart on a par with eyes and ears, it is clearly a sensing organ of a different type and scale than the other two. For one, the heart is dependent on impulses from the external senses to recognize its object. Moreover, love is an emotion that can come to preoccupy one to the utmost, whereas sensations that take shape in the eye and ear are momentary and can be disrupted through blocking the organs or turning away from the scene. As described in the allegory, beauty and its capacity to invoke desire and love in the heart are more complex matters than sight and sound pure and simple. To see some of the complexities involved here, I will treat hagiographic stories concerned with the operation of desire between men and between men and women.

Men as Subjects and Objects of Desire

The connection between beauty and desire is evident in stories where great Sufi masters are shown to have heightened sensitivity to beauty irrespective of the object's status. For example, ʿAli Hamadani's hagiographer states that the master himself related that when he was a young man traveling to find his vocation he lost consciousness when he saw a beautiful young man in the bazaar in Isfaraʾin and became a spectacle for the crowd. A disciple of the master Muhammad Azkani who was present there went and told him the tale of someone who had swooned upon seeing beauty. The master asked that Hamadani be brought to him immediately, and this message was delivered to him when he regained consciousness. That night Muhammad appeared to Hamadani in a dream and told him to take on oath on Azkani's hand, and, when Hamadani met the master the next day, Azkani told him that Muhammad had delivered him the same instructions. Hamadani and Azkani thus became joined by one Sufi understanding the other's spiritual capacity through the report on his reaction to beauty. Here the beautiful man himself has no relevance to the story apart from being an object with a remarkable external appearance.[11]

Other stories involve young men who are affected by beauty but have to be helped away from improper associations through masters' intervention. Abizi's hagiographer provides proof for the master's views on the heart as an organ I cited earlier by relating actual incidents, such as the case of a disciple who reported that he had become infatuated with a beautiful young man. One day when he appeared in front of the master after having spent time pining after this beloved, the master was angry and told him that he was going down his own path, which was negating his guidance. He then sat with the master and was, through his presence in his company, gradually relieved of his desire for the other man.[12] In a similar story, the master Shams ad-Din Ruji reported that once, when he had become a disciple of Saʿd ad-Din Kashghari, he fell in love with a beautiful man such that he could neither give up the infatuation nor get rid of his shame and embarrassment in front of the master for the situation. Eventually, Kashghari arrived in front of him by himself and absolved him of the love by putting his hands on his chest and working on his interior.[13]

Kashghari is himself featured in a story reported by his son Khwaja Kalan. It is said that when Kashghari was seven years old he accompanied his father on a trading trip where the party also included a most beautiful boy of Kashghari's own age with whom he became infatuated. One night when the lamps had been extinguished and the two boys were sleeping next to each other, Kashghari got the desire to take the other boy's hand and rub his eyes on it. But he had barely extended his hand when one corner of the room opened up to reveal a formidable figure with a lamp who came toward him rapidly, crossed over, and then disappeared into a cavity that had opened up at the opposite corner. Kashghari said that he was terrified by this experience and took it to be a warning that dissipated his desire for the relationship.[14]

Shah Qasim-i Anvar

In hagiographic materials relating to the fifteenth century, the most prominent case of relationships between Sufi men that are hinted at as being improper involve the master Shah Qasim-i Anvar, who is remarked upon as a man of high spiritual attainment but unable to properly control those attracted to him. The charges against his entourage are always left vague, and some of the criticism may reflect either inter-Sufi rivalries or Qasim's purported sympathy for the apocalyptic Hurufi movement that had him expelled from Herat after a failed attempt on the life of the Timurid ruler Shahrukh (d. 1447) in 1427.[15] A hagiography of Khwaja ʿUbaydullah Ahrar states that, even in his old age, this Naqshbandi master considered Qasim-i Anvar the most charismatic Sufi he had met in his life. He reported that whenever he had gone before him he felt "that the whole world circles around him to eventually descend into him and disappear [within him]."[16] Although he was clearly a remarkable man of his age, Qasim's hagiographic profile is marred by the fact that a number of authors pointedly criticize some of his disciples. ʿAbd ar-Rahman Jami writes that he had personally met some of Qasim's followers and considered them outside the pale of Islam altogether. One follower, whom Jami considered a worthy Sufi, told him that Qasim himself told him not to stay with him because of some of his other followers. Jami's explanation for the contrast between Qasim's own undeniable excellence and the waywardness of some of his followers is that he was too generous a person to shun anyone who came to him because of his innate attractiveness. People inclined to worldly pleasures took unjust advantage of this by deriving meanings from his words that he did not intend.[17] In Ahrar's words, as his hagiographer reports them, people explained Qasim's situation in two ways. They believed that he was either aware of his disciples' corruption, but suffered it as his fate, or these disciples were like the thorns put on top of walls around an orchard that keep thieves and animals away from the fruit. The prize protected by the thorns in this case was Qasim's true spiritual station, which he wanted to keep hidden from strangers.[18]

The same source that reports this provides the most detailed description of the activities of Qasim-i Anvar's followers. It reports that Ahrar said that once, when Qasim had come to Transoxiana, his followers got together and went around the bazaar to collect beardless young boys (*pisaran-i amrad*) with whom they began to establish relations. Their explanation for this behavior was that they were observing the beauty of God in the beautiful forms of these boys. As this was going on, Qasim asked after his followers by saying, "where have those pigs of mine gone?" Ahrar indicated that this meant that, to Qasim, these men appeared as pigs when he saw with his spiritual sight (*nazar-i basirat*).[19] The practice of contemplating young boys as beautiful forms that represent divine beauty is usually known through the term *shahidbazi* and has a controversial history in Sufi contexts. It is the chief defining feature of the work *Majalis al-'ushshaq,* which I have discussed earlier. While it is difficult to substantiate *shahidbazi* as a widespread social practice, such "looking" is a common feature of Persian poetic rhetoric. The theme is reflected also in the painting that is a part of an anthology and is accompanied by the verse of ʿAbd ar-Rahman Jami. (figure 5.3).

In Ahrar's view, to act amorously toward beings who were only outwardly beautiful was a grave error. As mentioned in the previous chapter, Ahrar's own story of attachment to the master Yaʿqub Charkhi involved falling in love with a master described as having a beautiful form. This, however, was a case of a person with a high spiritual station being able to control how he appeared to others in order to attract and guide them. His and others' criticism of Qasim-i Anvar's followers stems from the fact that they took physical beauty by itself as a legitimate object of love without reference to its deeper meanings. For a man to fall in love with a man deemed outwardly beautiful was not a problem in itself; the difficulty occurred only when the subject and object of desire were not part of a larger framework tethered to Sufi ideology.

While reports about Qasim absolve him from being responsible for the unnamed corrupt behavior of some of his followers, it is clear that he was seen as somewhat of a failure as a Sufi master. His attractiveness is remarked upon by one and all, but his unwillingness or inability to control the disciples is seen as at least an unwitting weakness. The ultimate cause for this was his incapability to manage the desires of those connected to him. His personal charisma was such that people were attracted to him, but unlike the truly consummate masters, he could not adequately control and manipulate the relationships established on the basis of this attraction. This flaw in his personality was at least in part responsible for the fact that he did not initiate a long-lasting Sufi community despite acknowledgment that he surpassed his contemporaries in charisma. This lack of a dedicated community meant that he never became the subject of an extended hagiography dedicated solely to his miracles and achievements, and narratives regarding him have to be culled from works devoted to others.

5.3   Men contemplating a beautiful youth. Shirvan, 1468. Opaque watercolor.
Copyright © The British Library Board. MS. Add. 16561 fol. 79b.

So far I have related stories in which handsome men are objects of someone's desire. A story regarding Ahrar provides a glimpse of the other side in the form of the haughty attitude adopted by a man known for his beauty. When the master returned to Herat after becoming attached to the Naqshbandi chain through Ya'qub Charkhi, he attended the house of an associate who was dedicated to the Khwajagan and greeted him with great respect. In fact, Ahrar's new association was so apparent on him that everyone present paid him great respect save one young man famous for his looks. On this occasion the host told Ahrar that although everyone had already eaten, if he was hungry food could be prepared. Before Ahrar could reply, the handsome man, who was used to being treated with deference, interjected to say that time for food was over. Noticing this rudeness, Ahrar indicated that he would teach him a lesson and proceeded to request that food be prepared for him. Then he worked on the handsome man's interior so that he fell in love with him and went out himself to make the fire for the food. His face became dirty from soot in the process, spoiling the beauty of which he had been so proud earlier. From that time onward, he forgot about his own beauty and became an absolute devotee of Ahrar. The story marked the triumph of the Sufi master's beauty over the attractiveness confined to external forms.[20]

Stories of attraction and love between men in hagiographic narrative indicate censure only in cases when lovers fall in love with beautiful beloveds whose status or moral attributes do not conform to Sufi values. The authors register no problem with the fact of a deep and abiding love between men who find each other physically attractive as long as they are appropriately positioned with respect to each other and are aware of beauty as an attribute for those truly worthy of being objects of love. This pattern contrasts significantly with cases when one of the parties is a woman not in such a relationship with a man where that would allow them unrestricted access to each other.

Desiring Women

A most emphatic example condemning a Sufi man's attraction for an unrelated woman is presented in the hagiography dedicated to 'Umar Murshidi. The master said that, during his youth in Kazarun, one day he went into the desert and on the way back heard a beautiful voice, which he greatly enjoyed. He felt tremendous desire to see the person to whom the voice belonged and could not get this idea out of his head even when he returned to his Sufi chamber and immersed himself in his religious pursuits. Then, when he was reading the Quran, he suddenly heard a voice commanding, "Look!" When he did this, he said, "I saw a woman, naked from head to foot, sitting and showing me her vagina, unhesitatingly and boldly, uncovering herself in a way that no wife would ever do in front of her husband." The voice then said, "This is the woman whose voice you had heard and taken pleasure from. Your hearing her voice is the same as seeing her vagina."[21]

This story implies the dangers of being led astray by sensory perception more strongly than anything present in narratives involving men alone. The Sufi's apprehension of a pleasant voice and the possibility of seeing a beautiful being leads to something indecent in a way never indicated for a handsome man. The critical issue that makes the difference here is that men's social relationships with women are subject to legal surveillance that does not apply to matters between men. What may seem like an extraordinary jump between Shaykh ʿUmar's hearing a woman's voice to her appearing naked in front of him is a direct reflection of Islamic legal ideology in which social intercourse between men and women is regulated according to the possibility, or lack thereof, of a lawful sexual relationship between them. Since Shaykh ʿUmar is neither married to the woman nor in a relationship that would make marriage impossible, his access to her has significant legal limitations. On this basis, the connection caused by her producing a sound and his hearing it laterally shifts the situation to the sexual domain immediately.[22]

A number of other, milder examples can be added to this story to make the point. A disciple of Amin ad-Din Balyani, another master from southern Iran, said that one day, when he was in the mosque, he heard a woman's voice and was intrigued to see her. As he was walking over to take a peek, a stone fell on his foot and rendered him unconscious. Later, when he went to see the master, he told him to be glad that he had not actually seen the woman. In that case the punishment would have come to his eyes rather than his feet and could have blinded him.[23] Similarly, a man said that before he came to ask Bahaʾ ad-Din Naqshband to become his disciple, he had spent time in an empty house with an unrelated girl with whom he talked and to whom he gave a kiss. When he expressed his intention of becoming a Sufi to the master, he replied that this did not seem to go along with his other recent behavior, which was illegal. The master's knowledge of the matter was one of his charismatic miracles.[24] Once when Khwaja Ahrar was instructing disciples on the necessity of averting the gaze from a woman because it would cause lust, a man asked what about a case where there is no lust. Ahrar got angry and said, "Even I cannot have a lust-free gaze; where have you come from that you can do it?"[25]

To these stories one can add a case involving Shaykh Safi of Ardabil, in which the direction of the gaze is inverted from female to male. As I mentioned in chapter 3, this master is known for spectacular dance when in the throes of ecstasy, during which he would leave the ground and sometimes hover over the whole assemblage. Once, when this occurred, the walls of the room picked themselves up from the ground and joined in as well, causing the sensation of an earthquake in the area. A woman, who was a sayyid and married to a nobleman, came out of her house to see what was going on. When people told her, she waded through the crowd to get to the mosque in order to see the shaykh for herself. However, as soon as her eyes alighted on him he sat down. Some people present there realized that this was because an unrelated woman had seen him, and they asked her to leave. She complied with the request and thought to herself, "If this audition were an effect of the carnal self (*nafsani*), it would have intensified with the gaze of a *na-mahram*. But, since it was an audition of the outpouring of divine secrets (*fayz-i asrar-i ilahi*), it became illegal with contamination from such a gaze." She then became a disciple of the master and gave away a part of a village to him.[26]

It should not come as a surprise that Sufi hagiographic representations pay close attention to legal strictures regarding male-female relationships. These texts are products of the religious literati who can be expected to adhere to established conventions in such matters. There is, however, no reason to take these legal strictures as literal descriptions of reality and presume that men and women interacted very narrowly in this context. Even hagiographic narratives do contain instances of unrelated men and women connected through gazes that do not merit censure. For example, once an old and decrepit woman came to see Khwaja Ahrar and sat down close to him. He asked her why she had come and she replied, "we have come to see your beauty." To make a joke of this, he turned to an associate and said, in a soft voice so that she would not hear, "and what do we get to see?"[27] Although rare, women do make it to pictorial representations of Sufi gatherings, as in figure 5.4, which shows one as part of the company assembled around a Sufi master. While homosociality can be presumed to have been a widespread norm, a larger range of interactions and attitudes become visible as we turn to other stories involving women.

In the allegory *Husn-o-dil*, the male and female main characters are separated and interact in stylized ways according to a particular gender ideology. Hagiographic representations differ from this in that both males and females can come to occupy the place of beauty and become seductive to the sight of a lover. Moreover, in the hagiographic sphere, seduction by beauty is ubiquitously subordinated to the legal framework in which male-female interactions are subject to far greater scrutiny than those between men alone. In the remainder of this chapter, we will attempt to see whether, and to what extent, representations of females show them in the position of the heart who seeks higher beauty in the form of the great Sufi masters and God, through its sight and other senses.

5.4 A Sufi gathering in a garden. Bukhara, 1520-1530. Opaque watercolor, ink, and gold on paper mounted on an album page, 22.1 × 14.2 cm. Arthur M. Sackler Gallery, Smithsonian Institution, Washington, DC: Purchase—Smithsonian Unrestricted Trust Funds, Smithsonian Collections Acquisition Program, and Dr. Arthur M. Sackler, S1986.216.

In the previous chapter I discussed stories regarding Shaykh Safi ad-Din Ardabili's early years, in which his mother figures prominently. However, the mother disappears from the narrative once Shaykh Safi becomes a disciple of Shaykh Zahid, and I argued that the transition from mother to master represents a changing of the guard with respect to guidance and love provided by a caretaker. This pattern is evident in a number of different places in hagiographic literature and can be regarded as the distinctive view on mothers of Sufi men in this material.

The interchangeability of the mother and the master is traceable in instances where the master is shown fulfilling a distinctly maternal function. One example of this that employs striking bodily imagery comes from the early life of Baha' ad-Din Naqshband. His main hagiographer relates that after Naqshband had entered into a relationship with the Khwajagani master Sayyid Amir Kulal, he was once passing through a village that was home to a Sufi master named Shams ad-Din. This master was suitably impressed by his potential and attempted to persuade him to stay with him rather than continue the journey. Naqshband's response, which convinced Shams not to pursue the matter further, was: "I am a child of others. Even if you were to put your breast of training (tarbi'at) in my mouth, I would not grasp the nipples."[28] The same metaphor is used in another work dedicated to Naqshband as well, albeit from a different angle. Khwaja Muhammad Parsa reports, when Naqshband finished his training with Amir Kulal, that the master told him, "I have dried up my breasts so that the bird of your spirit may come out of the egg of your base humanness. But your bird has gone much farther than [merely] this."[29]

A story that portrays the Sufi master in a maternal role and in competition with an actual mother of a disciple is given in hagiographies dedicated to Khwaja Ahrar. Ahrar himself related from the earlier master 'Ala' ad-Din Ghijduvani that he went to join the circle of Amir Kalan Vashi at the age of sixteen. This master instructed him in the Khwajagani path and told him that he must hide his Sufi affiliation from everyone, including people very close to him. He did as he was told, but it became difficult to hide his activity when he began to grow progressively weaker as an effect of bodily mortifications. His mother noticed the change and asked him if he was sick, which he denied. She perceived the answer as recalcitrance and, as a challenge, threw open her shirt to reveal her chest and said that she would not forgive him the milk he had drunk from her breasts if he did not come clean. He then saw no way out except to tell her the truth, and she herself decided to join the Khwajagani path upon hearing of the master's instructions. However, her decision caused 'Ala' ad-Din consternation because she had not been authorized by the master. He raised the matter with Amir Vashi, who said that it was fine and that he gave her the permission. Then one day, when he and his mother were alone at home, she asked him to get a pot of warm water. She did ritual ablutions from the water in front of him, prayed two cycles, and began doing Sufi exercises and shortly passed away.[30]

'Ala' ad-Din Ghijduvani's story matches that of Shaykh Safi in that the masters take control of the young men's bodies at the beginning of the Sufi path. In both cases women are shown as competing with the masters for their sons' affection and obedience, although they eventually acquiesce to the transfers. 'Ala' ad-Din's mother goes one step further by herself becoming a Sufi and being removed from the narrative completely through death. Both stories represent the future masters' mothers as having approved the sons' paths, even though this means losing their sons. There is no way to avoid this, however, since the young men's maturation as Sufis depends on being in love with the master over the mother.

The hagiography of Zayn ad-Din Taybadi presents a story with an alternative end to the mother-master competition over a young disciple. The author of this work relates from Zayn ad-Din's son Shams ad-Din that one day, a man unknown in the area appeared in Zayn ad-Din's gathering. The master asked him to sit down, but he first kept standing, lost in thought for some time, and then yelled loudly, fell down, and fainted. The master felt great pity for him and took care of him personally while weeping himself. When the man was completely recovered, he sent him away with the promise of remaining in touch, saying that he should go back to his mother because she greatly desired to see him. As he was leaving, people asked him how he had met Zayn ad-Din since no one had ever seen him before. He told them that he was from the region of Fars and that he had been saved when Zayn ad-Din had appeared miraculously somewhere at a moment when he had been in grave danger. He had been looking for Zayn ad-Din since that time and had realized that he had found him at the moment when he had yelled and fainted earlier.[31]

This story represents the rare case of a mother retaining her power over a Sufi son. Positing this story next to the ones I have related earlier highlights the fact that the earlier mothers are shown to have been willing participants in the paths undertaken by their sons and voluntarily gave up their control. The juxtaposition also underscores the fact that, under hagiographic conventions, a successful bond between a great master and an outstanding disciple is a fated event. When it occurs, a disciple is being incorporated into a Sufi group's self-articulation, and, when it fails to happen, the disciple is excluded from charismatic functions. The connection is essential for the continuation of the Sufi intergenerational chain of authority, which must remain unbroken in order to perpetuate a valuable mode of religious practice. The movement between the two types of love represented by the mother and the master is thus a necessary precondition for the functioning of the Sufi mode of perpetuation of religious authority.[32]

WOMEN MARRIED TO SUFIS

The vast majority of Persianate Sufi masters whose lives form the subject of hagiographic narratives are described as married men after the early years of Sufi searching in their lives. Equated with the commencement of heterosexual relations, marriage is avoided until the time when men are thought to have overcome sexual urges likely to lead them astray from religious pursuits. Stories relating the great masters' marital alliances provide a glimpse into the valuation of women as well as men. Such stories include cases where the women are shown to be worthy companions for the masters or situations in which they are seen as trials brought upon the masters to strengthen their religious resolve. Under both options, the masters are shown to have tied the knots to the spouses willingly, but women's purported actions have different repercussions for understanding the construction of gender in this context.

Sufi Wives

In literature produced during the fourteenth and fifteenth centuries, the most detailed example of a wife with the same values as her Sufi husband comes from a work concerned with the life of Fazlallah Astarabadi, the founder of the Hurufi movement. Written by one of his chief followers and successors, this work describes Fazlallah as a strict ascetic during the period he was just beginning to acquire fame as a master in Tabriz around 1370. His followers at this time included a vizier named Khwaja Bayazid Damghani, whose wife, also a devotee, was originally from the city of Astarabad and related to Fazlallah. This couple wished to arrange the marriage of their fourteen-year-old daughter to Fazlallah, and the mother approached him through one of his disciples. At first, she was told that the matter was difficult since the circumstances in which Fazlallah lived, incumbent on anyone who became attached to him, would be particularly arduous for a woman. She persisted by asking for the exact conditions and was told that the girl would be required to forsake all personal belongings upon leaving her parents' house; renounce any food or dress that could not be paid for by the small means of a dervish; determine never to take a single step out of the Sufi hospice where Fazlallah lived after entering it; adopt a bed made of sackcloth, a felt pillow, and a cotton dress; respect the religious community's practice of seclusion at night; and adopt the stringent collective prayers practiced daily by the community.

The prospective wife's mother was glad to hear these conditions and asked the girl what she thought of them. She wholeheartedly agreed because of the spiritual return she and her parents would attain as a result of the harsh life she would lead. She first spent four months in the house of another dervish, as a kind of trial to make sure that she could withstand the difficulties, and then married Fazlallah. Her entry to the dervish community was marked by the symbolic step of putting on the distinctive green dress worn by all of Fazlallah's dedicated followers. Besides the generally harsh living conditions, she also worked alongside other dervishes to sew caps that were sold to provide for the community's food and other bare necessities. In connection with this marriage, Fazlallah was asked about the permissibility of sexual relations, and he said that they were not spiritually harmful as long as the intention was procreation and not pleasure.[33]

We do not have any further representations of the activities of Fazlallah Astarabadi's wife in Hurufi literature. However, the same follower and hagiographer who provides the story about her represents one of his daughters named Kalimatallah Hiya al-ʿUlya as his main heir after his execution in 1394.[34] Historical and hagiographic sources external to the Hurufis state that this daughter remained active later on and that she and her husband gathered a considerable following in Tabriz, which led to hostility from the local community of scholars. The Karakoyunlu ruler Jahan Shah (d. 1467) was able to resist pressure from her enemies for some period but eventually gave in and issued the fatal order that led to both her death and the massacre of more than five hundred followers in 1441–42.[35]

A story similar to that of Fazlallah Astarabadi's marriage is related from the life of Shaykh Ahmad Bashiri, although here the woman makes numerous appearances in the narrative following her betrothal. The author relates that the master's associates included a man of high status who would come and visit him often. On one occasion he found the meeting so moving that he exchanged turbans with the master and was later made to understand by a friend that that indicated the development of a family relationship. He then approached Shaykh Bashiri, offering the hand of his twelve-year-old daughter Bibi Fatima. The master was initially reluctant to agree to the match because he wanted to remain celibate, but he then had a dream in which "men of the unseen" brought a woman to him and married her to him. He took this to be a command and acquiesced to the proposal. The marriage tie had an important effect on the lives of his parents-in-law as well. They did not have a male child and asked the shaykh for an intervention. They were soon graced with the birth of twin boys.[36]

Both Bibi Fatima and her mother, Amr Khatun, are mentioned a number of times in this work, the latter designated as Shaykh Ahmad's vicegerent among women. This work is exceptional in that it explicitly describes women as equal to men in their religious accomplishment.[37] The work iterates multiple times that women were a part of the master's inner circle of devotees throughout the various phases of his career.[38] The author mentions the procedure used for women when describing initiation into the group: at the point where the master is supposed to take the disciple's hand in his own, he offers his sleeve to the woman to hold in order not to cross the legal boundary that proscribes touching among *na-mahrams*. Interestingly, the oath of discipleship he is reported to have administered includes the promise on the part of the disciple not to look at a *na-mahram*, but this does not seem to have caused women to be excluded from Sufi guidance by the master.[39] In fact, the hagiographer makes the point that women and men dedicated to Shaykh Bashiri tended to lose their carnal desires completely: in one case, a woman who was married to a man for seven years had had so little real contact with him that she could not even recognize his face.[40]

Women as Burden

Some stories relating to the wives of famous masters show the men in states of vulnerability and powerlessness. These are rare situations since the hagiographic paradigm as a whole involves disciples and heirs representing the great masters as phenomenally powerful beings. Moreover, the total authority invested in images of masters works to justify the claims of the successors who either sponsored or wrote the hagiographies, making an indication of vulnerability counterproductive for their purposes. The way the narratives rationalize the masters' vulnerability provides an important view into the construction of gender as well as the social dynamics of Sufi communities and literary patterns in general.

The author of the *Rashahat* tells of a master named Tunguz Shaykh in Turkestan who belonged to the family of Ahmad Yasavi. A visitor to his place saw that his wife paid no attention to matters like cooking, usually associated with women. On this occasion, as Tunguz Shaykh was bending down to a fire that was refusing to light, his wife came in and gave him a swift kick such that his head went into the fire and his face was covered with ash. Much to the surprise of the visitors, he continued with his work and ignored this insult. When asked about his forbearance, he replied, "The knowledge and states that have become apparent to us have been due to our patience in putting up with the oppression of the ignorant."[41] In this instance the master's wife wholly personified the worldly burdens the Sufi must endure in order to acquire religious merits.

Detailed stories of a wayward wife of a prominent master relate to the Naqshbandi Shaykh 'Ala' ad-Din Abizi, who is otherwise portrayed as having been a tremendously powerful presence in front of his disciples. The hagiographer reports that he and his wife used to fight a lot, and once she hit him so hard that his forehead was bloodied. In his anger he grabbed her head and turned it so that it went halfway around, facing backward. Seeing this terrible condition, a child of theirs of five or six pleaded with the father, so that he restored the woman to normalcy. She was then grateful, feeling remorse, and gathered the area's notables to declare publicly that she forgave her dower and any other rights owed her.[42]

This incident did not resolve all Shaykh Abizi's difficulties with his wife. Later he again appeared in company with his collar torn and a bloody forehead, prompting someone to ask why he did not just divorce the woman, particularly since she had forgiven her dower and this would not even have monetary implications. He replied that she was a sayyida and that the fault had been his own because he had been rude to her. He then went and apologized to the woman. In his more extended explanation for his forbearance, he said that she was an affliction he knew and he was afraid that if he got rid of her something worse would alight on him. Going deeper than this, he also explained that putting up with this wife and taking care of children were necessary for him to stay in this world and obey God's commands. Otherwise he would be absorbed completely in the interior reality and would not be able to perform obligations like prayers and fasting. The hagiographer states that this explanation was akin to other stories of great men: a master would ask a servant to beat him whenever he experienced a great mystical state in order to keep him in the world. The author then suggests that these instances were equivalent to the famous report according to which Muhammad would ask his wife ʿAʾisha to intrude upon his thoughts by saying, "Talk to me, Humayra."[43]

The representation of the relationship between Shaykh Abizi and his wife presents important clues for understanding gender in the context. First, the male-female difference here maps exactly to the interior-exterior dichotomy critical to Sufi thought, enforcing the notion that women are tied to lower, material forms while men have the capacity to delve into the highly valued interior. This is, then, a case of the interior-exterior difference being carried into the social sphere in a way that gives the dichotomy greater power and naturalizes the gender difference and hierarchy. Taken at face value, women appear, like children, devoted to their carnal desires even when they are sayyidas. On the other hand, men wish to ascend out of the material world toward a more noble existence. By this token, men who do not live up to their potential are like women, as exemplified in a story about a master who got very agitated when he saw a religious scholar of questionable merit approaching him and asked his disciples to lead him away. When someone suggested that this man was knowledgeable, the shaykh responded: "In my eyes he was a naked black woman with drooping breasts, showing all manner of ugliness." While this master stated this

out in the open, Ahrar opined that the most upright masters cover up such matters when they become visible to them because of their special sight rather than
stating them in the open.[44] In this instance the interior-exterior division that
forms the basis of abstract Sufi thought is a matter enacted in social and textual
forms.

Beyond the arguments stated in the texts, stories about recalcitrant wives
married to Sufi masters contain important information when we consider the
frames within which they are set. The narrators are male Sufi adherents who
write from the positions occupied by men who question the masters about their
putting up with the women and not divorcing them. They are *murids*, those
who desire the master and cultivate deep love for him, thereby competing with
masters' wives and children for affection and emotional as well as material resources. One source asserts this explicitly, calling the disciple's transformation
into a new body after progressing on the Sufi path a birth that is the product of
a kind of marriage between the desiring disciple and the desired master.[45] My
suggestion throughout this book that hagiographic narratives be seen as textual
performances provides us a way to make sense of the stories that make powerful masters appear vulnerable through negative valuation of women attached
to them.

WOMEN AS ACCOMPLISHED SUFIS

The contrast between praiseworthy and troublesome wives in the stories discussed hinges on the question of whether the women in question are also Sufis.
When they are, their interests with respect to the masters are aligned with those
of other, mostly male, Sufis, leading to positive representation in hagiographic
narratives. And, when they are not Sufis, their needs and demands disrupt the
largely male-to-male world of Persianate Sufism. Given these strictures, we can
expect that the most laudable female characters to be found in hagiographic
narratives would be Sufi relatives of the masters, including wives, mothers,
sisters, and daughters. As we have already seen, this is indeed the case, and
women tend to become valuable particularly when they constitute crucial links
between men who are deemed important.[46]

Exchange of Women Among Men

When Shaykh Abizi fights with his wife in the stories previously discussed, one
of his reasons for later self-censure is the acknowledgment that the woman is
a sayyida and thereby deserving of special respect. This is particularly important since Abizi is not a sayyid himself and can allege kinship with the Prophet

only as an affine through marriage. Although Abizi's wife's relationship with the Prophet is very remote (she lived eight centuries after his death), the general respect accorded sayyids means that she occupies an intermediate role between two important men. This is the position in which we find many other women as well in hagiographic narratives.

A few examples of this pattern are helpful to make this point. Proceeding chronologically among masters discussed in the book, Shaykh Safi ad-Din Ardabili is shown to have thought explicitly along these lines. Once he had become a confidant of Shaykh Zahid Gilani, the master one day asked: "How is it that there is a master who has such a disciple that the master's station is because of his [disciple's] honor?" Shaykh Safi first thought that he was talking about the two of them, but then the master added: "The master gives his daughter to him, who gives birth to a child whose honor ratifies the station and glory of the father and the grandfather." Shaykh Safi then thought that the master was talking about another man who was his son-in-law, and he became especially attentive to him. However, at the age of seventy Shaykh Zahid eventually married another woman who gave birth to a son and a daughter. This daughter was Bibi Fatima, Shaykh Safi's future wife, who became the mother of the man who eventually became both his and Shaykh Zahid's heir.[47]

Continuing this pattern, it is reported that Baha' ad-Din Naqshband had four daughters, three of whom were married to disciples or their sons and became mothers to later members of the group.[48] Similarly, 'Abd al-Avval Nishapuri, one of Khwaja Ahrar's main successors, was also his son-in-law.[49] Importantly, Nishapuri also wrote a hagiography of Ahrar, indicating an overlap between kinship structures and textual production of the saintly figure's life. In hagiographic representations of exchanges of women, the relationship of love and desire is always between fathers-in-law and sons-in-law rather than either of the men and the woman through whom kinship is established. This characteristic reinforces the male-centeredness of the narratives in terms of both the regulation of an emotion as powerful as love and the ability to establish voluntary relationships.

Women as Exemplary Masters

Shaykh 'Umar Murshidi's hagiographer reports that the master said, when he traveled to Mecca to perform the hajj, that an old man told him an amazing story. He said:

> Once day as I was circumambulating, I saw a woman who was doing the same while skipping on one foot. I asked her about her condition. She said, "I have a suckling child still in the crib. I came from my own region in order to perform

the hajj with the intention to return. As I started the circumambulation, I heard the child crying, so I started moving the crib back and forth with one foot. With the other foot, I continued to go around [the Ka'ba] and also performed the rites of running between two hills (sa'i), in order that neither [obligation] would be forfeited." She said that there was three months' worth of distance between the two places.[50]

The principle exemplified in this story—that space can contract for the religious elect—is a widespread motif in Sufi literature and is discussed in chapter 7. The story provides an easy way to imagine the more restricted mobility allowed to women as compared to men in the societies in question. While God is shown to allow the woman to perform the great ritual because of her spiritual station, that that does not mean absolution from her maternal duties. The double burden on this woman as compared to men was in part responsible for women not becoming major players in the Sufi social world. In material I have surveyed for this book, there is one narrative that stands out for its exceptionality when it comes to discussing the possibility of women becoming full-fledged Sufi masters. There may well be other examples of female masters in sources not known to me at present, although a handful more would not negate the general point I am making. My example pertains to Kalan Khatun (literally, Elder Lady), daughter of Sayyid Amir Hamza, the son and chief successor to the Khwajagani master Sayyid Amir Kulal. What we know of this woman comes from a hagiography of the family written by her own son Amir Shihab ad-Din. This is a man who had legitimate free access to her, so that the case does not violate the rule of hagiographers not making unrelated high-status women subjects of discussion in the "public" hagiographic sphere.

Shihab ad-Din relates that when it came time for Amir Hamza's death he asked two of his nephews, one by one, to be his successor. The older of the two declined because he was a complete recluse, while the younger preferred to serve people in other ways than being a Sufi guide. He then turned to his own children and overlooked two of his sons in favor of his daughter, saying that everyone seeking him should seek her and that, just as some people are proud of their sons, he was proud of his daughter. Shihab ad-Din states that, while his mother was the subject of numerous miracles that were well known to her close relatives, he did not consider it appropriate to relate these in the open.[51] While his ostensible reasoning for this reluctance is that this would divulge the secrets of a Sufi, this clearly pertained only to women since he describes the miracles of men in great detail throughout the rest of the text. Such an attitude automatically restricts women from becoming recognized as prominent friends of God since public affirmation of the ability to perform miracles is a crucial aspect of being accorded this status.

After registering his reluctance, Shihab ad-Din does tell one story regarding his mother's spiritual powers. The particulars of this story are revealing in that they show the additional steps a woman needed to undertake so as to act as a full-fledged Sufi master in this context. He relates that some time after Kalan Khatun's accession to her father's mantle, the prominent Khwajagani master and author Khwaja Muhammad Parsa decided to go to Mecca for the hajj and came to Amir Kulal's shrine to ask his permission. After visiting the grave, he said that he must also ask permission from Kalan Khatun since she was Amir Kulal's heir and her father had said that whoever seeks him must seek her. He proceeded to her house for the visit, which occurred without the two ever coming face-to-face with each other. Upon his arrival, she sent some simple food to him to welcome him, and then he asked her servant to go and ask her permission for his journey. When she heard the request, she asked the servant to bring a plate, which she filled with plaited cotton and sent out to Parsa, who fell into a trance upon seeing it. When he regained consciousness, he told his companions that he had just learned something critical about himself and then he proceeded to Mecca. He performed the hajj normally, but when it came time to start the return journey, he asked the leader of the caravan to wait a couple of days. He then died in Mecca before leaving the holy city and was buried in the cotton that Kalan Khatun had given him at the time of his departure.[52]

The interaction between Kalan Khatun and Khwaja Parsa in this narrative contrasts interestingly with the majority of inter-Sufi relations that pertain only to men. In terms of her religious ability to lead disciples, Kalan Khatun appears as competent as her male counterparts: she is ratified strongly by her father, who was her own guide, and she can interpret Parsa's future to be able to guide him. She also provides for Parsa's future by giving him the cotton, knowing that he would pass away while traveling. Unlike the male masters, however, her interactions with Parsa are conducted through the intermediacy of another person (the servant) and an object (plaited cotton). Because as a *na-mahram* it is socially inappropriate for her to be face-to-face with Parsa, her ability to provide guidance requires an additional step. This requirement amounts to a restriction because it makes such a relationship cumbersome. Moreover, as discussed in the previous chapter, male masters' greatest power lay in their ability to establish love relationships with disciples that began with physical contact and ended with the bodies of masters and disciples merging into each other. In contrast, a woman could not display herself in public to become an object of love, and her female body was too different, both physically and socially, to meld with the bodies of male disciples.

Kalan Khatun's case presents important contrast with the way relationships between male Sufis are shown to have progressed in Persianate societies during the fourteenth and fifteenth centuries. The great Sufis among men became enmeshed in intergenerational chains and extended communities: they very often inherited their authority from multiple masters, and their power as religious and sociopolitical leaders derived from their ability to convey their charisma to large numbers of disciples through relationships described in the language of love. The constrained versus open potential in the two cases was, ultimately, a function of societal attitudes toward bodies: restricted from becoming objects of love, persons embodied female remained marginal to the massive expansion of Persianate Sufi social networks during the fourteenth and fifteenth centuries. This meant that any Sufi chain of authority likely to proceed through a female link was greatly disadvantaged from the start. Such a chain could be extended beyond the female master either through other women, with whom the female master could interact freely, or through close male relatives, such as father, husband, or son, who could have unproblematic loving relationships with her. It is then no accident that the only female master I have mentioned here is described as a Sufi with a public role in a hagiography penned by her own son. In contrast, most male masters were subjects of works written by men who were not consanguines. This fact severely limited a woman's capacity to lead a social network that included both men and women. It is, of course, possible that women had separate all-female Sufi networks that were led by women, as can be documented for modern Muslim societies. However, such networks remain obscure to us because all medieval Islamic sources at our disposal concern themselves exclusively with social arenas managed by men.[53]

I end this chapter by registering a twist regarding the story of interactions between Kalan Khatun and Khwaja Parsa that further illuminates the gendered nature of hagiographic narratives. Kalan Khatun is not mentioned in any work other than the *Maqamat-i Amir Kulal*, but two later Naqshbandi sources provide a story in which Khwaja Parsa interacts quite similarly with another *male* master. The author of the works state, on the basis of unspecified sources, that when Parsa decided to go on the hajj, he sent a messenger to Khwaja Daʾud, the maternal grandfather of Khwaja ʿUbaydullah Ahrar, to perform an augury (*istikhara*) regarding the auspiciousness of the journey. Khwaja Daʾud gave the messenger a fox's fur for himself and a pickaxe for Parsa. The man found the gift of the fur quite odd since this was during a time of warm weather, but he kept it with him, thinking that there must be something to it. Later he was once stuck in extreme cold and the fur saved his life. Parsa took the pickaxe with him to Mecca, also without knowing the reason behind Daʾud having sent it to him. When he died in Mecca, that instrument was the only thing people could find to dig his grave.[54]

The two "dueling" stories regarding Parsa demonstrate the mutually constitutive nature of gender, lineage, and the process of hagiographic narration in multiple ways. The narrators belonged to rival branches of the Khwajagani lineage—issuing from Amir Kulal in the case of Shihab ad-Din and Baha' ad-Din Naqshband in the case of Safi and Samarqandi—both of which regarded Parsa as an authoritative figure because of his literary fame. The ultimate aim of Safi and Samarqandi was to glorify Khwaja Ahrar, which made them especially attentive to Shaykh Da'ud, Ahrar's maternal grandfather. Their major difference lies in that the two stories involve important women, albeit in different roles. Kalan Khatun speaks and acts in Shihab ad-Din's version, while the unnamed woman who was Da'ud's daughter and Ahrar's mother is a critically important but silent presence in the story given by Safi and Samarqandi. Ahrar's hagiographies, in which the woman is silent, have been regarded as authoritative accounts of Naqshbandi-Khwajagani Sufi chains since the sixteenth century. Conversely, the work in which a Sufi woman speaks and acts authoritatively survives in an obscure modern lithograph edition and a handful of manuscripts. The historical fates of the texts mirror the ambivalence regarding women we see present throughout the materials that survive to give us a picture of Persianate Sufism. Concentrating on the way women are portrayed allows us to see the constructed nature of roles ascribed to female as well as male bodies.

6

MIRACULOUS FOOD

The hagiography of the rural Central Asian master Shaykh Ahmad Bashiri narrates the following incident between him and his wife:

> One day Bibi Fatima was sewing clothes and all the dervishes had gone off to work. His Eminence said, "all of you work and, in the midst, I alone am one who does nothing." Bibi Fatima replied, "Great Shaykh, we cannot possibly ask you [to work]." But his Eminence insisted, saying, "I will work, but sitting on the bed and with a pillow behind the back." Then within two or three days, a group of dervishes came to visit and brought four cows with calves as a gift for His Eminence and Bibi Fatima. Bibi Fatima then said to him, "Shaykh, this was your work. In springtime, milk and cheese are more important for us than anything else. This work that you have done was beyond everyone else."[1]

This seemingly unremarkable episode registers a critical but rarely commented upon aspect of Sufi masters' social role as it comes across in hagiographic narratives. It points to the fact that, in this discursive universe, these individuals perform critical work that is closely tied to the representation of other forms of labor and their expected fruits. Sufi masters' work is to perform miracles or charismatic acts (*karamat*) that defy the rules that govern material causality but bear tangible results that can be observed or enjoyed by their witnesses. Although extraordinary by definition, the ubiquitous presence of these miracles in hagiographic narratives makes them appear as an ordinary aspect of the social imagination of this historical context.

The dialogue between Bibi Fatima and Shaykh Bashiri shows three different types of work whose interdependency we must appreciate to understand the role of miracles in Sufi hagiographic narratives. Two of these are referenced within the story: the manual work performed by Bibi Fatima and the dervishes who have gone out to earn livelihoods and Shaykh Bashiri's work as a charismatic presence, which attracts goods to the household without apparent effort on his part. These two types of work are equivalent in their products—necessities and luxuries of life—but they differ on the basis of the preparation required to generate the expected outcomes. Although Shaykh Bashiri remains sitting on his bed with a pillow on his back, the text as a whole provides extensive details regarding the trials and travails he had undergone earlier in life in order to reach a stage of intimacy with God and other human beings to ensure the delivery of such gifts. As sketched by his hagiographer, his overall portrait is replete with evidence of his physical exertions, but these bear results cumulatively through the acquisition of a status that makes him a miracle worker rather than a manual worker such as a farmer or a taylor.

To notice the third type of work in evidence we must walk out of the frame in which the story is set. That is the work of producing the story of the miraculous act, without which Shaykh Bashiri would neither have acquired his special status in his times nor be known to us today through the hagiographic text. The author relates the story from an unnamed person who conveyed it to him by word of mouth as he went about collecting the materials to write the hagiography. This was a task, he says, he felt obliged to undertake on the basis of requests from Shaykh Bashiri's companions, who wanted to memorialize his extraordinary presence in the form of a text.[2]

It is critical to recognize that the process of generating, disseminating, and writing down stories regarding miracles attributed to Shaykh Bashiri was coextensive with the establishment of the Sufi master's reputation as a friend of God. That is, the very possibility of believing in a saintly figure who can perform miracles is predicated on the hagiographic process, making the work of producing and recording miraculous stories a constitutive element in the construction of the world we see reflected in the texts. Following this line of thought, I suggest that we should see miracle stories as a kind of payback for the benefits that are shown to emanate from the masters' extraordinary powers. Miracle stories and the material benefits mentioned in them are two halves of a circle: the story produces the miracle-working saints, and those who come to rely on the prestige of the saints generate more stories that legitimize their beliefs.

I would like to suggest that ordinary human work, miraculous work performed by saintly figures, and the work of storytelling are elements of a sociopolitical "economy" that forms the infrastructure of the world we see reflected in Persianate hagiographic texts produced in the fourteenth and fifteenth centuries.[3] The dialogue between Shaykh Bashiri and Bibi Fatima in the story cited in the beginning of this chapter indicates that Sufi masters' miraculous deeds were a tangible form of specialized work with exchange value that was correlated to other types of labor. The linchpin of this process was the narrativization of miraculous deeds in stories that circulated in oral or written forms, depending on the extent of the milieu in which the Sufi shaykh was active and influential. As a critical form of work, this storytelling was sponsored and performed by actors who participated in the economy's functioning. This is readily evident when we note that authors of literary hagiographies begin by stating that they felt compelled to write on their subjects on the basis of insistent requests of descendants or close companions of the persons who had manifested miraculous behavior. As heirs to great masters' charisma, these sponsors of hagiographies stood to gain the most in society from dissemination of such stories. Although certainly also literary and pious tropes, conventional beginnings of hagiographic narratives reveal the sociohistorical background to the genre's genesis and vitality: they highlight the value the narratives held in social, political, and economic relations and explain why such a large number of them came to be compiled during the period.

In the following pages I will concentrate on the representation of food in hagiographic narratives in order to illuminate the function of miracles in Sufi contexts. Food is by far the most common arena for Sufi masters' miraculous interventions in the lives of their disciples in this literature. Masters' control over food is closely tied to the production and maintenance of human bodies. This control extends to food's production, distribution, consumption, and absorption into the body, all of these being processes that implicate masters' social relationships within the world in which they are shown to act. In addition to being a necessity constantly flowing through the arteries of physical and social bodies, food is subject to Islamic legal taboos that can be deployed to include or exclude people from communities. Highlighting Sufi masters' control over food through miraculous interventions allows us a look into their roles as socioreligious arbiters at many different levels.

When examined closely, miracle stories concerned with food nearly always reflect the attempt to correlate individual bodies to the social body. Food is, of course, a matter related to corporeality irrespective of the question of miracles and this aspect will be amply in evidence in the stories I cite in this chapter. The examples I present (and many others that could be added) narrate the acts and behaviors of individual bodies with underlying messages that relate to the social sphere. This chapter's theme thus providess a powerful case in which the human body is invoked simultaneously as a material object and a symbolic system representing intellectual and social concerns of a given setting. The bodies we see here need food to continue physical existence; this material dependency is universally enmeshed in ideational and social imperatives that hold sway in the surrounding world. To discuss food, therefore, is to explore a critical arena in the conduct of social life and the intermingling of food and miracles provides us a way to canvass the social imagination of this context

THE MIRACLE AS SUFI LITERARY MOTIF

Miracles are a prominent leitmotif in stories about the lives of charismatic religious figures across various settings and are present as prominently in Islamic literatures as in materials stemming from Jewish, Christian, Buddhist, and other contexts.[4] In Islamic history, miracles attributed to Muhammad as a prophet became the first to acquire literary justifications in early Arabic literature. The status of his miracles received theoretical elaboration in rationalizing theologies generated in the early periods of Islamic history, and this practice remains a significant venue for pietistic elaboration to this day.[5]

Sufi authors usually divide miraculous events into three categories: prophetic miracles that are called *mu'jizat*; miracles performed by God's friends (meaning Sufis) that are referred to as *karamat*; and deceptions, known under the general term *istidraj*, committed by those without religious sanction.[6] The division between acts attributable to prophets versus those performed by Sufis stems from the status of the person performing the act and seems not to connote a difference in terms of what the two types of individuals are able to do.[7] Events under these three categories are alike in terms of their material effects, and the issue of the proper context in which to see them rests outside the fact of their miraculous status. 'Abd ar-Rahman Jami, the celebrated poet and Sufi author from the second half of the fifteenth century, writes in his extensive catalogue of Sufi luminaries *Nafahat al-uns* (*The Breaths of Intimacy*):

> There are very many types of events that disrupt conventions (*khavaraq-i 'adat*), such as making present something nonexistent and eliminating something existent; manifesting something hidden and obscuring something apparent; positive acceptance of invocatory prayer; covering the distance to a far-off place in a short period; knowledge of hidden matters, including sensory and [other] particular information; being present at different places at the same moment; bringing the dead to life and killing those who are living; hearing the speech of animals, plants, and minerals in praise [of God] and otherwise; presenting food and drink in a time of need without an apparent cause; and other performances of acts that break conventionality. . . . In general, when the Truth—may He be praised and exalted—renders one of His friends capable of exhibiting the totality of His creative powers, he is enabled to assert himself in

the created world in any way he wishes. This is, in reality, an effect and exertion of the Truth [Himself]—may He be praised and exalted—that appears in him [i.e., the miracle worker] without him being in the middle.[8]

This short description accurately conveys a sense of the range of events one finds attributed to famous Sufis in hagiographic narratives. While Jami's reference at the end defers to God the power that makes miracles possible, there is little question that to be God's agent in this manner is a primary identification for being an accomplished Sufi master. Therefore miracles occupy a prominent place in arguments about sanctity nearly universally in Sufi settings. Of the many possible miraculous events given by Jami, my focus in this book is on food in this chapter and bodily protection in chapter 7.

FOOD AND BODIES

Religious valuations of food and the body quite often go hand in hand.[9] Sufis' clear understanding of the idea that body and food are interdependent is expressed in stories related to the births of some of the great masters. An example comes from the hagiographic narrative devoted to Sayyid Amir Kulal, a particularly rich source for understanding the role of food in the construction of saintly personas. Amir Kulal's intuitive sensitivity to matters relating to food is shown to be active even before his birth. The text states that his mother reported that, while pregnant with him, she would get ill when she ate anything of questionable legal status.[10]

This theme is reflected in works on a number of other masters as well. Shaykh Ahmad Bashiri's hagiographer relates that once when Bibi Malakat, his mother, was pregnant with him she received some food from a neighbor. She ate it but then felt extremely sick, and her body refused to digest this particular food whenever she tried. It eventually came out that the food was not legally pure (i.e., it was made with ingredients acquired unjustly). Her inability to digest it came from the fact that it was inconceivable that any element of Shaykh Bashiri's growing body within her could be formed of unlawful materials.[11] Zayn ad-Din Taybadi's father reported that one day, while his wife was pregnant with the future master, he was passing by a flour mill when a plate of halva and two pieces of bread miraculously appeared fully prepared out of the mill's stone. A Sufi acquaintance of his who was walking by saw him with this food and asked him to share it. He put it in front of both of them, but the acquaintance withdrew his hand when he smelled it and said, "neither you nor I have a share in this food. You should take it home because this will give rise to a flower that will benefit the whole world."[12] The point of the story is that miraculous food was destined for Zayn ad-Din's mother, and her eating it was expected to convey it to the composition of his growing body within her.

A work on Khwaja Ahrar states that at the time of his birth Ahrar refused to take his mother's breast until she had stopped bleeding and had performed the ritual bath required after childbirth. This, however, took forty days, and the contention that he was able to survive for that long without nutrition was the first miracle associated with his life. Aside from the fact that, under normal circumstances, no child is expected to do what Ahrar did, this example is interesting in that, according to the technicalities of the law, Ahrar's mother's impure state could not have been conducted to him even if he had fed from her breast. Ahrar's alleged innate regard for legal requirements in this instance thus contravenes the general rule.[13]

The ultimate principle underlying these kinds of stories is explicated in the voice of Amir Kulal:

Know that the purity of heart, tongue, and body derives from the legally sound morsel. Think of the human stomach as a pool that contains pure water flowing out [to the rest of the body] in the form of streams. Every organ that comes into being from this pure water is pure itself and beneficial, according to the Prophet's saying that, whoever eats legally sound food for forty days, God opens the eyes of knowledge and wisdom on his heart and tongue and illuminates his heart. This becomes available when he turns himself into a person equipped with piety (taqva). Whoever is on the correct path in this world will be on the correct path in the next world.[14]

In this explanation as well as the stories, food is a substance that mediates between physical and metaphysical aspects of life. Its legal status inheres in it to the degree that it creates a permanent imprint onto the body and the being of which it becomes a part. Reflecting this attitude, Shaykh Bashiri is repeatedly shown telling his disciples that legal food is an absolute necessity for them to make any spiritual progress. His hagiographer reports that one of his disciples once saw a dream in which he was in paradise and flying from one tree to another. The Shaykh was asked what kind of a station this denoted, and he replied that this was someone who ate only legally sound food.[15]

MASTERING FOOD

Awareness of legal status and consuming as little as possible are the two most prevalent themes in hagiographic portrayals of Sufi masters' own intake of food. The restriction of amount is, of course, a part of the cultivation of an ascetic lifestyle, which comes across as a pervasive ideal, and the religious imperative for this could be translated into cultivating a particular corporeal posture. For example, Amin ad-Din Balyani, who steadfastly refused to eat meat because it suggested luxury, stated that the pleasure one may derive from it is not worth the trouble of having to use a toothpick afterward.[16] In one case Balyani is said to have told a disciple that his lack of progress on the spiritual path was a direct result of the fact that he had brought good food with him into the seclusion chamber while undertaking an extended exercise.[17] And in another instance he chastised those inclined to boast about their religious states by likening them to someone who eats meat one night and then displays a bone on himself the next day to show off.[18] Some masters seem to have objected to eating meat as well, on the grounds that animals have bodies much like those of humans and that killing them for the sake of consumption amounted to cruelty.[19]

Although sparse in their own intake of food, great masters are shown to possess unlimited powers to provide food for others. This pattern holds even in cases of antinomian masters such as Jamal ad-Din Savi who otherwise refused to participate in the reproduction of society at any level in a deliberate and calculated way.[20] For some masters, this ability is exemplified in events where they command the natural world to divulge its fruits or they miraculously multiply small amounts to feed large numbers. The *Maqamat-i Amir Kulal* relates that a man once brought Amir Kulal a lamb as a gift, and, just as he was handing it over to be killed for food, the animal escaped and ran away. The man starting to run after it, but Amir Kulal told him not to worry because the animal would submit voluntarily. A little later when the man was sitting in Amir Kulal's company, the animal came back and laid its head on the floor. The amir then asked that the animal be used to prepare a feast.[21] In a similar episode, Amir Kulal once got the desire to travel to Qaraman and requested his host, Shaykh Ibrahim Qaramani, to procure halal meat for him. The host replied that halal meat had become very rare in those parts and he did not know how to get it. Amir Kulal then asked him to go into the jungle and simply call birds to come to him. When he did this, all the birds of the area flocked to him and he chose a few for a meal. There could be no doubt that materials for this meal had been acquired fairly and that the animal had been prepared according to the legal requirements.[22]

In another story relating to Amir Kulal, a man put out some traps for geese with the oath that, if he were to catch some, he would gift two to the master. As it happened, he managed to ensnare them all and was determined to fulfill his vow when a local ruler came to his house and demanded that he kill the two particular birds he had chosen for the master because they were the fattest and equal to a "thousand lambs." The man said that they were already earmarked for Amir Kulal, but the ruler insisted and said that he could send just one over to the master. One of the two birds was eventually killed, but when it was cooked and presented to the ruler, intense heat came off of it and blinded him. He then sent a horse to Amir Kulal as expiation for his infraction, and his sight eventually returned after a few days. Although the author writes that the point of this story is that "one should never be rude toward God's friends," the critical issue is that the man who had captured the birds had been able to do so only because he had made a vow to Amir Kulal. The shaykh thus controlled food as a natural resource and could punish anyone's incursion in his domain.[23]

Amir Kulal's son and successor, Amir Hamza, was once passing by a recently sown melon field when the owner told him that he would have liked to have given some of them as a gift but they had not yet sprouted. Hamza asked him to look at the plants again, and he was astounded to see that not only had the fruit appeared, it had ripened and was ready to be plucked.[24] Shah Niʿmatullah Vali was similarly able to make an apple tree bear fruit by commanding it to do so,[25] and, in a different narrative devoted to this master, the author indicates that tables full of food were always made available to guests who came to visit him although no one ever saw the master himself partake of anything.[26] Bahaʾ ad-Din Naqshband is similarly shown to have directed people to the means for obtaining a large fish and other foods miraculously when receiving requests from groups of disciples who were hungry and without another ready resource.[27]

Reflecting a protective rather than productive theme, a companion of Zayn ad-Din Taybadi stated that once locusts arrived in Taybad, leading to illness and danger to the food supply. People then appealed to Shaykh Zayn ad-Din, and he first performed two cycles of ritual prayer and then looked to the heavens and importuned God to take away the trial he had sent. As a result, the locusts descended on the mosque where he was sitting, and one of them came to sit on his lap. The shaykh told it that the time to leave had come, and it as well as all the others flew away for good.[28] Taybadi is also credited with numerous miracles of multiplying a small quantity of food to make it enough for a large group. He once presented a piece of bread and a lamb to Timur that never diminished despite being consumed by the conqueror's whole entourage.[29] In another instance, he made it possible for a single piece of bread and a pomegranate to suffice for four hundred people.[30] Similarly, Bahaʾ ad-Din Naqshband made a single dish of dough suffice to make bread for multitudes of guests over a two-month period when he decided to visit and stay in the house of a disciple. Naqshband told the man never to tell anyone about this, and as long as he kept the secret even after Naqshband's departure, the dough kept at the same level. But when he went against the master's wishes and told others about the miracle, it lost its extraordinary quality.[31] This case is particularly interesting in that it indicates a transfer between a miracle's material benefits and its efficacy as a story that goes to establish the master's reputation. Together with the reference to a staple such as dough, this anecdote exemplifies the interdependency of all three types of work I described as forming an economy in the beginning of this chapter.

The hagiography of Amin ad-Din Balyani reports that the area where he lived was faced with a severe drought in the year 705 AH (1305–1306 CE). People petitioned him to do something about the calamity, and he asked a man present there to go and procure the innards of an animal (*jigarband*) that could be cooked by the dervishes. At the time when the man came back with the meat, there was no sign of clouds in the sky, but, from the moment they started to cook the meat, clouds began to appear, and the sky was completely overcast by the time the job was complete. Then it began to rain as soon as all in the group started eating, and the rest of the day it rained more intensely than anyone could ever remember. In the end, that year turned out to be one of the wettest and most bountiful in memory, and the man whom the shaykh had commanded to fetch the meat became known as a source of auspiciousness in the region.[32] In this story the human procurement, preparation, and consumption of food proceed in exact parallel to developments in the sphere of nature. Perhaps the emphasis on the animal's innards—which undergo the further process of crossing into the insides of the bodies of the humans who eat them—reflects the fact of the master working on the interior of the cosmos in a way that leads to the rebalancing of its exterior. The overall effect of the story is to naturalize human work as a part of the cosmos, with the Sufi master acting as the guarantor of balance and proper functioning.

An emphatic assertion of the idea that masters provide rather than consume food can be seen in another story related to Amir Kulal. The text states that a man asked Amir Kulal to bless a dwelling and said that he would cook a feast to mark the event. The amir told him to make arrangements for the meal and come and tell him when everything was ready. He went home and made preparations for three days and then came back to say that it was time for Amir Kulal and his whole entourage to come and have the meal. When pressed, he insisted that he had cooked enough for more than a hundred men. Amir Kulal then asked him to take one of his close companions, a certain Mawlana 'Arif, with him and see if he could be satisfied. The man did this, although complaining that the amount of food available was much beyond the capacity of a single person. When presented with the food, 'Arif finished off the whole feast and then asked if he had anything more to offer. Looking incredulously at 'Arif's stomach—which had not distended in the least despite his eating spree—the man became fearful of Amir Kulal's power and went back to ask forgiveness for any infractions he may have committed. The amir told him that there was nothing to worry about and that he had accepted the gift the man had wished to present.[33] The morals of these stories are captured in verses Ni'matullah Vali is said to have recited when he was invited to a meal by Timur:

If you wish to be host to Ni'matullah,
    you must stretch an eating cloth across the world from end to end.
To make a guest house worthy of him,
    you must put up four walls around the earth's seven climes.[34]

The close connection between food and Sufi masters' status as social media-tors is implied in the occasional complaint about those who did not make it a point to provide for their devotees or visitors. A prominent example of this is to be found in a hagiography of Khwaja Ahrar, who was immensely wealthy in later life and prided himself on being able to provide for others.[35] He had spent substantial time traveling as a poor Sufi in his youth and related to his hagiog-rapher that once, when in Herat, it was hard for him to keep his head covered properly using the tattered piece of cloth he could afford. At one point a beggar asked him for food, and all he could think of was to offer this embarrassing head cloth to a food seller in exchange for a meal for the man. He said that, compared to this, the master Baha' ad-Din 'Umar, who was well established, never offered his visitors much despite being prosperous enough to do so. Ahrar visited him two or three time a week during his five-year stay in Herat and was offered food only twice in the whole period: once this was because food had been prepared for someone else and they could not exclude him; the second time he was offered apples. The fruit turned out to induce more pain than plea-sure because his teeth were hurting at the time and were not helped by eating something hard.[36]

Khwaja Ahrar's critique of other masters on this question can be connected to his general ambivalence regarding the spiritual benefits of restricting food intake. In a hagiography written by one of his closest disciples, he is shown to say: "Although the restriction of food and hunger can induce substantive mysti-cal unveilings, the person who sees these can sometimes be lead into error. This is why some of the greats have called [hunger] a treacherous place on the path. The Khwajagan have not recommended restricting food out of fear that it may constrain [rather than aid] the wayfarer."[37] The fact that this view was shared by some others is reflected in 'Umar Murshidi's hagiography, which reports that someone once asked him why another respected master ate sumptuously while he subsisted on barley meal alone. He responded: "He is an ocean, and an ocean never becomes polluted or contaminated." When they asked the same question of the man who ate well, he replied: "[Murshidi] is a royal falcon, and a falcon never sullies its beak with carrion."[38] The fact that the men justify each other's practice through metaphors without portraying their own variant attitude as an opposite or conflicting case indicates that both options were tenable Sufi positions in the context.

FOOD AS SOCIAL RESOURCE

Although concerned with food as a physical necessity for human existence, all the stories I have related so far have a social import built into them. Masters' ability to function as caretakers of their communities through being recognized as providers of food can be substantiated with stories that directly articulate this theme.

Amir Kulal's innate concern for the communal value of food as a resource is reflected in a story from his youth. One day his mother cooked a stew of fish and gave all the children their due share. Amir Kulal did not touch his portion for a while, and when she asked him the reason he said that he found it unfair that a share had not been reserved for one of his brothers. This brother was, however, on a trip to do the hajj at the time, and his mother took him to the pot to show that a portion was left in there. Amir Kulal asked that this be given to him so that he would convey it to the rightful owner. Then he took the food, went away, and was back in an instant. Upon being queried, he said that he had traveled to Mecca in that moment to deliver the food. People then wrote down the exact date and time when the incident occurred, and when the brother returned from the pilgrimage he confirmed that the incident occurred exactly at the time that had been recorded at home.[39]

Another story regarding Amir Kulal deploys food to mark the level of intimacy between the master and his disciples. The text relates that once Amir Kulal was gifted a lamb when he was accompanied by Baha' ad-Din Naqshband, who in this narrative is presented as equal parts his disciple and his rival. At the time this occurred, Naqshband had been congratulating himself with the thought that he was Amir Kulal's closest companion. Seeing the lamb, he thought to himself that it would have been great if Mawlana 'Arif were here to roast it. Intuiting this thought, Amir Kulal told him to go outside and call 'Arif to come and do the job. Naqshband responded that that made no sense since they knew that 'Arif was in a different town at the moment and it was impossible to reach him no matter how loud he called. But the amir insisted, saying that there was no need to travel and he could call the man in ordinary voice. When Naqshband went outside and called the man very softly, standing in a corner, the desired man showed up and said, "Why did you call thrice—I heard you the very first time!" He then went inside to do the job, and Amir Kulal admonished Naqshband by telling him that he had other companions who were even closer and that a Sufi should worry about his own works rather than ruminating over his level of proximity to the master.[40]

The particular emphasis on food as communal resource in *Maqamat-i Amir Kulal* is observable in the account of the end of the master's life and in stories relating to his descendants. As he lay on his deathbed worrying about the subsequent well-being of his disciples, a voice from the unseen world (*hatif-i ghaybi*) spoke into his ear: "Amir Kulal, we cast our mercy on you, your friends, and all those who have a connection to your kitchen."[41] After taking charge of the community, his son and successor Amir Hamza initially became worried about how he would feed the large numbers who had become attached to the family. One day he came into the house brooding over the problem of providing food and saw his wife doing her prayers. When she was done she told him that just as he had accepted the charge of taking care of things outside, she would be responsible for serving from the inside of the house. Then he went out and came back to see that a lot of food had been prepared and was ready for serving. He fell into prostration to God in thankfulness and then asked his wife about the source of the food. She replied, "Amir, although they are not Mary herself, the connection of friendship and obedience between Muhammad—may God exalt him and grant him peace—and [members of] his community is such that they can acquire Mary-like qualities." This reference to the description of the Quran (3:37) where God sends food to Mary miraculously as she is about to give birth to Jesus convinced Hamza that he would never lack in food when attempting to provide for his followers.[42]

Hagiographic narratives regarding Baha᾽ ad-Din Naqshband contain a particular emphasis on his use of food as the means to mark the community. He is said to have participated in cooking food himself and troubled to teach people in his entourage the proper etiquette for eating. He is reputed to have been able to tell, and refuse, food cooked by someone who had been gripped by a negative emotion at the time of cooking. He thus treated the mental state of the one who cooks as an ingredient in the resulting meal.[43] On the side of consumption, he explained that the taste of any given food depends on the state one is in when one eats it. For example, the same food tastes different when one is in a state of spiritual expansion (*bast*) versus being in the state of constriction (*qabd*).[44]

Naqshband's hagiographic portrait contains a number of other instances where the bond between the master and the disciple is seen to be established or broken through food. After hearing tales of his miracles, a man named Baba Sahib Samarqandi decided to go and meet him in person near Bukhara. On the way he had the notion that when, according to custom, the master gives him the top cream of milk (*sarshir*) to welcome him, he would like not to share it with anyone. When he arrived at his destination, a noble-looking man came up to him, addressed him by name, and asked him about things in Samarqand. He was astounded by this since he had never met him but then realized that this was Naqshband himself and his fore-knowledge was a miracle. Later, he placed bread and top cream in front of him and said, "Eat, this is a share in which no one will be your partner."[45] In another instance Naqshband became very happy when some disciples came to visit him while he was ill, roused himself to get lambs, and cooked a feast.[46] A man became his disciple when he accosted him working in his field and asked him to share his watermelons. When he complied, Naqshband told him that they should go to his house since his wife was cooking such and such food, which turned out to be the case, convincing the man of Naqshband's special knowledge (201).

The most dramatic stories to illustrate Naqshband's control over his community through food involve moments of conflict or censure. Once a man who was cooking kebabs for everyone sneaked one for himself before the meal was offered. As Naqshband went to distribute the meat to the company, he refrained from giving any to this man, who thought to himself that this was strange. Intuiting his thought, Naqshband said aloud that he could not lust after both the food that he had stolen and what he expected to get from the master (226). In a more extended story, Naqshband asked a seller of drinks whether he had any work that could be assigned to someone without remuneration. The man replied that he needed his icebox to be cleaned, and Naqshband first told two of his disciples to do the work and then told the seller that he gave them over to him on the condition that he would not give them any food. It was a rough day, and the two disciples worked very hard until they could barely move. The seller took pity on them and said that he realized that they must be hungry but was afraid to go against the master's wishes. Eventually, he could not resist and sent one of them to get food for the two from the bazaar. Although scared of the consequences, he went and got some bread, but, on the way back, Naqshband suddenly appeared, took the food away, hit him on the neck, and said, "No one besides me can give you food; you must work hungry." He then returned to work until the afternoon prayers (*namaz-i digar*) and tried to get food at that time, having seen the master enter the mosque to perform his prayers. But, just as he was returning with the food, Naqshband appeared again to take it away and said, "Plans like these are not going to go forward." One of them then tried to run the distance to the bazaar but was still unsuccessful. Eventually, they had to ask Naqshband's father to intercede on their behalf so that they received food as well as access to Naqshband's company (374–76). This story emphatically asserts disciples' dependence on the master for food.

Naqshband's control over his disciples' intake could in fact go to the extent of contravening ordinary religious injunctions. Once when a follower brought a cooked fish to him, one among the company happened to be fasting. Naqshband told him to partake of the food with the others, but he declined. The master then again asked him to eat, saying that he would become responsible for any sin issuing from the breaking of the fast. When the man still refused, Naqshband commented that this was a case where fasting had become a worldly fetish. His refusal to be a part of the community by eating the food was marked as a case of rudeness and from then onward he was deprived of being associated with the master. Following the narrative of another incident, in which Naqshband asked a disciple to break his fast for the sake of participating in a community meal, the master is supposed to have said, "Those who are our companions are obligated to obey us. Without obedience, a dervish cannot be said to have attained affiliation with us" (122–23).

In similar stories told of Khwaja Ahrar, a disciple said that one day an acquaintance invited him to his house for a meal but said bad things about the master on the way. When they got to the house, the disciple was unable to touch the food because he found it instinctively repulsive, and the host himself was gripped by a swelling of his throat such that nothing could pass through to his stomach. He eventually died after a week because of this illness, which had come upon him because of his rudeness toward Ahrar.[47] One day Ahrar was meditating when he suddenly came out of it and showed signs of being perturbed. He told his companions that very soon a bitch with milk-laden breasts would make an appearance along with nine puppies. Just as he was saying this, ten people could be seen approaching him from afar. These were the famous astronomer Mawlana ʿAli Qushchi (d. 1474) and nine of his disciples who had come to see Ahrar. As soon as they sat down, Ahrar got up and left on the pretense of looking after food for them. Then he sent food out but did not return to the public space until they had eaten and left.[48]

A disciple of Ahrar said that there was a scholar named Mir Jamal in Tashkent known for logic and mathematics. He cultivated the habit of a Qalandar, wearing a woolen robe, refusing to perform ritual prayer, and using hemp. One day he ended up near the disciple and started taunting and ridiculing Ahrar, saying that he could not discern much at all and that he would prove this by showing up in his company and consuming hemp in front of him without being detected. The disciple resisted replying to this rudeness in any way, and, when he went toward Ahrar, Mir Jamal followed along with three of his companions. Once seated, he extracted a measure of hemp from a hidden pocket in his robe and put it in his mouth to prove his point. But the hemp got stuck in his throat, blocking his windpipe, until Ahrar ordered that someone hit his neck with a fist. This dislodged the hemp, which went flying out into the company, causing the assembled to laugh at him. Completely deflated and humiliated, he and his companions then left Ahrar's place.[49]

Stories regarding Sufi representations of food reflect a deep sense for the desirability of commensality between masters and disciples as well as among people at the same level of religious achievement. Tales of the miraculous regarding food are therefore rooted in particular cultural patterns that reflect the valorization of the sharing of food as a marker of intimacy between human beings. We can see this in stories such as Khwaja Ahrar's relating that once the master Shah Qasim-i Anvar gave him his own half-eaten bowl of soup and said that the whole world would some day be under his cloak.[50] Similarly, Safi ad-Din Ardabili's master Shaykh Zahid liked pomegranates and melons, and, when he died, Ardabili vowed that he would never again eat these fruits. Later, when he fell sick on two occasions and doctors recommended these fruits as medicine, he refused until Shaykh Zahid appeared to him in dreams and asked him to eat them for his sake and not his own.[51] The potency of sharing or not sharing food is also reflected in Shaykh Bashiri's advice to his disciples that they must never eat food left over by an unknown person because food absorbs something from the self of the person eating and can affect the person who eats what remains.[52]

In a chapter devoted to Shaykh Safi ad-Din Ardabili's favors and kindnesses, his hagiographer describes a number of instances where he shared something from his mouth as a mark of special favor. Once when he was in a condition of spiritual tasting and expansion (*bast va zawq*), he met a simple Turkish boy who had grown up in the wild. He took part of a mixture of herbs that were in his mouth and placed them in the boy's mouth, causing him to go into a mystical state (*hal*), his face becoming agitated. After that, religious secrets opened up to the boy so that he could examine the whole world without a barrier; he could go anywhere he wished and was able to subdue horses that would not come under anyone's command; he eventually became a great man of the world.[53]

In another incident, while traveling, Ardabili chose as his hosts a poor couple who presented him with the bread, meat, and honey they had available. He took some food and then, when he cast a glance of kindness on the man, he went into a state and felt himself alchemically transformed. He then called out to his wife that he was no longer the man he had been and saw himself as an entirely different being. She replied that she was no longer who she had been either. The man later came to Ardabil after wandering everywhere and said that he heard zikr and God's praises from every hair on his body. The shaykh then pointed to a log in the room's roof and said that it would happen so that he heard it from even this dried wood. The log then promptly started reciting the zikr, and the man could hear it.[54] Similarly, Ardabili once put some of his saliva in a man's mouth three times, and he lost consciousness. When he woke up he could suddenly recite the whole Quran by heart even though he was illiterate. Once he sent food to some men and women who had been unable to visit him; upon eating it they immediately became religiously devout.[55]

As we see it cumulatively in these stories, food had a central role in the formation and perpetuation of Sufi communities. Sufi masters attracted devotees to themselves through food, and they later used it to maintain their affective and coercive bonds. The provision of food was the chief element in making the abode of a Sufi shaykh a hub for gatherings within particular localities as well as across regions. In addition to these material considerations, food was a tool to define community boundaries through asserting its legality or otherwise. In the sphere of ethics, hagiographers show Sufi masters to have had a particular concern with the proper distribution of food among those who could assert a right. Similarly, masters are shown to exercise control over their disciples' corporeal existence through providing or restricting food based on their perception of what would aid in their spiritual progress. The satiation of physical bodies in these instances correlates directly with religious progress, with starvation denoting lack thereof. Since material objects become food by crossing into the body's hidden interior, Sufi masters' control over it marks them as guardians of the interior-exterior boundary.

KNOWLEDGE AND POWER

I have cited a wide array of episodes regarding food in order to provide a general sense of the types of miracle stories that are found in hagiographic literature. In this section I would like to go back to the issue of the social purpose of such stories, besides the basic principle that they bolster Sufi masters' roles as actors in the lives of their disciples. For this purpose, I will focus on a single theme in one particular work that can be related to the milieu in which the work was produced. This intratextual examination will allow us to bring the matter into high relief.

Haydar Badakhshi's work *Manqabat al-javahir* is dedicated to the life of Sayyid ʿAli Hamadani and was compiled more than fifty years after the Kubravi master's death. It contains a number of episodes that exemplify the master's ability to detect the legal status of food presented to him. Moreover, in these episodes, Hamadani is shown to be competing with worldly rulers and non-Sufi scholars, whom he vanquishes on the basis of his special knowledge. This competition between different types of authorities highlights the fact that one of the main purposes of miracle stories is to assert Sufi masters' influence in society. While the stories are about ʿAli Hamadani, taken collectively, they represent the interests of his successors, whose social legitimacy rested on Hamadani being acknowledged as a great miracle worker by as wide a circle as possible. In both Hamadani's own context and that of his successors, the stories helped to concretize the authority of the master and his lineage by showing these to be superior to other holders of power in society.

A Dog, a Cat, and a Pig

The *Manqabat al-javahir* relates three stories in which various opponents attempt to harm Hamadani by trying to feed him meat from animals forbidden for consumption. The three stories' variant contextual parameters indicate the different ways in which Hamadani could deploy his knowledge of food.

One case begins with the story of a king, proceeding from India to Transoxania, who bore a particular enmity toward Sufis. Hearing of his intentions, many Sufis migrated to other places to save themselves. However, Hamadani remained in the area, and one night he had a dream in which Muhammad told him that when he was taken in front of the king he should pray for his wellbeing and wish nothing bad for him. Hamadani found these directions puzzling but agreed to see the king when invited. Prior to his arrival, the king decided that the best way to seal his fate would be to kill a dog and present it to him as a meal. If he knew that it was unlawful meat and decline eating, he would be killed for refusing the king; if he did eat it, then religious scholars could be assembled to have him condemned for having partaken of a forbidden animal. Either way, the trick of dog meat would allow the king to eliminate the master.

The king's retainers procured a dog, and when they killed it they realized that it had been pregnant. They cooked the dog and the four puppies inside it and presented them as a meal to Hamadani and his entourage. The king himself was standing close by behind a curtain at this time, and when the servants went to take the covers off the dishes, Hamadani called out to the king to uncover himself as well. The king appeared, and Hamadani told him that he had unjustly killed some living beings. When the king pretended not to understand, Hamadani lifted the covers off the dishes and everyone saw there the dog alive with the four puppies. This caused the king to be ashamed, though he refused to believe in Hamadani's special status and proclaimed that the servant who had prepared the dog had told the master about the plan in advance. He then had this man killed, but Hamadani was able to bring him back to life when he heard about the matter. The king then tried to trick him in other ways as well but failed.[56] The two salient symbolic elements of this story are the equating of the king with the dead dog hidden under the covers and the assertion that Hamadani's power over living beings far exceeded what was possible for a king.

In the second story, a close disciple of Hamadani reported that a messenger came to the master one day with a letter, to which he wrote a reply. When asked about this, he said that it was a request from some seekers of knowledge (*talib-i* 'ilman). This was actually a trap that some non-Sufi scholars were trying to set for Hamadani, and they were disappointed that his response did not provide them a pretext for criticism. To obtain their objective, they then decided to kill a cat and prepare it as food for the master. He was invited for a meal, and, when the cat was placed in front of him, he lamented these scholars' stupidity in unjustly killing the cat. They pretended to get angry at the suggestion and said that this was not the case. To prove them wrong, the master ordered the cat to rise; the animal reconstituted itself from the cooked meat and walked away. This finally shamed the scholars, and Hamadani left for his hospice.[57]

The third story of this type involves a king trying to feed a pig to the master. One day as Hamadani sat in his hospice having a discussion with disciples, a messenger from the king of Bukhara appeared with a letter inviting the master and his friends to the court to answer religious questions. The master agreed to do this and gave the messenger a piece of bread for food for his return journey. The king was glad to hear this and, although he was positively inclined toward the master, he consulted his viziers to come up with a suitable trial to test his knowledge. In the meantime, Hamadani told his followers to get ready for the event but instructed them not to partake of any food until they saw him doing it first. On the first occasion, the master and his followers ate the meal, but then the king decided to put Hamadani to the test and had a pig killed and cooked for presentation to the party. When the food was being offered, the dish that contained the pig began to boil as soon as Hamadani's gaze fell upon it, despite the fact that it was not very hot when brought in. The king saw this happening and became fearful of the master's powers. Hamadani then recited the Quranic verse that forbids eating pig's meat and eventually had the meat reconstitute itself into the animal and come alive again, to the astonishment of the assembled. The king grew ashamed of what he had done, and Hamadani hit him on the back three times. The king himself and a large number of others then became Hamadani's devotees, and the master stayed in the area for four months before leaving for Baghdad.[58]

These stories of Hamadani's ability to tell unlawful foods apart stand in contrast with a case where some scholars tried to poison him in order to get rid of him. While on the way to an invited meal with these men, Hamadani twice ran into the ever-living master Khizr, who told him to avoid the event. But the master went, nevertheless, seeing it as his obligation to disseminate knowledge. At the meal itself, the hosts presented him with a sweet drink, and he imbibed it, not realizing that it contained poison. He then had to rush out of the hosts' place and rid himself of the poison through vomiting and diarrhea. In later years he would say that his body had acquired a certain weakness from the experience of having been poisoned in this way (393a–394a). The fact that Hamadani was unable to tell the presence of poison while having no trouble recognizing forbidden meat marks legal proscription as the sphere of his powers. His knowledge pertains to the requirements of being a law-abiding Muslim rather than providing him protection from things that might be personally harmful.

Countering Injustice

While these stories represent Hamadani's ability to exclude foods that are taboo according to Islamic dietary laws, other incidents show his knowledge of food forbidden as the result of having been acquired illegally. In one such case a king decided to test Hamadani's claim of never having eaten anything unlawful by inviting him to a meal and asking his servants to procure food unjustly from someone. They went to the bazaar and confiscated a woman's possessions, which included a lamb, some flour and rice, and all the spices needed to make these materials into a meal. The food was cooked and presented to Hamadani, who proceeded to eat it without any qualms. The king then taunted the master for having broken his vow of never eating forbidden food, but Hamadani replied that that was not the case. When the woman was presented to the king, she said that she had been carrying all the food to present as a gift to Hamadani; therefore his having eaten it did not constitute a legal infraction. Seeing this, the king fell down in front of the master to ask forgiveness, but he refused to accept the apology, knowing that the king's heart was fundamentally corrupt (374b–375b).

In a more extended case of this type, Hamadani's disciple Muhammad Shami related that once, when he was in charge of distributing food in the hospice, he found himself in a perplexing situation. The usual order of business was that food would be sent to everyone in the evening and then the empty bowls would be collected from Sufis' chambers the next morning for cleaning and re-use. On this occasion Hamadani himself angrily refused to eat the food, and Shami found out that no one else had touched the food that had been provided the previous evening. He then went to see Hamadani, who told him that the flour and rice he had purchased from the bazaar for the meal had been tainted because they came from a woman being taxed unjustly by the king. Shami was ashamed to hear this and resolved never to acquire any food without guidance from Hamadani. He then arranged for the food to be thrown into the river since it was not fit for human consumption. The next day, he saw a vision in which a fish was presented for food and some dervishes ate a part of it. Then he saw himself requesting Hamadani to tell the rest not to eat it because it had consumed the food that had been thrown in the river. When he awoke from the vision, he went to see Hamadani, who told him that this was a lesson to show him how a simple mistake could cause drastic contamination of the whole food chain. From that day onward, he made a point of calling upon Hamadani whenever he purchased any food, and, if there was ever any doubt about its source, the master would appear and stay his hand before the purchase could be made (430a–431b).

In these stories we see the master triumph over other authoritative figures because of his superior abilities to tell things apart from the inside. As seen in the last story, this knowledge pertains to food as a material that becomes imbued with certain properties based on it being a part of transactions that happen between human beings. The food's materiality is affected by social action, making the figure of the master all the more important because he can interpret the situation as well as intervene to make things right.

Coercion and Voluntary Submission

Stories of Sayyid ʿAli Hamadani being able to resist tainted food directed at him by rulers and scholars contrast with an instance in which the master is able to provide food without any outward effort. Haydar Badakhshi relates that one day, as Hamadani was sitting with his followers, the city's king arrived to be with him and ask that he pray for him. The master complied, and, as the king got ready to leave, he asked him to stay, saying that a banquet was ready. The other dervishes were surprised to hear this since no preparations had been made for a banquet and they became fearful that this would weaken the king's confidence in the master. As time went on, the master asked a servant to spread the eating cloths, and, as he hesitated, the master gave him an angry look to make him move. When he got up and went outside, he was astounded to see a whole group of people standing there with dishes of prepared food in their hands. The eating cloths were spread, and there was much food left over, even after everyone present had been fully satiated. The people who had brought the food then took the dishes and disappeared as suddenly as they had arrived.

When the king praised the food as being immensely delicious, Hamadani replied that it had to be so given the effort someone had spent on it. He then explained that there was a man in the city of Tus who had been collecting food-stuffs for seven years with the aim of sending them to Hamadani. When he had finally prepared all the laborers and camels to deliver them, an unjust king heard about the matter and came, confiscated the food for himself, and had it sent to his kitchens to be made into a feast. Knowing all this, Hamadani had asked his servants in the unseen world (muwakkalan) to carry the food over from the king's kitchens to the waiting company as soon as it was cooked. The king was amazed to hear this story, and later it was all proven to be true when the devotee from Tus and the unjust king both appeared in front of the master and confirmed the details. The unjust king told Hamadani that the night after the incident he had had a dream in which he was standing in front of Muhammad with bound hands and the Prophet was issuing an order for him to be executed. Before this could be carried out, Hamadani appeared on the scene and interceded to save his life. He then decided to make the journey to ask Hamadani's forgiveness and become a disciple. The master forgave him, and the incident caused both kings to acknowledge his greater authority (409b–412b). Most significantly in this story, Hamadani is shown able to carry out justice and provide food for a king. He thus stands above those who possess worldly power.

This story parallels the incident with which I began the chapter. There Shaykh Ahmad Bashiri provides for his household because of the voluntary devotion of his followers, here Hamadani acquires the gift meant for him when he needs it despite the adverse efforts of a king. In both cases the masters' miracle-making work marks them as legitimate intermediaries through whom material resources such as food are distributed within society. Masters' charismatic personalities compel others to direct the material resources toward them voluntarily, a fact that stands in contrast with the coercive behavior of some kings to eventuate the same result. The masters' miraculous power is constituted by their knowledge of where food is to be found and how it can be circulated while respecting principles of legality and justice. Kings who acquiesce to the masters' judgments are represented as fair while those who do not are seen as condemned competitors. The eventual result of these processes is to show the masters as authoritative figures of the world responsible for social balance and material equity.

The representation of contrast between Sufis and kings is a popular theme in Persianate painting such as figure 6.1.[59] Dated to circa 1490, this painting occurs in a Turkoman manuscript of Muhammad Assar Tabrizi's *Mihr-o-mushtari*, an allegory for love of the type of Fattahi's *Husn-o-dil* that I have discussed in chapter 5. The text surrounding the image describes the scene of two worldly characters arriving at the abode of a Sufi resident in a deserted place and treating him with great deference. The image itself shows the interaction between two different worlds, represented by contrasting elements, such as a rocky versus verdant landscape, and the Sufi's drab dress versus the colorful and embroidered robes worn by the visitors. Such paintings are notable because they were produced for political elites but show Sufi masters dominating the kings. The iconography thus represents acceptance of the Sufi critique of royal authority in the self-image of the elites. This pattern indicates that, in the Persianate sphere, Sufi masters acted as power brokers on a very large scale, beyond their communities of dedicated disciples.

Stories of miracles attributed to Sufi masters raise a hypothetical question that can help us see the narratives' social purposes: given that the masters seem to have infinite power to manipulate the material world, why do they not go ahead and just eliminate injustice and danger from the world altogether? The answer to this lies in the fact that masters are shown to manipulate causality by performing miracles in only two particular situations. They do so either when

6.1   A royal party visiting a Sufi master in a cave. From a copy of 'Assar's *Mihr-o-mushtari*. Reproduced by courtesy of the university librarian and director, John Rylands University Library, The University of Manchester. MS. Ryl Pers 24, fol. 15a.

they need to demonstrate their powers to vanquish their competitors, be they kings, non-Sufi scholars, or rival Sufis, or when they aid those who have become attached to them as devotees. Miracle stories never show masters transforming the world as such to respond to abstract notions regarding justice or suffering. Rather, these stories are narrative performances within particular contexts. When seen from within the viewpoint of hagiographic literature, the world is presumed to be unjust and cruel without the possibility of wholesale change. The purpose of the miracle narrative is to importune the reader to believe in particular Sufi masters whose miraculous powers are the critical resource that allows one to survive in the face of adversities and the anomie of life. The master's role as a miracle worker marks him as the crucial patron one needs to make it through life.

When considered within the context of the period, stories of miracles were meant to compel people to become attached to the great masters and their legatees. During the lifetimes of the masters, the stories usually circulated orally, providing the momentum for the creation of communities based on collective belief in the masters' miraculous powers. After their deaths, these stories were collected by their successors to form hagiographic compilations that served the interests of those who inherited the communities' leadership and needed the masters' charismatic presence to continue exercising its effects beyond their physical demise. It is no accident that a great number of miracle stories in hagiographic literature relate to food, a necessary and ubiquitous concern in human affairs. Through their miraculous mastery over food, the great Sufis became involved in mundane matters in the lives of their devotees. Conversely, by attributing the control of their daily necessities to the masters, ordinary people in society came to see the narratives of their lives as being entwined in the works of great Sufis and those who continued their legacy. The functioning of these social mechanisms was made possible by the work of storytellers who conjoined the performance of miracles to the interests of the beneficiaries on both sides of the line that divided ordinary people and political and religious elites.

7

CORPSES IN MORTICIANS' HANDS

The title of chapter 7 refers to a Sufi dictum that uses a highly corporeal metaphor to advocate disciples' total voluntary submission to Sufi masters. According to manuals for proper conduct, the oath of discipleship requires aspiring Sufis to submit themselves to unconditional manipulation by the master, becoming like inert corpses in morticians' hands.[1] Many stories I have related here testify to the significance of this metaphor's underlying message as an aspect of Sufi rhetoric in Persianate societies. In the present chapter I concentrate on hagiographic representations of direct enactment of masters' control over the bodies of others.

I aim to utilize the image of corpses in morticians' hands in two ways. First, it refers to stories that show masters manipulating and repairing disciples' bodies in protective as well as coercive contexts. As hagiographic stories indicate implicitly and explicitly, disciples' voluntary submission is one side of a bargain in which they acquire protection from powerful beings. However, as this occurs, the limbs and sensory functions of disciples' bodies are shown to become subject to masters' wills. Representations that convey masters' powers in this arena make them appear as "hypercorporeal." They are able to appear in multiple places at the same time to protect their dependents, and they are shown to intervene upon disciples' phenomenological experience by assuming control over their senses. Episodes that exemplify these processes provide symbolic ballast to the notion that masters' bodies extend far beyond the confines of their own skins, becoming identical with social bodies formed from their circles of influence.

My second use of the corpse and mortician metaphor relates to the authorship of hagiographic narratives. While masters are certainly the manipulating morticians and disciples the corpses within the internal thrusts of stories, the positions invert when we recall that hagiographic narratives are the products of disciples' hands and represent portraits of the masters as seen from the vantage point of their successors. Masters' powerful performances highlighted in these texts do not represent their own claims about themselves. Instead, they are witness reports from those who are protected or coerced by the masters. Given that virtually all hagiographic texts at our disposal were compiled after the deaths of the masters they glorify, the stories they contain can be read as disciples' morticianlike manipulations of masters' bodies. In the context of trying to understand the ideological underpinnings of this literature, hagiographic compilations contain details of masters' lives selected with an eye toward being serviceable to their successors.

In the discussion that follows I underscore the second meaning of the corpses metaphor by concentrating on narratives concerned with the deaths of great masters. Depictions of the dissolution of masters' powerful bodies constitute optimal locations to see the socioreligious logic of hagiographic narratives. These deaths are portrayed as cataclysmic events and as moments when authority transfers from masters to their successors. Both these themes go toward clarifying the underlying ideological interests of those who wrote or sponsored hagiographic texts.

A consideration of masters' deaths leads also to the way their bodies are memorialized after their disappearance from the physical world. I see this occurring in three places: in the bodies of their descendants and disciples, through the efficacy of shrines constructed over their gravesites, and through the compilation of hagiographic narratives that promulgate stories about their corporeal performances. Masters remained available to those invested in their charismatic presence through their descendents and close disciples who had formed love relationships with them during their lifetimes. These groups represented corporeal continuity since the descendants were physical products of the masters' bodies, and, as I have shown in chapter 4, disciples often promoted their spiritual inheritance with the claim that their bodies had become indistinguishable from those of their erstwhile teachers by the time the masters died.

In addition to human heirs, the charisma of great masters became physicalized through the construction of shrines at their gravesites, which were places for pilgrimage as well as elite sponsorship. Royal and other patronage of Sufi shrines and their associated communities is a major feature of the architectural history of Central Asia and Iran during the fourteenth and fifteenth centuries. Visiting the graves of the religiously eminent and elite sponsorship for the construction of elaborate structures over them influenced religious ideology as well as social and economic patterns in this historical context.

In my view, stories depicting great Sufi masters' corporeal exploits were the most critical element in promulgating the memory of their powerful presence after their deaths. Such stories allowed disciples and descendants to memorialize masters' earthly lives as well as present their own claims for authority, which often went hand in hand with the establishment of shrines. Hagiographic compilations that contain these stories can be regarded as orchestrated sedimentations of memories of great masters' presence in the flesh during their lifetimes. To become known as God's powerful friends, Sufi masters needed such stories to be told about them during their lifetimes. After their deaths, the aggregation of stories into spiritual biographies exhibiting varying levels of coherence enabled their descendants and successors to continue to benefit from their reputations. Over larger spans of time, stories concerned with many masters were grouped together according to categories such as genealogy, lineages, or geographical location. Stories about Sufi masters' extraordinary powers were a critical element in the process through which these men became focal points for the establishment of communities and networks in Persianate societies during the fourteenth and fifteenth centuries. By highlighting these themes in this chapter, I aim to bring together the arguments regarding hagiographic literature I have put forth in the course of this book.[2]

THE LIVING AND DEAD BODIES OF SUFI DISCIPLES

The fact that discipleship to a Sufi master demanded total corporeal subservience is a common theme in Persianate Sufi literature. The author of the Khwajagani work *Maslak al-'arifin* contextualizes such submission with respect to its benefits by stating that when disciples acquiesce to the desires of a master completely, all the organs of their bodies start performing zikr. This indicates a total reorientation of sensory functions since it means that the eye stops seeing individuals classified as *na-mahram*, the ear stops registering that which is not beneficial to the person, and the whole body becomes involuntarily obedient to the shari'a so that the fear of God becomes totally dominant in the person.[3] The oath of discipleship acts like protective armor around the body, allowing disciples to maintain their religious obligations in adverse situations as well as be protected from outside harms. While disciples are required to show obedience, the same imperative obliges masters to spread themselves through time and space in order to be able to provide protection to multitudes of dependents.

Manipulation and Control

In the hagiographic context, masters' control over disciples' bodies is shown to operate in a number of different dimensions. Relatively straightforward cases involve incidents in which disciples are asked to alter themselves based on their affiliation with a master. For example, Amir Kulal is said to have forbidden a new disciple, who had earlier been a Qalandar, from the practice of shaving his beard with the explanation that it now belonged to the master rather than the man himself.[4] In addition to requests or commands, masters are also shown to have the ability to affect others without verbal articulation. A report in the *Safvat as-safa* states that, in the beginning of his career, Safi ad-Din Ardabili's gaze held such intense power that it could imprison people, disenabling them from exercising control over their own bodies without knowing what had caused this condition to come upon them.[5]

Masters' control over bodily functions extended to religious experiences, so that disciples were not free to pursue their own agendas without the master's advice and agreement. This was justified by the idea that disciples required, for the sake of their own safety, appropriate and adequate preparation before being allowed to experience intense states. The seriousness of this issue is reflected in the story of a disciple of Shaykh Ahmad Bashiri who died right after experiencing an ecstatic state. The master's explanation was that, for the state to be beneficial rather than fatal, the effort he had expended should have been combined with the master's permission and guidance.[6]

These stories about masters asserting their rights over disciples' actions represent an amalgamation of protection and coercive control. Taken on face value, masters' authority is a protective mechanism that is being implemented for the benefit of those who are being restrained. But the deadly consequences of cases where disciples fail to submit mark these stories as threats that allow Sufi authoritative figures to assert their domination over their subordinates. The double function of these narratives can be seen repeated in the context of stories that reflect inter-Sufi and other rivalries articulated through the question of proper religious practice. In these instances masters are able to regulate their disciples' sensory functions in such a way as to have the acts of their own bodies become proxies for the social body under their control.

As discussed in chapter 2, the master Baha' ad-Din Naqshband was a stringent advocate of silent zikr that interdicted the use of the tongue or other parts of the body. His primary hagiographer shows him in conflict with those who would use music and dance in their gatherings. He states that when Naqshband was visiting the home of a disciple in the vicinity of a palace one evening, the prince who lived there had invited a party of singers (*qavvalan*) who were performing loudly accompanied by dance and ecstatic cries from the audience.

Naqshband told his disciples that the wanton behavior was unlawful and the sounds should not enter one's hearing. He indicated that the solution was to stuff the ears with cotton. As soon as he put cotton in his own ears, the whole company assembled before him stopped hearing the sounds. Later some neighbors inquired of Naqshband's disciples as to how their group had managed to pass the night in the house, given their opposition to music. When they told the neighbors what had happened, they were so impressed by Naqshband's powers that they decided to join the ranks of his devotees.[7]

The hagiography of Shaykh Ahmad Bashiri mentions a case that also involves hearing, but from the opposite direction. This master is shown to have experienced opposition from other Sufis, belonging to a Yasavi lineage, who represented the area's established Sufi authority. On one occasion his opponents decided to track the master down and cause him physical harm, thinking that they would be able to find his community by hearing their vocal zikr. As it turned out, however, they were miraculously disabled from hearing the sound of the zikr and could not intrude upon the community as it performed its religious exercises.[8]

While these stories reflect masters' control over the faculty of hearing, an incident regarding Khwaja Ahrar registers the idea that a person can speak only that which a powerful master is willing to hear. This story pertains to the conflict between Zayn ad-Din Khwafi and his disciple Ahmad Samarqandi, which is discussed in chapter 3. Ahrar's hagiographers relate that this master had been sympathetic toward Samarqandi in the context of the fight because of both ideological empathy and the fact that he enjoyed Samarqandi's eloquence from the pulpit at the Friday mosque in Herat. However, one day, as Samarqandi was giving the sermon, he began to aggrandize himself by talking about his abilities to be persuasive. Khwaja Ahrar found this distasteful since, in his view, the truth was that his ability to articulate things well stemmed from the fact that eminent Sufis were willing to hear the sermons. To prove this point, Ahrar put his head inside the neckline of his garment so that he would not see the man, placed fingers on his ears, and held his breath. Samarqandi was then suddenly dumbstruck, unable to utter a single word no matter how hard he tried. He realized the source of this restriction but was unable to lift it and had to walk away from the pulpit ashamed. No one aside from Samarqandi knew what had come to pass, and Ahrar was able to teach him a lesson by manipulating his hearing rather than his tongue.[9]

The issue of control brought Sufi masters and disciples into mutually affective relationships. The idea that what was seen and learned in such situations was a subjective experience, limited to the two people involved, is illustrated in a story given by one of Khwaja Ahrar's hagiographers. He tells of a man who felt slighted by his master because he would ask other disciples to be his confidants but not him. After many complaints, the master eventually told him to come meet him at night in order to participate in a special mission. When he got to the master, he saw him with his hands and feet covered in blood, carrying a sack. He told him that he had just killed such and such a disciple and that now they had to go and bury the body in a secluded place. The man obliged, but, the very next day, he went to the victim's father and told him the whole story. The father went to the king, and, when they investigated, the body turned out to be that of lamb. The man who had supposedly been killed came forth as well. The master then cut off his relationship with the beseeching disciple because of his inability to submit to the master and keep their mutual relationship confidential.[10]

In these stories masters are shown to cause their disciples to submit in many different ways: by verbal comment, by the nonverbal exercise of power as in the direction of a gaze, by the displacement or stoppage of sensory functions, by control exerted through a refusal to be the recipient of effort emanated from the bodies of disciples, and by deceiving their senses and mind in order to enforce the larger point of the submission due them. Between these various modes, hagiographers represent great Sufis as absolute masters controlling the bodies of others through the extension of their own corporeal powers.

Mending Bodies

In addition to cases of control over the sensory functions of others' bodies, Sufi masters are shown to have the ability to heal and mend the bodies of those dependent on them. This is in fact another form of control, extending the masters' reach from affecting sensory faculties alone to the actual physical shape and working of limbs and other body parts. The most straightforward cases of these include instances such as when Amin ad-Din Balyani was approached by a man whose fingers were paralyzed, and he restored them.[11] Similarly, a lame man came to Ahmad Bashiri saying that he was tired of his disability, and the master restored his leg.[12] In a more extended form, healing properties could be a significant feature of a master's overall profile. For example, 'Umar Murshidi's hagiographer reports:

> When people got headaches, his Eminence—may his Secret be sanctified— would write an amulet (ta'viz) and tell them to cover it in wax and keep it with them. That was extremely effective. He wrote the same amulet for eye injuries, as has come in the Sahih Bukhari and Muslim. He said that in the case of a pregnant woman close to delivery, when she was ready to begin the birthing process, this amulet was to be dropped in water while covered in wax. Then she was given the water to drink and the amulet was tied to her left thigh. Under this condition, she would give birth without any difficulty.[13]

In all these cases, masters act to provide relief from bodily hardships to those who are their committed religious dependents.

Instances of healing also include situations where masters' powers are presented as acting on the social body through the intermediacy of an individual body. In this regard, Amir Kulal's hagiographer tells a poignant story that encapsulates miracles' symbolic capacity to bridge the gap between a person and the community. He states that while Amir Kulal was a disciple of Khwaja Muhammad Sammasi, some people in the village of Sammas had a fight in which a man lost a tooth. The injured party's group initially thought to take the matter to a judge in order to seek compensation for the injury, but then decided to seek Sammasi's council. Sammasi asked to see the tooth and handed it over to the young Amir Kulal with the words "My son, do something so that these people get over their conflict." Amir Kulal took the tooth, placed it in the correct place in the man's mouth, and prayed to God and sought aid from the spirits of deceased masters. The tooth became attached exactly as it was before the fight, which astonished the injured man and compelled him to forgive those who had assaulted him. The miraculous restoration of the tooth led to the healing of the rift within the community.[14]

Protection, Multilocation, and Hypercorporeality

Masters' ability to protect their disciples in far away places without leaving their own abodes is a pervasive theme throughout hagiographic literature. Great figures such as Safi ad-Din Ardabili, Baha' ad-Din Naqshband, 'Ali Hamadani, and Shah Ni'matullah Vali are all shown to have preserved their disciples' bodily integrity in crises such as animal attacks, being lost while traveling, and being caught in storms while at sea.[15] This can be seen pictorially in the painting in figure 7.1 illustrating the story of a Sufi riding a tiger while using a snake as a whip, from a copy of the *Bustan* by the great moralist Muslih ad-Din Sa'di. In the text surrounding the painting, the man riding the tiger advises the one questioning him about his powers to become like the submissive tiger and snake in front of authority that deserves to be obeyed.[16]

The Mongol and Timurid periods were marked by widespread wars and political instability throughout the Persianate region, and masters are sometimes shown extending protection during sieges and conquests of cities, which involved significant loss of life. In fact, it can be argued that political instability and the associated lack of personal security helped to elevate Sufi masters' political roles during the fourteenth and fifteenth centuries. This can be seen directly in the case of a man such as Khwaja Ahrar, who controlled substantial economic resources and acted as a political arbitrator and sometime kingmaker

7.1 A man riding a tiger using a snake as a whip. From a copy of Saʿdi's *Bustan*. 1525, Herat, Iran. Opaque watercolor, ink, and gold on paper. Text and illustration: 20.6 × 13.7 cm. Arthur M. Sackler Gallery, Smithsonian Institution, Washington, DC: Purchase—Smithsonian Unrestricted Trust Funds, Smithsonian Collections Acquisition Program, and Dr. Arthur M. Sackler, S1986.36.

in Central Asia because of his vast influence. The record of his letters to rulers, viziers, and other governmental officials show him working in the capacity of his community's protector and a guarantor of justice in general. In these letters he is at times solicitous and at others censorious of official behavior, treating his addressees as equals rather than with the tone of an ordinary subservient subject in front of royal authority. His protective role over ordinary people he represented is marked by the fact that they are referred to as servitors (*mulazi-man*), reflecting an overlap between their religious allegiance as disciples and their status as political and economic clients in need of his sponsorship when required to deal with ruling authorities.[17]

Like other great masters, in hagiographic narratives devoted to him, Khwaja Ahrar is also shown to be a miraculous protector. In his case, then, the ordinary protection of a powerful political figure is intertwined with the extraordinary security that could be provided by a miracle-working friend of God. Although we do not possess much documentary or archival evidence similar to Ahrar for all the great masters, it can be presumed that the pattern we see in his case applied to them as well, according to the levels of influence they enjoyed among the political elites of the environs in which they operated.[18]

When it came to providing protection, the theme of Sufi masters' miraculous ability to multilocate stands out as being emblematic of the situation of Persianate Sufism. While the idea that masters can move and transform their bodies to be present in multiple locations at the same time has roots in early Sufi literature, the possibility was particularly useful in a context where Sufi communities were expanding rapidly and individual masters were considered responsible for the well-being of multitudes of disciples and others. Episodes that depict masters deploying this power most often lead to the cementing of Sufi intergenerational bonds.

In most cases of the use of this theme, male masters are depicted as able to transport themselves long distances instantaneously and be present in multiple locations synchronically in order to carry out their protective duties. Amin ad-Din Balyani's hagiographer tells the story of a dervish whom the master told explicitly that when a man starts calling people to God his disciples are never absent from him; wherever they go, he aids and protects them. The dervish was somewhat skeptical about this assertion until he decided to go to the Hijaz. One night in Basra, on the way, he went to sleep after a meal, neglecting to use a toothpick or clean his hands and mouth. Close to morning, he saw a dream in which Balyani appeared to him and gave him a toothpick along with the injunction to make up for his lack of proper care of the body prior to falling asleep. He then awoke to find the toothpick with him and realized that "in all situations, the shaykh is never absent from us; being far or near, or present or absent [from view], are all the same to him."[19]

The narratives I am utilizing provide varying accounts of the place of masters' bodies while interacting with those far removed from their own locations. For example, a story about ʿUmar Murshidi shows him become absent from his location while on such a mission. Once when a group from Kazarun was visiting him, he retracted his head into his shirt below the neckline and kept it there. The men, who were not Sufis, began arguing with each other, some saying that they should leave because he had fallen asleep while others maintaining that it would be rude to depart without taking formal leave. They then probed his robe and turban to realize that these were empty. A little while later, his head appeared from his neckline once again, now with water dripping out from his sleeves. When pressed, he explained that when he retracted his head, Muhammad appeared to him and told him to go to Baghdad to aid four orphan children who had some sheep that were about to drown in the river. He then proceeded to save the sheep and returned them to their owners before returning to his original location.[20]

Most stories concerned with masters' long-range abilities portray them with the capacity to be visible in multiple locations at the same time. A story concerned with Naqshband presents this directly when a group of dervishes split up to go various places after being in his company. As it happens, each of the subgroups sees him when they arrive at their destinations and thinks that he must have traveled there from a different route. When they meet up again they become very confused about where to go in order to find him, since people seem to have seen him in many different places. Then a servant arrives asking that they come back to where they had first met with the master. He tells them he had been in the same room with the master the whole time after they'd left, adding yet more mystery to the matter. When they all return to Naqshband and ask him about what they had experienced, he smiles and says, "It is related that one evening during Ramadan, his Eminence [the Khwajagani master] ʿAzizan [Ramitani] was asked to be at thirteen different places and he honored each request."[21]

While in this case disciples known to each other witness Naqshband's abilities, another prominent theme relating to multilocation is the idea that masters have disciples present in various localities completely unbeknownst to one another. In Naqshband's case a man reported that when traveling through Simnan he heard of a man known to be a devotee of the master. He made the effort to meet him and asked him how he had acquired his affiliation. The man replied that he had first seen a dream in which Muhammad had pointed to a man of great spiritual form and had told him Naqshband's name along with the advice to follow him. He had noted this man's appearance in detail and had written it down in the back of a book along with the date of the incident. Then, many years later, one day, as he was sitting in a shop, a spiritual-looking man appeared, and he was able to recognize him based on the description he had written down. He then asked Naqshband to grace his home by going there. He agreed and walked to it without being told the way and, when there, he proceeded to pick out the book that contained the written description and asked the man about it. Thoroughly convinced of this master's extraordinary knowledge, the man asked to become his disciple, and the wish was granted.[22]

The extraterritorial influence represented in this story is a particularly prominent theme in the hagiography of Amir Kulal. During this master's lifetime, one day a good-looking young man came and sat down at his gathering without a greeting or any other word passing through his lips. After a while, Amir Kulal raised his head and said, simply, "This is the end." The stranger replied, "There was one hollow left and now that is also hidden." He then remained in the company for some time, and, when he finally went out to leave, people gathered around him and asked about his rudeness, not asking for leave before his departure. He replied that he had come from Anatolia (Rum) and that Amir Kulal had been building a mosque there and had asked to be informed when it was complete. The disciples showed surprise at this, saying that the master had not been to Anatolia in recent times. He replied that everyone in the vicinity where he lived was a disciple of Amir Kulal and prayed behind him every Friday. He also explained that his greetings and other conversation with the master had been from the heart rather than the tongue. The fact that the locals had not been privy to the possibility of such communication marked them as deficient in knowledge.[23]

Moving to a different corner of the world, a group from Turkestan once came to Bukhara and began talking about Amir Kulal. The locals asked them how they had heard about the master, given that he'd never traveled there. They said that the master was extremely famous in their parts and that they were all his disciples, had been initiated by him, and would call upon him whenever they encountered any difficulties in life. After his powers had saved them many times, they finally asked who he was, and he replied with his name, leading to further affirmation of their relationship. They then praised Amir Kulal in ways the locals had never considered until this time.[24]

In a third instance of this sort, the hagiographer relates that after Amir Kulal died a group of Sufis from Mecca and Medina arrived in Bukhara and headed to Sukhari, the master's abode, asking for him. When people told them he had died, they said they would go and see his children. There they were asked how they had known Amir Kulal since he had never traveled to the Hijaz and they had never before been to Sukhari. They said that they were disciples of Amir Kulal, as was everyone else in Mecca and Medina, and had followed behind him circumambulating the Kaʿba for thirty-two years. This year he had not come to lead them, which had compelled them to seek him. They then visited his grave, mourned his passing, and eventually took leave of his descendants. In parting, they expressed the regret that no one in Amir Kulal's vicinity quite understood his greatness.[25]

These stories about Amir Kulal have two particular lessons built into them that reflect the deployment of the multilocation theme. By invoking the idea of masses of followers in Anatolia, Turkestan, and the Hijaz, the stories overcome the master's handicap, that he spent his whole life near the city of Bukhara in Central Asia. This must have been an important concern for those who sponsored the hagiography since, by the time the text was produced, the pace of institutionalization among Sufi communities in Central Asia had increased considerably. Particularly in comparison with competing groups such as the followers of Baha' ad-Din Naqshband, it was in the interest of Amir Kulal's successors to show him as having a following that extended far beyond the confines of his abode during his life. Simultaneously with this projection into the field of inter-Sufi competition, all the visitors are made to chide those who had spent their lives in the vicinity of Sukhari for not adequately appreciating Amir Kulal's powers and spiritual worth. These stories can then be read as injunctions to the audience to evince greater confidence in the patronage on offer from Amir Kulal's descendants.

It is important to note that, in these stories, masters are shown to present themselves physically rather than merely extending their protection by manipulating the environment to affect disciples or avert danger for someone. This power to multilocate is an especially advantageous hagiographic device when arguing for the breadth of influence of particular masters while constructing their hagiographic personas. Acknowledging masters' powers to project themselves through space and time in this way allows them to override limitations placed on ordinary bodies.

Life and Death

Accomplished Sufis' ability to kill and resurrect human beings represents the most dramatic enactment of the theme of corpses in morticians' hands in hagiographic sources. This is a fairly common subject in the literature, and the power is attributed quite unproblematically to the famous masters. Narratives that show masters exercising this ability are invariably concerned with a larger point having to do with ideological or social matters. As I argued at the end of the last chapter, hagiographic representations of masters' abilities to perform miracles never depict them overturning material causality in the abstract. They are shown to exert such powers either while asserting themselves against rivals, or in the context of specific relationships with other individuals whom they are obligated to protect or chastise. This pattern is equally true for miracles of bringing the dead back to life and the provision of food.

ʿAli Hamadani is shown to have traveled widely throughout the regions that are today classified as Middle East and Central and South Asia, and is regarded, to this day, as the force behind the Islamization of Kashmir. His hagiographer Haydar Badakhshi tells a story that includes the theme of bringing the dead back to life in conjunction with conversion to Islam, although the venue for this is described as a Christian habitation near the "Land of the Franks" rather than India. When passing by this village he is shown to inquire from the inhabitants as to why they had not converted to Islam. They reply that they considered their religion superior because their "prophet," meaning Jesus, could make the dead come back to life and that if they ever came across someone able to do this in their own times they would convert to the religion of that person. As Hamadani hears this, an unseen voice (*hatif*) tells him that he might have this power if he wished. He proceeds to the graveyard and is able to rouse dead bodies, which leads the village to convert to Islam.[26]

While this story affirms Hamadani's role as a proselytizer, a different narrative in the same source deploys the theme of quickening a dead body in the arena of interpersonal relationships between a master and a community. One day, as ʿAli Hamadani was sitting inside a mosque, the dead body of member of the local nobility was brought into the courtyard for funeral prayer. Someone in the party went in to see Hamadani and asked him to lead the prayer for the sake of the man's afterlife. The shaykh replied that there was no reason for this because the man was still alive. The man remonstrated that he had died the night before, and, by the time Hamadani went outside to check, the funeral prayers had been performed and people had taken the body away to the grave. Upon reaching the graveyard, Hamadani had the people reopen the grave and then told the dead man to rise, which he did immediately, walking away. When people asked the man the meaning of it all, he told them that the members of his family were disciples of Hamadani, but he had spent his whole life committing sins. The angel of death had then appeared and taken away his life before he could repent his bad deeds. Hamadani brought him back to life since no disciple of his could be fated for eternal punishment. To fulfill this destiny, the man lived for twelve more years and spent every moment in acts of worship.[27] This story illustrates the notion that Sufi masters' reputations and the acts of their disciples were thoroughly interdependent matters.

The full cycle from life to death and then back to life is represented as being under the control of a great master in some instances. Khwaja Parsa reports that Baha' ad-Din Naqshband told him that while he was still a novice on the path, he once went into the desert with another dervish where they discussed many things. At one point, the conversation came to the quality of servitude (ʿubudiyyat) and abandoning one's self (fida) that can characterize a Sufi. The dervish asked about what the limit of such dedication could be, and Naqshband replied that if a dervish is told to die, he dies instantly. After he said this, he was overcome by a feeling and looked at the dervish, commanding him, "Die!" Instantly the man fell down, and his spirit left his body. From morning to midday, the dead body lay there in the sun while Naqshband himself went off to find shade because it was a very hot day. When he went to see the body, it had begun to change color because of the heat. Then another feeling came over him, and he commanded the body, "Come alive!" After he said this three times, the man's limbs began to move and he raised himself, fully alive. Naqshband then went to Amir Kulal, his master, and told him this story. When Amir Kulal inquired as to why he had eventually told the body to come back to life, he replied that he had been compelled by an intuition (ilham).[28]

Among prominent shaykhs, Naqshband comes across as being particularly adept at giving and taking life. In the story I have just recounted, his command establishes the credentials of the second man by showing that he could implement servitude to the point of death. In other stories Naqshband is depicted as punishing disciples by commanding them to die. He once asked a disciple a question, but the man failed to respond. Becoming angry, Naqshband then shot him a look that made the disciple fall down and die. Other disciples present at the moment felt pity for the man and interceded on his behalf. Naqshband then made him come back to life by putting his feet on the dead man's chest. He repented from his rudeness, and the master asked him to jump into a pool of water. When he did so, he said he saw his whole field of vision saturated with light.[29]

Naqshband once made a dead man come alive by simply telling the body, "Come to life, Muhammad." Exerting greater effort on another occasion, he put his feet on the chest of a dead man to bring him back and later said that he had had to travel to the fourth heaven to catch up with the man's spirit and bring it back down to earth to unite with the body.[30] Extending the theme of giving life in a different direction, Naqshband is, like other masters, credited with being able to grant people's request for children. Once someone came to him who had had ten children die from various causes. Naqshband offered prayers that led to the birth of a daughter who, however, became very sick. The master then asked the parents to provide a sheep as a kind of substitute for the child's life, after which she recovered and lived a long life.[31] Similarly, a woman once asked her husband to give Naqshband some coins to distribute as alms without indicating a direct wish. Upon receiving these, Naqshband smiled and told the man they exuded the smell of a child and he would soon have one. The hagiographer reports that a child was indeed born and was actually present in company when this story was related to him for the sake of including in the hagiographic text.[32]

Between the stories I have related so far in this chapter, Sufi masters are shown to be able to affect all the different functions a human body is presumed to possess while being present in the world. They can control disciples' sensory perceptions, heal or regenerate limbs and organs, guarantee the integrity and dignity of their bodies under adverse circumstances, willfully take away and endow life to bodies, and extend their presence in the world by granting children. Seen from the side of masters, these processes imply the capacious abilities of their own bodies to intervene on others' experience of being in the world. But when seen from the side of disciples, these themes imply the tying up of their individual bodies to that of a master able to extend himself simultaneously in multiple arenas. Since disciples are the ones who composed hagiographic literature, highlighting this theme shows the texts as annals of their own corporeal submission at the hands of the masters. In the remainder of this chapter, I explain why Sufis in the Persianate context found it useful, and even necessary, to portray themselves as hapless corpses in the hands of masters.

MASTERS AS CORPSES

The hagiography of Shaykh Ahmad Bashiri tells a story involving death positioned at the beginning of the master's Sufi career. The author states that the master himself said that once, during warm weather, he acquired an unrecognizable disease that made his body start to smell extremely bad. The odor was so horrendous that even his relatives gave up coming near him, and he found himself sitting in the wilds under the sun, not possessing enough strength to move to shade. All who walked by would cover their noses with their sleeves, and no one would give him any water or food. He then sensed that he had no one left near him, whether in the exterior or the interior world, and he passed out, losing any sense of the difference between night and day. But he eventually recovered from this illness and realized that it had caused him to become completely free of the created world. The experience meant that everything had washed away from his heart save God.[33]

This and other similar stories told of Sufi masters convey their acquiescence to Muhammad's command to "die before you die." The prophetic injunction is aimed at advocating a separation from the cares of the world and can be interpreted metaphorically, as is usually the case, or enacted physically, as seen in Shaykh Bashiri's example. Inasmuch as great masters are supposed to have reached ultimate Sufi goals, stories such as these imply that they are to be seen as beings who have undergone deaths and rebirths within their lifetimes. The working of this process is, in part, what makes their bodies special: their extraordinary powers, exhibited through miracles, derive from the fact that they are seen as being dead in ways that ordinary bodies are alive and living in ways that other bodies are dead.[34] If such is presumed to be the case, hagiographic narratives that describe moments when masters leave the physical world for good hold special interest as points of analytical concentration for understanding the metaphysical and social functions of saintly bodies.

As studies of death and bereavement have highlighted, the passing away of a human being is a thoroughly social event that implicates multiple bodies. Save for situations of mass death, the presence of a dead body has a profound effect on those who surround it.[35] At the moment of his permanent death, the Naqsh-bandi master ʿAlaʾ ad-Din Abizi is said to have briefly regained consciousness and heard the weeping of women. When told that they were doing so because of his condition, he is said to have told them to rejoice instead since, for someone like him, death represents final union with God and is a moment of accession to the greatest happiness.[36] A man named Shams ad-Din Bukhari is described as having prepared himself for his death by wearing his best clothes and digging his own grave before telling his companions, "The time for my departure has arrived; when I go into seclusion, stay close until I say 'O He' three times; after that, start the work of washing the body and putting on the shroud."[37]

The different processes that are put into motion upon death are presented in a painting with very fine details that dramatizes a story in Farid ad-Din ʿAttar's classic *Conference of the Birds* (figure 7.2).[38] Here a Sufi master counsels a man lamenting at the funeral of his father to the effect that death is inconsequential in the larger scheme of things and that it is more significant to concentrate on what one does while one is alive. The painting contextualizes the dead body, hidden inside the coffin, by surrounding it with living ones of various ages and comportments. Whether in this image or in the stories I have cited earlier, the narration of death conjoins the state and perspective of the dying person with the actions and attitudes of those who are to live with the fact of the death. Although the narratives provide a contrast between the two sides, the texts and the painting convey varying investments held by the dying person's successors.

I will discuss hagiographic representations of death by concentrating on narratives regarding Safi ad-Din of Ardabil and Khwaja Ahrar. These two cases are exemplary, but for different reasons. The work *Safvat as-safaʾ*, concerned with Ardabili, contains the most extended account of a master's death, encompassing themes that are found piecemeal in other narratives. And Khwaja Ahrar's death is represented in three different sources with slight but highly meaningful variations. Juxtaposing these narratives highlights the fact that, in representations of death as in other cases, awareness of the eyes and pens that mediate the event for later observers makes a significant difference for analyzing hagiographic material.

7.2 A son being consoled at his father's funeral. From a copy of ʿAttar's *Mantiq at-tayr*. Bihzad, circa 1487–88. 19.7 × 14.6 cm. Image copyright © Metropolitan Museum of Art, New York. Fletcher Fund, 1963 (63.210.49).

The author of the *Safvat as-safaʾ* narrates Shaykh Safi's last illness and death by relating accounts by a number of different prominent disciples. His chief witness is the master's son, Shaykh Sadr ad-Din, who not only succeeded his father as the head of the religious community but was also the specific sponsor of the hagiographic compilation in question. Shaykh Safi is said to have endured a protracted final illness of bladder constriction, which the hagiographer links to his youthful habit of holding urine for weeks at a time so as not to exit a state of ritual purity. His master, Shaykh Zahid, is said to have told him to desist from this practice, because it would likely cause great pain in his old age, but he is shown to have continued it.[39]

The significant duration of Shaykh Safi's illness allows the hagiographer to depict him interacting with a number of people, providing details of the transition occasioned by his demise. The author relates, from Sadr ad-Din, that when his father had been ill for a year and two months, he thought to himself that perhaps he was not close to his death since it was reputed that the passing away of great masters threw the world into imbalance because of the vacuum left behind them. When he inquired of his father, he replied, "My son, after me you will see things that no eyes have seen before and hear that which no ear has heard before." This was proven after his death with a number of calamities: a famine came to grip the world and people were driven to eat cats, dogs, and dead bodies; political upheaval led most of the population of Azerbaijan to be exiled and villages and cities to be destroyed; a plague devastated the population for many years such that many thousands of dwellings stood empty for want of owners.[40]

In the personal sphere, Sadr ad-Din is shown to say that he was absolutely distraught over his father's death, thinking that all his relatives and friends would turn against him and he would lead a miserable life without any supporters. As a result of these thoughts, he contemplated eating poison to destroy himself, but the father divined his troubles from his face and told him that if loneliness and trials did come, they would be a kind of patrimony for him since his father and (maternal) grandfather had not led an easy life. He also pointed to his own illness as a case in point, saying that whenever physicians were able to lessen his pains God sent more terrible ones since this kind of affliction was the mark of his status as an ardent lover of the divine.[41]

For the last two days of his life, Shaykh Safi had nothing but Quranic phrases on his tongue. The death itself occurred after the morning prayers on Muharram 12, 735 (September 12, 1334 CE). As the body lay on his bed, his wife Bibi Fatima, who was the daughter of his own master, asked to see him for the last time and gave the men her father's waistcoat and two turban sashes she had woven to be put on the body before it was buried. Eighteen days after the master's death she herself passed away as well. As the body was prepared for burial, it exhibited miraculous powers like lifting the arms by itself, and one person carrying the coffin to the grave realized that it was being held up by itself in air without burdening anyone. He was buried in the room where he used to dance during musical auditions since this is where his body had gone into ecstasies while he had been alive. Even before Shaykh Safi's death, people reported having seen thousands of spiritual beings (*ruhaniyyun*) sitting outside this room waiting for its eventual sanctification with the body's interment.[42]

Hagiographic narratives regarding Shaykh Safi present his son Shaykh Sadr ad-Din as the sole preeminent successor to the great master's mantle. Among episodes I have cited, Sadr ad-Din's desire to destroy his own body while seeing the gradual demise of that of his father makes the two appear fundamentally connected to each other. Shaykh's Safi's statement that bodily pain of the type he was undergoing at the time was a kind of inheritance for both of them emphasizes this identity even further. The close connection between the narration of death and succession can be seen even more clearly in a case such as that of Khwaja Ahrar where we have testimonies from the perspective of many different disciples.

Successors at Deathbeds

Ahrar's son-in-law, disciple, and hagiographer ʿAbd al-Avval Nishapuri relates that the master, a few months before his ninetieth birthday, was stricken with acute diarrhea, which caused severe weakness and forced him to be bedridden while in Samarqand, away from home. During three months of illness, he made special efforts not to miss any prayers despite his fragile condition. On the last day, as Nishapuri sat next to him, he opened his eyes and asked who was there. When someone else who was present said Nishapuri's name, he extended his right hand and grabbed him. Nishapuri says that, in hindsight, that was his parting handshake. He died toward the end of Rabiʿ al-Avval 895 (February 1490).[43]

In the second narrative regarding Ahrar's death, Mawlana Shaykh reports that, on the last day, the master wished to issue a testament. When this occurred Nishapuri was sitting on one side of the room, Ahrar's son Khwaja Kalan was on the other side, and the narrator himself was behind the head side of the bed so that Ahrar could not see him. He raised his head and asked who was there. People responded that it was the Khwajagan and nobles (*amiran*). He then asked who else was there. They then said Mawlana Shaykh's name, and Ahrar insisted that he come in front of him rather than sitting behind. He then proceeded to give very detailed financial instructions regarding the construction and maintenance of a *madrasa* that had been in planning stages at the time. The author writes: "From the beginning of the testament to the end, this wretch was his addressee. It occurred to me that the Khwajagan and nobles may not like it that all this was said to me. Becoming aware of this [thought in my mind] from his great nobility, he [Ahrar] screwed up his face and said, 'Now they are with us as well; whatever comes to someone's mind he should say it.' No one knew why he said this, but the reason was that the thought had arisen in the mind of this wretch."[44] As in Nishapuri's case, this account is constructed carefully to show the closeness between the master and the narrator. First, he places himself at the location and shows that Ahrar was able to discern his presence, even though he could not see him physically. Then the testament is addressed to him. Finally, the special connection between the two is shown through Ahrar's ability to divine his thoughts to the exclusion of others who were present.

The third account of Ahrar's death available to us comes from *Rashahat-i 'ayn al-hayat,* whose author, Fakhr ad-Din Safi, does not represent himself as having been present by the master's side when he passed away. The first part of his report is virtually identical with the account of Nishapuri previously discussed, except that he attributes the words to a disciple named Mawlana Abu Sa'id Awbahi, who is described as having been his companion throughout the illness and the last moments. Safi makes no mention of the presence of Nishapuri or Mawlana Shaykh at the scene. He then goes on to say that, right at the moment when Ahrar died, the city of Samarqand witnessed a severe earthquake, and those who were aware of Ahrar's illness knew immediately that this was an indication of his death. Those present where he lay said that just before his spirit left the body they saw an extremely bright light come out of the space between his eyebrows and completely overshadow all the candles burning in the house. The rulers of the area rushed to the scene to aid in preparing the body for the funeral, and Ahrar's descendants constructed a lofty shrine over the grave after the burial.[45]

The most interesting information to be gained from comparing these accounts of Ahrar's death has to do with the bodies of the authors rather than the dying man. Nishapuri was an intimate companion of the master, and his account emphasizes the latter seeking corporeal contact with him before life escapes his body. This is not a mere incidental detail, because Safi's report is identical, save that it makes no mention of Nishapuri's presence or the handshake with Ahrar. Moreover, Nishapuri's account conveys the impression that he alone was present at the critical moment, whereas Mawlana Shaykh shows the presence of a large group that includes Ahrar's son and the author himself. Clearly, then, Nishapuri's version is carefully constructed to emphasize his own position relative to the dying master as well as the survivors. His portrayal of the matter constitutes an argument aimed at legitimizing his own claims as a successor.

Mawlana Shaykh was not as close a companion to Ahrar as Nishapuri, but he is also compelled to insert himself in the scene. As the author of a text on the master, his presence at the time of his death is an important factor for legitimizing his narrative. Moreover, of all hagiographic works concerned with Ahrar, his work provides the greatest amount of details on the master's economic engagements. This emphasis gets reflected in the death narrative as well, since Ahrar is shown giving very precise instructions regarding a major public project. His modulation of the death narrative is therefore closely tied to the general tenor of his work.[46] Similarly, Safi's account also matches the overall purposes of his work. The *Rashahat*'s extensive description of Ahrar's life is keyed to portraying him as an extraordinary man of the age and contextualizing his life within the Naqshbandi lineage. Safi eschews espousing the cause of any particular successor, showing, instead, Ahrar's significance as a cosmic figure and one whom society's elite felt compelled to honor.

Themes found in narratives concerned with the deaths of Shaykh Safi and Ahrar appear piecemeal throughout Persianate hagiographic literature.[47] The two most prominent features of these accounts are the idea that masters' deaths cause imbalance in the world and that those designated to succeed to the master are present at moments of death to show transfers of authority. Both these aspects of death narratives contain ramifications for the authors and sponsors of these texts. The issue of imbalance begs the rise of someone who can correct it so that the hierarchy of God's friends readjusts and remains the mechanism through which God maintains the world. There can be no better substitute for the dead master than someone who can claim to be his direct successor. For the succession to be fully valid, however, it has to be ratified through close connection to the master, which is best shown by placing the two bodies in question in close proximity as one ceases to live and the other takes its place.

Narratives about great masters' deaths are optimal places to see disciples handling masters' dying or dead bodies, metaphorically as well as physically. As I suggested earlier, the idea that disciples are the real morticians applies to the whole hagiographic genre, including the stories where masters are shown as great and powerful beings. However, the permanent death of a master's body marks a significant transitional moment within hagiographic narratives' internal logic. To see this, we will consider, quite briefly, the functioning of Sufi shrines in the Persianate context.

Embodiment and Enshrinement

The foundation of the city today known as Mazar-i Sharif in northern Afghanistan is an intriguing episode in the religious history of Persianate societies during the fifteenth century. The city's name means "the noble shrine," referring to the purported grave of Muhammad's cousin and son-in-law ʿAli, which became "manifest" at this site first in the twelfth century CE and then again toward the end of the fifteenth century. This is somewhat enigmatic since ʿAli died in Iraq and his shrine in Najaf has been a well-known place of pilgrimage from early Islamic times.

Historical improbability notwithstanding, the surprising appearance of a second grave in 1135 CE is said to have led to the construction of a shrine, which had fallen away from the public eye by the fifteenth century. The grave's rediscovery in 1480–81 precipitated the construction of a new shrine under the patronage of the Timurid king Husayn Bayqara. This fifteenth-century shrine is commemorated in the city's name and has been central to the settlement that has continued on to the modern city. The shrine has already received significant academic attention, and, for the present purposes, I will focus on representations found in a short treatise on the rediscovery written by ʿAbd al-Ghafur Lari.[48] A disciple of ʿAbd ar-Rahman Jami, Lari also wrote a hagiographic text on his master that was meant to continue Jami's own extensive dictionary of Sufis.[49] Lari's contextualization of ʿAli's shrine in a Sufi idiom provides a useful example to understand the formation and functioning of such monuments in the Persianate world during the fifteenth century. I have chosen to highlight narratives about this shrine in particular because of the way they illustrate the *discontinuity* between bodies and shrines.

Lari begins his work with extensive praises of ʿAli and then goes on to state that, in the reign of Husayn Bayqara, the grave was discovered through the mediation of Shaykh Shams ad-Din Muhammad, a descendant of the great Sufi master Bayazid Bistami. This man had found a book in a library in India that contained the story of the original discovery of the grave. According to this, in 1135 CE, four hundred people saw dreams in which Muhammad told them that ʿAli's grave was located in the village of Khayran, in the Balkh region. The dreams compelled the local ruler to consult scholars, of whom all except one gave the opinion that the dreams must be true because Muhammad is reported to have said that Satan does not have the power to impersonate him in dreams. The one naysayer protested that ʿAli had died in Najaf, very far from the region, and it was impossible that the body could have been brought there for burial. However, the next night this jurist saw himself beaten and berated by sayyids under ʿAli's own supervision in a dream, causing him to change his point of view. The ruler of the times then ordered an engraved epitaph prepared for the site and had a building constructed over the grave. This grave and epitaph reappeared in 1480–81 when Shaykh Shams ad-Din was able to convince the governor of the region, who was a brother of Husayn Bayqara, that the site should be reexcavated. The shrine's location was rationalized through the idea that, although ʿAli had died in Najaf, the body had been moved to the location in Khayran around the middle of the eighth century in order to protect it from possible desecration by enemies of ʿAli and his descendants, the Umayyads.[50]

Once the news of the manifestation of the shrine spread, it became a major center of pilgrimage for people, coming from near and far, who poured offerings into the hands of the shrine's caretakers. Lari's florid verses in praise of the shrine state:

> Noble tomb, to you belongs the sanctity of all sanctuaries.
>> Your location is the *qibla* of Arabs, the Kaʿba of non-Arabs.
> Compared to its brilliance, the sun and the moon are mere candles.
>> Heaven's back stoops as it bends down to kiss its lights.
> In its spirit-nurturing dust are inscribed cures,
>> its spirit-scattering floor the place to smash all sorrows.
> Creation takes refuge at its threshold.
>> Time swears by the dust of its court.
> From the manifestation of this garden, abode of the angel of Paradise,
>> dust of the earth of Balkh has become the Garden of Iram.
> What to say of a human being who comes to this noble place,
>> a speechless stone would lose its fault of being dumb.
> For anyone who has passed through this sacred shrine,
>> the sky is a feeble lamp, equivalent to twilight.[51]

This description emphasizes the shrine's status as a place of cosmic significance, deserving to be treated as the focal point of rituals. It also bears a close connection to corporeal well-being because of its healing qualities. And, in the manner of the description of other mausoleums in the Islamic context, the shrine is portrayed as a piece of heaven on earth because of the special character of the person buried in it. Immediately after providing the poetic tribute, Lari writes that, once the shrine's miraculous powers had been confirmed through the appearance of a continuous stream of extraordinary events, the king Husayn Bayqara himself went to the shrine and circumambulated it, treating it with the greatest deference. The king's decision to do so is memorialized in a verse by Lari that inverts the normal order of things by presenting those who are living as dead and the abode of the dead body as the fount of life:

> Jesus has become apparent, why should I be dead?
> I am a blooming tulip, why should I appear wilting?[52]

In later years, Bayqara's government relied heavy on revenues generated by the shrine and also promoted it as a pilgrimage site preferable to Mecca for the region's inhabitants.[53]

As presented in Lari's work and corroborated by other sources, the phenomenal efficacy of ʿAli's shrine at Khwaja Khayran derived from the confluence of three elements: the promulgation of a story regarding the site that was justified through textual referents, the attribution of healing characteristics to its physical constituents, and investment in its reputation on the part of religious and political elites that made the shrine a source of legitimacy as well as revenue. Notably, what was needed for the shrine to be established was not a freshly dead body but *narratives* about a body whose prestige mattered to those who sponsored the shrine and were its patrons. In physical terms, the earth and buildings surrounding the grave seem to have held powers similar to those ascribed to the bodies of great masters during their lifetimes. The deployment of these powers now depended on those who held religious and temporal authority over the shrine's physical space. There is, therefore, a close connection between stories regarding shrines and the interests of caretakers, which parallels the case of the contents of hagiographic texts and the interests of their sponsors.

A great number of shrines were erected over the graves of dead Sufis during the fourteenth and fifteenth centuries in the Persianate area, including most of the great Sufi masters I have discussed in this book.[54] At least in part, the efficacy of the sites where these were constructed derived from the notion that sanctity had seeped into their physical elements through the masters' presence. One source likens this to the practice of some masters even during their lifetimes: before assigning a room to a disciple, they would go and pray in it themselves to make the space favorable for the disciple's endeavors.[55]

It should be noted that there is no absolute one to one correspondence between the reputation of a master and the scale of a shrine built for him immediately after his death. If and when shrines would be constructed and become focal points for visitation and patronage depended ultimately on the confluence of masters' reputations and the interests of those willing and able to sponsor them. Overall, then, what matters is that shrine construction and visitation were significant cultural preoccupations in this historical context as a whole. As in the case of the great masters' personalities, the reputation of a shrine depended, in the last instances, on the production of narratives about the site that could well add to the posthumous reputation of masters but were also independent venues for socioreligious elaboration. The shrine of ʿAli at Khwaja Khayran exemplifies this since its rejuvenation as a pilgrimage site did not require the presence of a dead body. What mattered was the production of a compelling narrative, backed up by the interests of those in power. The shrines can then be seen as new physical manifestations—new "embodied" forms—that were first justified through narratives about their material connection to saintly persons' bodies but then took on lives of their own in new symbolic and ritual contexts.

Figure 7.3 contains a painting from a mid sixteenth-century copy of the *Divan* of the famous poet Ahli Shirazi (d. 1535–36) that depicts the types of corporeal behaviors one could expect to see around great Sufi shrines. Two couplets surround the painted panel that contains the grave:

(*top*)
On the threshold of his value, the realm of Mulk is less than dirt.
Its measure is the value of earth in comparison with the heavens.
(*bottom*)
The world is nonbeing, I see him as being.
In front of that being, I see the sky in prostration.

In the image, the grave hides a body that is deemed more precious than the multitude of living bodies that surround it. The grave is separated from the main chamber by a grill, over which hang various vessels. Behind the grill, two men and two women touch the grave and hold their hands in praying postures. In the main chamber, eleven male figures are shown praying, prostrating, reading, and sitting respectfully. The words of the verses invert the value placed on life versus death by tying the matter to apparent versus hidden truths, the dichotomy central to Sufi ideology. The inscription and the scene together present a community in which the living are tied intimately to the dead through devotion directed at the shrine.[56]

Scenes such as these correlate to hagiographical stories in which the great Sufi masters are shown continuing to act upon the world after their deaths. In some such narratives, masters expect visitation to their graves from disciples in the way this should have happened during their lifetimes. Once when ʿAlaʾ ad-Din Abizi agreed to undertake an errand while on the way to visit the grave of Saʿd ad-Din Kashghari, the dead master complained to a later visitor that Abizi had not come exhibiting complete devotion.[57] From a different angle, when Mawlana Qazi visited a shrine without permission from Khwaja Ahrar, his living master, he felt he was about to die because of being guilty of incomplete faithfulness.[58] In both cases, the stories emphasize obedience due to the masters, dead or alive, whom one has chosen as one's guide.

We can observe the underlying social functions of such stories by considering an episode from the extensive section (running to ninety printed pages) devoted to Shaykh Safi ad-Din Ardabili's posthumous actions reported in his hagiography. The general tenor of the material given here can be seen from the following story: a disciple of Shaykh Safi reported that a man in the vicinity of Ardabil had started an unjust dispute with Shaykh Sadr ad-Din, Shaykh Safi's son and

7.3 Prayers inside a shrine. From a copy of the *Divan* of Ahli Shirazi. Circa 1550, Shiraz, Iran. David Collection, Copenhagen. No. Isl. 161.

successor. At the time, another man saw a dream in which Shaykh Safi asked him to tell the disputing man to desist from his actions or he would be made to resemble an obedient buffalo with his eyes popping out of their sockets and all his relatives abandoning him. However, the man paid no heed to this warning and continued with his fight. Soon thereafter, all the organs of his body began swelling up so that he began to resemble the form of a buffalo. This caused such tremendous pain that he was incapable of even using a knife to end his own life despite having the desire to do so. All his relatives abandoned him, and, eventually, the swelling and pain reached such dimensions that his eyes fell out of their sockets, causing his death.[59]

This story illustrates what I have argued about the interrelationships between dead masters and their successors and hagiographers. The exemplary punishment meted out by Shaykh Safi is meant to benefit his successor, the man who commissioned the hagiography that is our source. Inside the story, Shaykh Safi is able to transform a living body at will, although he is himself no longer present in an embodied form. But seen from a sociopolitical perspective, the story advances the interests of the successor. We can surmise, therefore, that the hagiographer sponsored by the successor is utilizing the memory of Shaykh Safi to affirm the authority of his successor, who is his own benefactor.

Throughout this chapter, I have attempted to elicit the power relations observable in Persianate hagiographic literature by considering narratives from within as well as without the frames of their internal logic. From the inside perspective, masters' miraculous power to give, preserve, and withdraw life while defying space and time is a significant feature of this literature. This is precisely the quality of the literature that is responsible for its dismissal by historians as a repository of information that could be valuable for representing the past. However, as I have shown through my interpretations of narratives about the deaths and afterlives of the great masters, hagiographic representations contain significant information when we see them as expressions of authors' particular interests. Stories like the one in which Shaykh Safi causes the destruction of the body of a recalcitrant person show the exercise of power between multiple generations of men. By treating the theme of corpses in morticians' hands as a discourse concerned with power relations, we can appreciate these materials as important sources for understanding the development of ideas as well as communities in a social context where Sufism was a deeply influential paradigm.

EPILOGUE

This book is an effort to utilize stories related in words and depicted in paintings to understand societies that existed many centuries ago. In the process of writing it, I have been asked many times to tell the story that I have found especially interesting or entertaining. Most often, my response to this has been to relate a very short one that has stayed with me from the time I first began working on this project. It comes from the famous Naqshbandi work *Rashahat-i 'ayn al-hayat*: Khwaja 'Ubaydullah Ahrar said, "I went into the presence of Shaykh Baha' ad-Din 'Umar quite often. He would say to me, 'Come here, shaykhzada, and massage my shoulders.' I massaged his shoulders frequently, and sometimes I would pull off his socks from his feet. I have never smelled a more pleasing odor than what came off from his stockings."[1]

The thought of smell coming off of stockings provokes a visceral reaction. By remarking upon it as beautiful, the author of this work is able to convey the idea of a particularly intimate devotional relationship between Ahrar and 'Umar without requiring an intellectual gloss. The immediacy of the author's imagery collapses the differences of time and space that would ordinarily distance us from having an intuitive understanding of relationships between Central Asian Sufis who lived nearly six centuries ago.

This story has stayed with me because it encapsulates the promise I felt when I first contemplated focusing on corporeal themes to interpret Persianate texts and paintings from the fourteenth and fifteenth centuries. It seemed quite logical that matters related to bodies would enable me to overcome the strangeness of ways of being and expression long past. This could, in turn, allow me to recover a social imagination that is otherwise difficult to grasp. Although I believe some part of my initial instinct has been borne out, the process of writing the book has led me to consider carefully the particularities that must be taken into account when interpreting images whose meanings seem self-evident from their surfaces. While the smell of soiled stockings—or the practice of shaking hands with which I began this book—may need little explanation to be meaningful, understanding why such matters are evoked in Persianate Sufi hagiographic literature requires consideration of socioreligious patterns that are not intrinsic to the evocative images in and of themselves. In stories, matters that are familiar can provide the first points of access to the narratives. But it is crucial to inquire further, for the significance of images and stories resides in the interrelationships between them far more than in their isolated impacts.

The smell of socks one registers when one reads the story related above is emanating from a narrative rather than a piece of cloth. Within its own point of articulation, the smell belongs in the relational space between three men: it legitimates claims of intimacy between Khwaja Ahrar and Baha᾿ ad-Din ʿUmar, and between Ahrar and the narrative's author. The story's original addressees were Sufis who relied on Safi, the author, to learn about Ahrar's intellectual attitudes and bodily comportment in order to emulate him. Despite its readily appreciable materiality, the story is no simple exercise in realism. It constitutes a strategic deployment of a theme within a highly formalized and typological literary form. The story has to be unpacked from its nesting place in between the social relationships that connect these Sufis, to whom it mattered as a meaningful narrative both personally and socially. Such unpacking leads to the kind of story I have constructed in this book to represent Persianate Sufism.

When we read hagiographic narratives or observe paintings in a straightforward way, they appear as flat and two-dimensional accounts of a fantastical worldview. But when we take seriously both their representational content and the contexts of their production, the images contained in them acquire movement in three dimensions. Here the questions of who produced these materials, and with what apparent and latent purposes, are our keys to unlocking their historiographic potential. These narratives and paintings represent, simultaneously, the memory of great Sufi masters and expressions of social and political interests of those who held authority in Sufi communities. Historiographic "meaning" in these sources is to be found in the middle of these two matters that constitute the reasons behind their production. From this perspective, my thematic explorations of these materials substantiate processes that were central to the functioning of Persianate Islamic societies during the fourteenth and fifteenth centuries.

These considerations corroborate my argument that, far from being an insurmountable hindrance, the highly stylized nature of representations found in hagiographic narratives and miniature paintings is a valuable datum for understanding sociocultural matters pertaining to pre-modern Islamic societies. However, mining these texts and images as historical sources requires that we ask questions regarding their origins, rhetorical purposes, social uses, and intended audiences. Seen through such lenses, these materials become major venues for reconstituting the social imagination at work in them. In particular, these sources are indispensible for understanding matters such as the articulation of religious and social authority, intergenerational transfers and negotiations surrounding gender, contextual meanings ascribed to affective forces that activate love and desire, and sociopolitical relationships between narrators and their subjects, sponsors, and audiences. By paying attention to these topics we can illuminate intellectual and social worlds that are impossible to access from any other types of sources available from medieval Islamic societies. If I have been able to demonstrate this to the satisfaction of readers, I would consider myself to have met the objective I set for myself in writing this book.

NOTES

INTRODUCTION: SHAKING HANDS

1. Awbahi, "Risala-yi musafaha," 475.The text in question does not include the name of the author, but the editor argues convincingly that it is Awbahi on the basis of very strong contextual evidence. Awbahi's formulation regarding the handshake reflects the combination of two different strands connected to transmission of hadith that seem to have been current in Central Asia in the later medieval period. The notion of long-lived companions ratifying statements ascribed to Muhammad originated early in Islamic history and remained relevant through the centuries (cf. G. H. A. Juynboll, "Mu'ammar," s.v. EI^2). Acquiring salvation through shaking Muhammad's hand was a popular idea in North Africa from the fifteenth century onward as well. The only scholar to have investigated the theme suggests that it was an extension of a hadith from the canonical collection of Tirmidhi where Muhammad guarantees salvation for someone who sees the person who had seen him (cf. Katz, *Dreams, Sufism, and Sainthood*, 224–31). A systematic excavation of hadith literature to trace the text cited by Awbahi is beyond the scope of my present interest. Apart from the short work on handshakes, Awbahi is best known in history as the possible author of a dictionary of Persian poetic terms (cf. Awbahi, *Farhang-i tuhfat al-ahbab*). For arguments against Awbahi's authorship of this work see Sadiqi, "Aya *Farhang-i tuhfat al-ahbab* az Hafiz-i Awbahi ast?"

2. For a useful discussion of the significance of paying attention to the interlacing of various measures of time in historiography see Koselleck, "Time and

History." For Islamic contexts, this theme has received some attention with a focus on Arabic sources (Azmeh, *Times of History*). I hope to expand my brief comment on the question of time here in forthcoming work.

3. For a lucid account of historiographic debates on these issues see Clark, *History, Theory, Text.*

4. Nawshahi, "Du risala dar isnad-i musafaha," 477–79.

5. For literature pertaining to the deployment of this idea in early Islamic history see C. Gilliot, "Tabakat," s.v. *EI²*.

6. We have one textual witness to Awbahi exercising his intercessory prerogative. In his dictionary of poets, Nisari writes that he shook hands with Awbahi at the latter's deathbed, when he gave him his work on handshakes and advised him to memorize it (Nisari, *Muzakkir-i ahbab*, 180).

7. Badakhshi, *Khulasat al-manaqib*, 62–63. The text cites 830/1426–27 as the year of the meeting, which surely represents a scribal error since ʿAli Hamadani died in 1385 and the author of the text in question is himself said to have died in 797/1394–95.

8. Badakhshi, *Manqabat al-javahir*, 353b–356a. There is some confusion in the dates here since, if he was twenty-two in 713 AH, ʿAli Hamadani would have been an improbable ninety-five at the time of his death in 786.

9. Nawshahi, "Du risala dar isnad-i musafaha," 477–79.

10. Palaspush, "Risala-yi musafaha," 482.

11. Ibn al-Karbalaʾi, *Rawzat al-jinan va jannat al-janan*, 2:170–72. Aside from Jaʿfar Badakhshi's *Khulasat al-manaqib,* all Kubravi sources I have mentioned belong to the Zahabi branch of the Kubraviya that goes back to the prominent master Sayyid ʿAbdallah Barzishabadi (d. 1468).

12. Cf. Arjomand, "From the Editor."

13. Some studies on other Persianate contexts that are in part comparable to my perspective include: Eaton, *Sufis of Bijapur*; Lawrence, *Notes from a Distant Flute*; Le Gall, *Culture of Sufism*; Suvorova, *Muslim Saints of South Asia*; Wolper, *Cities and Saints.*

14. For a perceptive discussion of the modern creation of "Sufism" as a discrete aspect of Islamic societies see Ernst, *Shambhala Guide to Sufism*, 1–25.

15. The prescriptive nature of *tasawwuf* within Sufi usage is evident from the fact that all definitions of it in major early Arabic sources revolve around the following three issues: *tasawwuf* represents cultivating an ascetic lifestyle combined with yearning for God; it connotes conducting oneself with proper manners (*adab*)—including elements such as humility, patience, generosity, etc.—in the course of all one's social interactions with respect to those who are above or below one in spiritual attainment; and it indicates acquiring intuitive knowledge, which cannot be learned from books, and progress along stations that draw one closer to God (cf. ʿAjam, ed., *Mawsuʿat mustalahat*, 177–84).

These are all recommendations for behavior rather than neutral descriptions of a mode of life.

16. My use of the term *Sufism* is relatable to what Jonathan Z. Smith has advocated about *religion* in general. He argues that religion "is not a native term; it is a term created by scholars for their intellectual purposes and therefore is theirs to define. It is a second-order, generic concept that plays the same role in establishing a disciplinary horizon that a concept such as 'language' plays in linguistics or 'culture' plays in anthropology. There can be no disciplined study of religion without such a horizon" (*Relating Religion*, 193–94).

17. Cf. http://www.ibnarabisociety.org/. For Rumi's place in contemporary Western culture see Lewis, *Rumi Past and Present*.

18. For a recent example, see Ishaan Tharoor, "Can Sufism Defuse Terrorism?" *Time*, July 22, 2009. For some detailed studies of these issues, see Dressler, Geaves, and Klinkhammer, *Sufis in Western Society*.

19. Cf. Masuzawa, *Invention of World Religions*, 197–206; De Jong and Radtke, *Islamic Mysticism Contested*.

20. Trimingham's *Sufi Orders in Islam* continues to be the standard source to refer to these Islamic institutions despite its considerable tendency toward essentialism and excessive schematization. In this book, I avoid the term *order* because of the Christian baggage it brings and hope that some of what I am suggesting about the way these networks functioned will supplant Trimingham's representations.

21. For overviews of this political environment with attention to religious and cultural issues see Bernardini, *Mémoire et propagande à l'epoque timouride*; Manz, *Power, Politics, and Religion in Timurid Iran*; Subtelny, *Timurids in Transition*; Jackson and Lockhart, *Cambridge History of Iran*.

22. For a number of different Sufi definitions of the *awliya*ʾ and *walaya* (Persian: *valayat*) in classical Arabic sources, see ʿAjam, *Mawsuʿat mustalahat*, 1051–59.

23. See, particularly: Radtke, *Concept of Sainthood in Early Sufism*; Chodkiewicz, *Seal of the Saints*; Cornell, *The Realm of the Saint*, and McGregor, *Sanctity and Mysticism in Medieval Egypt*.

24. For recent surveys of the study of embodiment see Lock and Furquhar, eds., *Beyond the Body Proper*, and Latimer and Schillmeier, *Un/knowing Bodies*.

25. For a recent illuminating exploration of how these issues have figured in philosophical and literary discourses, see Heller-Roazen, *Inner Touch*.

26. For a more extended treatment of my views on how the body matters in Islamic studies, see Bashir, "Body."

27. For an exploration of this theme see Stern, "Dystopian Anxieties Versus Utopian Ideals."

28. Turner, "The Body in Western Society," 17.

29. Langer, Merleau-Ponty's "Phenomenology of Perception," 32. My understanding of Merleau-Ponty's view of the body is guided by Langer's commentary and Kelly, "Merleau-Ponty on the Body." For useful critiques of Merleau-Ponty see Leder, "Flesh and Blood"; Shusterman, "The Silent, Limping Body of Philosophy"; and Butler, "Sexual Ideology and Phenomenological Description."

30. Merleau-Ponty, Phenomenology of Perception, 88–102. See also Heller-Roazen, Inner Touch, 253–70.

31. Langer, Merleau-Ponty's "Phenomenology of Perception," 34.

32. In his own somewhat more abstruse formulation, Bourdieu equates habitus to "systems of durable, transposable *dispositions*, structured structures predisposed to function as structuring structures . . . objectively adapted to their goals without presupposing a conscious aiming at ends or an express mastery of the operations necessary to attain them and, being all this, collectively orchestrated without being the product of the orchestrating action of a conductor" (Bourdieu, *Outline of a Theory of Practice*, 72).

33. Ibid., 87.

34. Spiegel, "History, Historicism," 77–78.

35. Ibid., 84–85.

36. Cf. de Certeau, *Writing of History*.

37. For a perspective that does presume that all stories about Islamic saintly figures across time periods and geographical contexts can be treated together, see Renard, *Friends of God*, and Renard, ed., *Tales of God's Friends*. I find this approach analytically and historically untenable and see it as being too closely tied to the promotion of particular Islamic perspectives to allow for an adequately critical assessment of materials.

38. Persianate Sufi hagiography was written in two forms: collections of short notices containing pithy lessons, such as Farid ad-Din ʿAttar's classic *Tazkirat al-awliyaʾ* and ʿAbd ar-Rahman Jami's *Nafahat al-uns*; and works devoted to individuals or lineages that provide extensive biographical details. This book is based primarily on the significant number of texts of the second variety produced during the period 1300–1500. For earlier Persian works of this variety see Ibn al-Munavvar, *Secrets of God's Mystical Oneness*; Moayyad and Lewis, *The Colossal Elephant and His Spiritual Feats*; Mahmud b. Usman, *Vita des Scheich Abu Ishaq al-Kazaruni;* Arberry, "The Biography of Shaikh Abu Ishaq al-Kazaruni."

39. I should acknowledge that many sources I am utilizing remain to be treated carefully as parts of particular textual lineages and that some of my contextual comments may need revision as specialized scholarly works are published in the coming years. I hope that my thematic treatments in this book will prove useful for such efforts by highlighting the works' potential as sources for Islamic history.

40. For recent treatments of these questions see Grabar, *Mostly Miniatures*; and Roxburgh, *The Persian Album*. The paintings I cite belong to Timurid, Turkoman, and Safavid styles. In my analyses, I focus on the paintings' representational content alone with citations to studies that situate them with respect to historical and formalistic concerns.

41. In this context see Renard, *Friends of God*; Amri, *Les saints en islam*; and Kugle, *Sufis and Saints' Bodies*. These studies contain much valuable information and analysis, with the more or less explicit aim of promoting the cause of Sufis in comparison with other Islamic groups.

1. BODIES INSIDE OUT

1. The division of the cosmos into interior and exterior aspects is neither unique to Islam nor limited to Sufism within Islam (cf. Hannegraf, *Dictionary of Gnosis and Western Esotericism*). Besides Sufism, Shiʿism in its Twelver, Ismaʿili, and Ghulat forms represents the other prominent Islamic tradition rooted in the apparent/hidden difference. Sufism and Shiʿism have a lot in common and a kind of rapprochement between them occurred in precisely the period that is the main focus of this book. Shiʿism is distinguished from Sufism by a genealogical claim that vests knowledge of the interior world as well as religious and political authority in certain lines of descent from Muhammad. For the overlap between Sufism and Shiʿism in Persianate societies, see Babayan, *Mystics, Monarchs, and Messiahs*, and Bashir, *Messianic Hopes and Mystical Visions*.

2. Anvar, *Risala-yi suʾal va javab*, in *Kulliyat-i Qasim-i Anvar*, 390.

3. Cf. Abul Fadl Mohsin Ebrahim, "Biology as the Creation and Stages of Life," s.v. *EQ*.

4. Musallam, "The Human Embryo in Arabic Scientific and Religious Thought," 37. The acceptance of this idea meant rejecting Aristotle's theory that only male semen causes conception and that the female contribution to the embryo is limited to "passive" menstrual blood.

5. Ibid., 41–42.

6. For the significance of this work in Islamic medical history see Gul A. Russell, "Ebn Elyas, Mansur b. Mohammad," s.v. *EIr*, and Newman, "Tasrih-i Mansuri."

7. For Lahiji, see Bashir, *Messianic Hopes and Mystical Visions*, 173–75. The *Gulshan-i raz* itself has been translated into English (Shabistari, *The Garden of Mystery*).

8. Lahiji, *Mafatih al-iʿjaz*, 207-9. This description is very close to what Basim Musallam describes from the work of the Hanbalite scholar Ibn Qayyim al-Jawziyya (d. 1350) (Musallam, "The Human Embryo in Arabic Scientific and Religious Thought," 40–41).

9.   Lahiji, *Mafatih al-iʿjaz*, 210.

10.   For a general description of the history and ideology of the Hurufi sect, see Bashir, *Fazlallah Astarabadi and the Hurufis*.

11.   Anonymous, *Risala*, 102b-104a. This work is a summary of Fazlallah Astarabadi's ideas, found in different forms in works such as *Javidannama*, *ʿArshnama*, etc.

12.   Hurufi comparison between reading the body and the Quran hinges also on wordplay characteristic of the movement. The word *jild* means both skin and the cover or binding of a book, following from the fact that such bindings were usually made of leather.

13.   It is interesting to note that, in contrast with human reproduction, which requires two parents, two major Sufi hagiographical works relate the idea that Iblis, the devil, generates offspring through intercourse with itself. Iblis is depicted as having a penis on one thigh and a vagina on the other, which copulate to bring forth more members of the species that go out and corrupt the world (Badakhshi, *Khulasat al-manaqib*, 156; Safi, *Rashahat*, 1:290).

14.   Parsa, *Fasl al-khitab*, 358–59. Parsa's wide-ranging erudition in the Islamic sciences is evident from the surviving information about his library: Muminov and Ziyadov, "L'horizon intellectuel d'un érudit"; Dodkhudoeva, "La bibliothèque de Khwâja Mohammad Pârsâ."

15.   For an extended discussion of these issues see Lahiji, *Mafatih al-iʿjaz*, 404–12.

16.   Mahmud b. ʿUsman, *Miftah al-hidayat va misbah al-ʿinayat*, 93. A similar description of the spirit's imprisonment in the body is given in an influential Sufi guidebook by Najm ad-Din Razi Daya (d. 1256–67) that was a standard textbook for Sufi training during the later medieval period (Daya, *Mirsad*, 111–25, and, *The Path of God's Bondsmen*, 132–48).

17.   Mahmud b. ʿUsman, *Miftah al-hidayat*, 152.

18.   Hamadani, "Risala-yi darvishiyya," 490.

19.   Ibid.

20.   Safi, *Rashahat*, 2:484.

21.   Cf. Samarqandi, *Silsilat al-ʿarifin*, 215–16. For background on the concept of the imaginal world and its later elaborations in Islamic thought, see Bashir, *Messianic Hopes and Mystical Visions*, 117–19; Rahman, "Dream, Imagination, and ʿAlam al-mithal"; and Corbin, *Alone with the Alone: Creative Imagination in the Sufism of Ibn ʿArabi*.

22.   Mahmud b. ʿUsman, *Miftah al-hidayat*, 162–63.

23.   Cf. Chittick, *The Self-Disclosure of God*, 353.

24.   Badakhshi, *Khulasat al-manaqib*, 174.

25.   Farghanaʾi, *Hasht hadiqa*, 26b–27b. For the provenance of this work, see DeWeese, *An "Uvaysi" Sufi in Timurid Mawarannahr*, 14–20.

26. For the details of Nurbakhsh's ideas on this issue and their repercussions in the historical context, see Bashir, *Messianic Hopes and Mystical Visions*, 97–102.

27. Musha'sha''s theories about the body as a veil derive from views earlier expressed in Shi'i sects known as the Exaggerators (Ghulat). For references to such notions, see Bashir, "The Imam's Return."

28. In addition to Nurbakhsh and the Musha'sha', the ideology of the Ahl-i Haqq sect that took concrete shape in this period in Iran contains full-fledged belief in metempsychosis, according to which each spirit can have up to seventy-two different corporeal manifestations. For a review of literature on this sect see Bashir, "Between Mysticism and Messianism," 60–73.

29. The term *nafs* is also often translated as "soul," a usage that is better suited to discussions on Islamic philosophical discourses. See, for example, Druart, "The Human Soul's Individuation"; Black, "Psychology."

30. For an array of Sufi statements on *nafs,* see 'Ajam, *Mawsu'at mustalahat,* 969–89. For variant understanding of *nafs* in Islamic thought more generally see I. R. Netton, "Nafs," s.v. *EI².*

31. Kashani, *Lata'if al-i'lam fi isharat ahl al-ilham,* 568–69.

32. For a substantiation of this theme in Persianate Sufism during the period before the centuries that concern me, see Ballanfat, "Théorie des organes spirituels chez Yûsuf Hamadânî."

33. Anvar, *Risala-yi su'al va javab,* 388–89.

34. Daya, *Mirsad,* 189–90, and *The Path of God's Bondsmen,* 203.

35. Badakhshi, *Khulasat al-manaqib,* 183.

36. Bukhari, *Maslak al-'arifin,* 103a–b. For the significance of this work, see Paul, "Maslak al-'arifin."

37. Daya, *Mirsad,* 192–93, and *The Path of God's Bondsmen,* 205–6.

38. Ibid., 195–98; ibid., 208–10.

39. Such mappings of the body do appear in manuals dealing with poetic usages of the body. See, for example, the translation of Sharaf ad-Din b. Muhammad Rami's *Anis al-'ushshaq* in Huart, *Anîs el-'ochchâq.*

40. For the ideology behind this substitution see Bashir, *Fazlallah Astarabadi,* 69–73. The correspondence between the *lam-alif* and the human form figures in aspects of Islamic figurative art as well (cf. Grabar, *Mediation of Ornament,* 86–89).

41. Ishaq, *Risala.* Bektashi Sufis in the Ottoman Empire who were influenced by the Hurufis from the sixteenth century onward used these ideas to develop a form of figural art in which human bodies were constructed out of the letters of the names of important religious beings such as God, Muhammad, 'Ali, Hasan, and Husayn. For examples of such figures, see Zarcone, *Secret et sociétés secrètes en Islam;* Atalay, *Bektashilik ve Edebiyati.*

42. Mourad, *La Physiognomonie arabe*, 60–61. For general discussions of Islamic ideas about physiognomy, see the introduction to this work and, more recently, Hoyland, "Physiognomy in Islam."

43. Mourad, *La Physiognomonie arabe*, 6–7.

44. Parsa, *Risala-yi qudsiyya*, 20.

45. Nurbakhsh, *Kitab-i insan-nama*, 8a, 11b–12a. For six other manuscripts of this work see Bashir, "Between Mysticism and Messianism," 261.

46. Nurbakhsh, *Kitab-i insan-nama*, 9a–11a.

47. Ibid., 21b.

48. Ibid., 23b–25a.

49. For greater context for understanding this painting see Milstein, "Sufi Elements in Late Fifteenth-Century Herat Painting," 366.

2. BEFRIENDING GOD CORPOREALLY

1. Corporeal management as mandated by law has been the subject of a number of recent studies. Particularly useful examples include Reinhart, "Impurity/No Danger"; Katz, *Body of Text;* and Maghen, *Virtues of the Flesh.*

2. Among Persianate Sufi groups, Naqshbandis are well known for emphasizing their commitment to the sharicʿa in their internal rhetoric. My reading of the material does not mark them as being different from most others in this respect and my choice here has to do with the strength of the material to illustrate the point alone.

3. Bukhari, *Anis at-talibin*, 325.

4. For the relationship between Naqshband, Parsa, and other masters who formed part of this prominent Sufi circle see Paul, *Doctrine and Organization.*

5. Parsa, *Fasl al-khitab*, 305.

6. Ibid., 309–10. A similar explanation for the relationship between the intellect and the shariʿa is given also in Jaʿfar Badakhshi's hagiography of ʿAli Hamadani. Here the shaykh is supposed to have said that the intellect is like food and shariʿa is like medicine; both are necessary for people to stay alive and get to their religious destinations (Badakhshi, *Khulasat al-manaqib*, 109). The editor's note states this formulation can be traced to works by Muhammad Ghazzali and Ibn al-ʿArabi.

7. Bukhari, *Maslak al-ʿarifin*, 73b.

8. Ibid., 13b–14a.

9. Ibid., 16b.

10. Charkhi, *Kitab-i maqamat va slisila-yi Khwaja Naqshband*, 146a.

11. For reviews of legal literature on ablutions see Katz, "The Study of Islamic Ritual"; and Maghen, "Much Ado About Wudu'."

12. Charkhi, *Kitab-i maqamat va slisila-yi Khwaja Naqshband*, 150b–152a. Such a recommendation is obviously quite problematic in the case of women, since menstruation and bleeding following parturition are involuntary processes. Charkhi clearly presumes the standard reader to be male, for whom the full bath is necessary only after ejaculation.

13. Ibid., 154a–155a.

14. Jami, *Nafahat al-uns*, 457.

15. Ardabili, *Safvat as-safa*, 975–76.

16. Safi, *Rashahat*, 1:355–56.

17. The great Sufi theoretician Ibn al-ʿArabi is an important exception to this statement. For his extended explanations of the various Islamic rituals, see his own *at-Tanazzulat al-Mawsiliyya*, and Chodkiewicz, *An Ocean Without Shore*, 109–115.

18. Ishaq, *Risala*, 76a.

19. Bukhari, *Maslak al-ʿarifin*, 30b.

20. Shihab ad-Din, *Maqamat-i Amir Kulal*, 10b–11a.

21. For issues pertaining to the use of asceticism as a category in the study of religions see Clark, "The Ascetic Impulse in Religious Life" and Flood, *Ascetic Self*.

22. For a full consideration of the manuscript that contains this painting, see Soucek, "The New York Public Library *Makhzan al-asrar*."

23. For further contextualization of this image, see Soudavar, *Arts of the Persian Courts*, 97. For the possible iconographic significance of the doorway in this painting, see the discussion of figure 1.2 in chapter 1.

24. The phenomenological basis for the relationship between pain and religious endeavors is discussed in Glucklich, *Sacred Pain*. For other treatments of this theme in Sufi literature see Feuillebois-Pierunek, "La maîtrise du corps"; and Ferhat, "Le saint et son corps."

25. Badakhshi, *Khulasat al-manaqib*, 49.

26. See, for example, *Bukhari, Anis at-talibin*, 106.

27. Safi, *Rashahat*, 2:400, 407; Samarqandi, *Silsilat al-ʿarifin*, 112.

28. Mahmud b. ʿUsman, *Miftah al-hidayat*, 8–11. Balyani's inclination toward severe austerity is also reflected in a letter to a disciple attributed to him that recommends absolute abjection in front of the master and complete denial of all pleasures and pastimes other than the Sufi path (cf. Balyani, "Maktub-i Amin ad-Din Kazaruni beh Darvish ʿAli Hajji Rashid," in Muhaddis, *Twenty Philosophical-Mystical Texts in Persian and Arabic*, 121–24).

29. Vaʿiz, *Maqsad al-iqbal-i sultaniyya*, 48.

30. Kirmani, *Tazkira dar manaqib-i Hazrat Shah Ni'matullah Vali*, 41; Ni'matullahi, *Risala*, 165; Va'izi, *Risala da siyar-i Hazrat Shah Ni'matullah* Vali, 284.

31. Ni'matullahi, *Risala*, 159. A similar ability to maintain the state of ritual purity is reported for Amir Kulal's son 'Umar as well (Shihab ad-Din, *Maqamat-i Amir Kulal*, 54b).

32. Murshidi, *Ma'dan ad-durar*, 29.

33. Ibid., 30–31.

34. This master is also reputed to have practiced severe asceticism during his stay in Mecca while performing the hajj (cf. ibid., 45–46).

35. Karamustafa, *God's Unruly Friends*.

36. This painting is dated to the middle of the sixteenth century. However, it is based on earlier prototypes, including one attributed to Bihzad, circa 1480–85 (cf. Bahari, *Bihzad*, 56).

37. For a recent assessment of the sources available for understanding antinomian Sufi groups in the Persianate sphere that includes numerous samples, see Kadkani, *Qalandariyya dar tarikh*.

38. Farsi, *Manaqib-i Jamal ad-Din Savi*, 31, 43, 48–50.

39. Ibid., 79–85.

40. For more detailed evaluations of antinomian Sufism along this vein, see Karamustafa, *God's Unruly Friends*; Watenpaugh, "Deviant Dervishes"; and Ewing, *Arguing Sainthood*.

41. Badakhshi, *Khulasat al-manaqib*, 195–96.

42. For a general review of zikr as a Sufi practice see: Ernst, *Shambhala Guide to Sufism*, 81–119; Netton, *Sufi Ritual*.

43. *Bukhari, Anis at-talibin*, 145; Charkhi, *Kitab-i maqamat va slisila-yi Khwaja Naqshband*, 156b. The historical picture of Khwajagani-Naqshbandi positions on zikr is quite complex and the product of gradual evolution involving much internal debate and contestation. The silent zikr eventually became the most prevalent practice, based on the example of Naqshband himself. However, for earlier advocacy of silent zikr among the Khwajagan, see Bukhari, *Maslak al-'arifin*, 47a. Naqshband's perspective on zikr and other matters of Sufi practice is traceable to the early Sufi movement called the Malamatiyya or the "Path of Blame," whose members shunned public affirmation of their religious vocation and sometimes sought active condemnation from society to prove that they had given up care for the material world. For Naqshband's possible indebtedness to this perspective see Algar, "Éléments de provenance Malamati." For the practice of vocal zikr among branches of the Khwajagan not deriving from Naqshband see DeWeese, "The Legitimation of Baha' ad-Din Naqshband."

44. Safi, *Rashahat*, 1:43–44.

45. Ibid., 1:129. For the translation of a later, and somewhat different, description of the Naqshbandi zikr that is clearer about its referents to human physiology, see Netton, *Sufi Ritual*, 80.

46. Kurani, *Rawzat as-salikin*, 22a–b.

47. Ibid., 103b–104a.

48. Bukhari, *Anis at-talibin*, 146. As reported in a later work, Naqshband's concern with numbers in this instance pertained both to keeping track of the times one did the zikr and the number of times the formula was repeated in a single breath (Safi, *Rashahat*, 1:48).

49. Safi, *Rashahat*, 1:87.

50. Ibid., 1:164; Samarqandi, *Silsilat al-ʿarifin*, 202.

51. Safi, *Rashahat*, 1:328–29.

52. Badakhshi, *Khulasat al-manaqib*, 42–43. A later hagiography devoted to Hamadani gives the story differently: the author states that Hamadani first had the dream about Muhammad and then saw his teacher performing the zikr when he went to him seeking an interpretation. The eventual result is the same in both versions in that Hamadani ends up as a disciple of Mazdaqani (Badakhshi, *Manqabat a-javahir*, 349a–350a). It is worth noting that evidence from Hamadani's own works is divided on whether he preferred the silent or the vocal zikr. One work advocates the silent zikr ("Risala-yi zikriyya," 540), while the *Risala dar bayan-i adab-i mubtadi va taliban-i hazrat-i samadi* gives the practice as in Badakhshi's description (MS. Add. 1684, British Library, London, 202a). These varying opinions were a point of discussion among later generations of Hamadani's lineage (cf. Badakhshi, *Manqabat a-javahir*, 397a, 423b).

53. Badakhshi, *Khulasat al-manaqib*, 101. For citations for other versions of the Kubravi zikr, see Bashir, *Messianic Hopes and Mystical Visions*, 140.

54. Badakhshi, *Khulasat al-manaqib*, 197.

55. Ibid., 169.

56. H. T. Norris, "The *Mirʾat al-talibin*," plate 2 (facsimile). My translation of the text differs from that given by Norris (62–63).

57. Badakhshi, *Khulasat al-manaqib*, 46–48.

58. Hamadani, "Risala-yi zikriyya," 542. The notion of competition between the senses is a theme represented in imaginary dialogues between them as well. See, for example, Tabrizi, "Munazara-yi samʿ va basr." Here, hearing and sight, and the bodily organs that enable them, describe themselves as whole bodies with their own organs that get deployed to do their tasks.

59. For general surveys of samaʾ as a Sufi practice see Lewisohn, "The Sacred Music of Islam"; Fritz Meier, "The Dervish Dance: An Attempt at an Overview," in *Essays in Islamic Piety and Mysticism*, 23–48; Gribetz, "The Samaʿ Contro-

versy"; During, *Musique et mystique*; and Molé, "La danse extatique en Islam."
For a crititque of the use of music and dance in religious practice, see Michot,
Musique et danse selon Ibn Taymiyya.

60. Ardabili, *Safvat as-safa'*, 643–45. Similar vigorous dance is described as the
practice of Shaykh Ahmad Bashiri (Farghana'i, *Hasht Hadiqa*, 67b–68a).

61. Ardabili, *Safvat as-safa'*, 650.

62. Abarquhi, *Sama' dar khanqah*, 299–300, in Hiravi, ed., *Andar ghazal-i khvish
nihan khvaham gashtan*. Hiravi's volume contains a combination of twenty-
six small treatises or excerpts from larger works in Persian on the topic of
sama'.

63. Samarqandi, *Silsilat al-'arifin*, 53.

3. SAINTLY SOCIALITES

1. Bukhari, *Anis at-talibin*, 72. These verses are reported in a later text without
attribution (Farghana'i, *Hasht hadiqa*, 85a).

2. For a summary of this theme in Sufi literature, see Feuillebois-Pierunek, "Maîtres, disciples et compagnons."

3. Kashani, *Misbah al-hidaya va miftah ul-kifaya*, 153–59. This work is a Persian
adaptation of Shihab ad-Din Suhrawardi's famous Arabic guidebook for Sufis
entitled *'Awarif al-ma'arif*. For an extensive description of the duties incumbent upon masters, see also Samarqandi, *Silsilat al-'arifin*, 68–72, 75–82.

4. Kirmani, *Tazkira dar manaqib-i Hazrat Shah Ni'matullah Vali*, 28.

5. Safi, *Rashahat*, 2:391–92. For a treatment of the common hagiographic theme
of the refusal to play see Hagen, "'He never took the Path of Pastime and
Play.'"

6. Safi, *Rashahat*, 2:409–10.

7. Khabushani, "Adab-i darvishi," 112–13. Following this statement, the author
goes on to describe in detail the etiquette for performing solitary retreats. For
an extended description of such rules, see also Samarqandi, *Silsilat al-'arifin*,
72–75, 82–90.

8. Safi, *Rashahat*, 2:449–50.

9. For another depiction of an ordered group surrounding a master see figure 5.4.
For further description and color reproductions of the painting shown in fig-
ure 3.3, see Bahari, *Bihzad*, 60; Soudavar, *Art of the Persian Courts*, 100; Barry,
Figurative Art in Medieval Islam, 188–89.

10. Bukhari, *Anis at-talibin*, 240.

11. Murshidi, *Ma'dan ad-durar*, 89.

12. Anonymous, *Malfuz-i Hazrat Zayn ad-Din Taybadi*, 27a–b.

13. Cf. Hujwiri, *Revelation of the Mystery*, 212–16.

14. For a discussion of Ibn al-ʿArabi's understanding of the hierarchy that was very influential in the Persianate sphere, see Chodkiewicz, *The Seal of the Saints*.

15. Hagiographic sources usually refer to their subjects as the poles of their times without placing them in a diachronic sequence spanning Islamic history. A rare exception (which, in any case, falls outside the time period that concerns me in this book) is the hagiography of Shaykh Nur ad-Din Basir (d. 1249), whose author calls his subject the fourteenth pole in history and provides the names of the preceding thirteen (cf. Abu l-Hasan b. Khwaja Sayf ad-Din, *Maqamat-i Shaykh Nur ad-Din Basir*).

16. Badakhshi, *Khulasat al-manaqib*, 68.

17. Ibid., 81–84.

18. Kirmani, *Tazkira dar manaqib-i Hazrat Shah Niʿmatullah Vali*, 7.

19. Samarqandi, *Silsilat al-ʿarifin*, 221.

20. Badakhshi, *Manqabat al-javahir*, 441a. Khizr and Elias were sometimes considered interchangeable figures (cf. John Renard, "Khadir/Khidr," and Roberto Tottoli, "Elijah," s.v. *EQ*).

21. For a narrative mapping of various lineages and sublineages in Central Asia during the fifteenth and sixteenth centuries see Schwarz, *"Unser Weg schließt tausend Wege ein."*

22. Bukhari, *Anis at-talibin*, 80.

23. While Naqshbandi sources do acknowledge Amir Kulal as Naqshband's master, it is clear from the *Maqamat-i Amir Kulal* that Kulal's hereditary successors did not see him as the chief successor. The Amir Kulal version of the continuation of the chain represents Naqshband as a rather self-indulgent disciple (Shihab ad-Din, *Maqamat-i Amir Kulal*, 24a–25b, 33b).

24. Safi, *Rashahat*, 2:390.

25. Ibid., 2:387.

26. Nurbakhsh, *Risalat al-huda*, 109.

27. It is noteworthy that Amin ad-Din Balyani's hagiographer was also the translator, from Arabic, of the hagiography of Balyani's lineal forbear Abu Ishaq Kazaruni (d. 1035), who is regarded as the first Sufi master to organize his followers into a Sufi community. As such, it is likely that the hagiographer's detailed description of initiation reflects a heightened concern for formal rituals of the type in this particular community (cf. Mahmud b. ʿUsman, *Vita des Scheich Abu Ishaq al-Kazaruni*).

28. Mahmud b. ʿUsman, *Miftah al-hidayat*, 22–24.

29. Badakhshi, *Khulasat al-manaqib*, 190–91.

30. Ibid., 193–95.

31. In a later hagiography, Hamadani is himself shown to receive these three instruments from Muhammad in a dream while he is visiting Medina. When he

wakes up, he finds himself in possession of the items (Badakhshi, *Manqabat al-javahir*, 416b).

32. Bukhari, *Anis at-talibin*, 88–91; Parsa, *Risala-yi qudsiyya*, 8–9. For a detailed discussion of the many ways in which Naqshband and other Central Asian Sufi masters are legitimized in hagiographical narratives, see DeWeese, "The Legitimation of Baha' ad-Din Naqshband."

33. Farghana'i, *Hasht hadiqa*, 3b–4b.

34. For the details of Muhammad's night journey and its status as a model for later Muslims, see Colby, *Narrating Muhammad's Night Journey*; and Gruber and Colby, *The Prophet's Ascension*.

35. For more detailed discussions of the Uvaysi element in the story of Ahmad Bashiri and other related figures, see DeWeese, *An "Uvaysi" Sufi in Timurid Mawarannahr*; and Bashir, "Muhammad in Sufi Eyes."

36. Cf. Gerhard Böwering, "Baqa' wa fana'," s.v. *EIr*.

37. Bukhari, *Anis at-talibin*, 95. For another extensive example of corporeal transformation through initiatory experiences see, Murshidi, *Ma'dan ad-durar*, 12–18. For an attempt to understand the general functions of vision in hagiographical narratives see Bashir, "Narrating Sight."

38. To see particular details of internal contestation in a text devoted to this issue, see DeWeese, "Khojagani Origins and the Critique of Sufism."

39. Ahrar has been the subject of studies concerned with the considerable sociopolitical and economic influence he wielded for much of his life. For details, see works by Jürgen Paul and Jo-Ann Gross listed in the bibliography as well as 'Arif Nawshahi's introduction to his editions in *Ahval va sukhanan-i Khwaja 'Ubaydullah Ahrar*.

40. Safi, *Rashahat*, 1:203.

41. Stories showing competition are present in other sources on the life of Ahrar as well, although the authors of these works are not as systematic as Safi in creating the image of the master's early life.

42. Safi, *Rashahat*, 2:418.

43. Ibid., 2:421; Samarqandi, *Silsilat al-'arifin*, 237.

44. Safi, *Rashahat*, 2:426–27; Samarqandi, *Silsilat al-'arifin*, 253–54.

45. Safi, *Rashahat*, 2:425.

46. For summary assessments of Ibn al-'Arabi's reception in later centuries, see William Chittick, "Ebn al-'Arabi," s.v. *EIr*; Morris, "Ibn al-'Arabi and His Interpretors"; and Knysh, *Ibn 'Arabi in the Later Islamic Tradition*. Knysh's work is limited to the discussion of Ibn al-'Arabi solely in Arabic-speaking Islamic societies.

47. Bakharzi, *Maqamat-i Jami*, 95. For reports on 'Abd ar-Rahman Jami's defense of Ibn al-'Arabi in this work, see also Bakharzi, *Maqamat-i Jami*, 90–93, 254.

48. Fairly extensive secondary scholarship is now available on Ibn al-ʿArabi's place in the thought of these and other Persianate authors. The eminent historian of Sufism Najib Mayil-i Hiravi has indicated his intention of publishing an assessment of Ibn al-ʿArabi's place in Persianate Sufism under the title *Ibn-i ʿArabi dar Iran va sharq-i jahan-i Islam*. As far as I am aware, the book has not yet appeared (cf. Hiravi, *In bargha-yi pir*, xxxi, note 1).

49. Anonymous, *Malfuz-i Hazrat Zayn ad-Din Taybadi*, 38a.

50. Isfizari, *Rawzat al-jannat fi awsaf madinat Herat*, 207.

51. Jami, *Nafahat al-uns*, 494–95.

52. Safi, *Rashahat*, 1:179–80; Nishapuri, *Malfuzat-i Ahrar*, 175–76; Samarqandi, *Silsilat al-ʿarifin*, 107–8.

53. This reports relates directly to the question of "oneness of being," reflecting the difference of opinion regarding the extent to which God and the created world, including humanity, share in the same being. Khwafi's work *Manhaj ar-rashad* is a detailed refutation of Ibn al-ʿArabi and those whom he considered his antecedents and followers (for an edition of this work with extensive notes see Hiravi, *In bargha-yi pir*, 485–579). For explorations of oneness of being with reference to the development of Persianate Sufism see: Lahiji, *Mafatih al iʿjāz*, 460–63; Chittick, "Wahdat al-wujud in Islamic Thought," and "Sadr al-Din Qunawi on Oneness of Being."

54. Safi, *Rashahat*, 2:427–28.

55. For a reproduction in color, see Bahari, *Bihzad*, 94. Bihzad's significance as a cultural figure is discussed in Lentz, "Changing Worlds: Bihzad and the New Painting"; and Sadri, *Kamal ad-Din Bihzad: Majmuʿa-yi maqalat-i hamayish-i bayn al-milali*.

56. Bahari, *Bihzad*, 36–38. Zayn ad-Din Vasifi's *Badayiʿ al-vaqayiʿ*, an extensive work on the cultural life of Herat under Navaʾi's patronage, contains an episode where Bihzad is said to have brought the vizier a portrait of him, set in a garden, with him leaning on a staff. For reflections of cultural life among the Timurid elite, see Lentz and Lowry, *Timur and the Princely Vision*; Golombek and Subtelny, *Timurid Art and Culture*; Thackston, *A Century of Princes*.

4. BONDS OF LOVE

1. For summaries of Sufi understandings of love for God, see Ernst, "The Stages of Love in Early Persian Sufism"; Abrahamov, *Divine Love in Islamic Mysticism*; Daylami, *A Treatise on Mystical Love*. For the question of love in Islamic literature in general, see Bell, *Love Theory in Later Hanbalite Islam;* and Chabel, *Encyclopédie de l'amour en Islam*.

2.   What I am suggesting here regarding Sufis naturally applies to poets as historical actors as well. My comment is, therefore, limited to poetry as a genre and is not meant to suggest that poets simply reproduced their paradigms without active engagement with their historical contexts.

3.   There is extensive literature now available describing the characteristics and ethos of medieval Persian poetry. The most useful examples, which provide in-depth analysis in addition to surveying major figures, are Meisami, *Persian Court Poetry*; Losesnsky, *Welcoming Fighani*; de Bruijn, *Persian Sufi Poetry*; Feuillebois-Pierunek, *A la croisée des voies célestes*; Tourage, *Rumi and the Hermeneutics of Eroticism.*

4.   An immense amount of Persian poetry was produced in the period being considered in this book. An assessment of the literary qualities of the work of the many major and minor poets is beyond the scope of my topic, and the few examples highlighted represent figures well known both as poets and Sufis. For a summary description of the poetic scene that includes references to other studies see Subtelny, "A Taste for the Intricate."

5.   Jaghata'i, *Divan-i Hilali Jaghata'i ba Shah-o-darvish va Sifat al-ʿashiqin-i u*, 284. For Hilali's significance as a poet and a cultural figure in Herat during the late Timurid and early Safavid eras, see Michele Bernardini, "Helali, Astarabadi Jagata'i, Mawlana Badr al-Din," s.v. *EIr.*

6.   For more details of the internal mechanics of the relationship between desire and love see chapter 5.

7.   Qasim-i Anvar, *Kulliyat-i Qasim-i Anvar*, 104–5.

8.   The fullest and most elaborate discussions of properties associated with love that I have tried to summarize here are found in allegorical narratives. For examples in Persian from the period that concerns me, see the discussion of *Husn-o-ʿishq* in chapter 5 as well as Abivardi, "Kitab-i anis al-ʿashiqin."

9.   Samarqandi, *Tazkirat ash-shuʿara'*, 350.

10. For the details of the manuscript that contains this painting see Robinson and Gray, *Persian Art of the Book*, 11–12.

11. For the transformation of the Safavids from a Sufi lineage to a dynasty see Aubin, "L'avènement des Safavides reconsidéré." Religious aspects of the transformation as they pertain to corporeality are discussed in Bashir, "Shah Ismaʿil and the Qizilbash."

12. For a history of this text, including the production of the modern edition I am utilizing, see Mazzaoui, "A 'New' Edition of *Safvat al-safa.*"

13. Ardabili, *Safvat as-safa'*, 80.

14. Ibid., 91–92.

15. Ibid., 94–95.

16. Ibid., 106.

17. Ibid., 109. Wearing felt indicates Safi ad-Din's adoption of an ascetic lifestyle.

18. Ibid., 113. It is tempting to interpret the incidence of wet dreams during the journey in modern psychoanalytic terms as an indication of Safi ad-Din's latent sexual desire for the master. In the context of the original narrative, however, it is clearly an aspect of the emptying of the disciple's body, on par with the negation of his senses prior to his arrival at the master's door.

19. Ibid., 115.

20. Safi, *Rashahat*, 2:428–30, 2:577; Nishapuri, *Malfuzat-i Ahrar*, 187–88.

21. Safi and Samarqandi also state that a different Naqshbandi shaykh by the name of Husam ad-Din Parsa Balkhi attempted to convince Ahrar to take an oath with him while he was on the way to see Charkhi. Ahrar declined this invitation since he had already made up his mind to meet Charkhi (Safi, *Rashahat*, 1:166; Samarqandi, *Silsilat al-ʿarifin*, 244).

22. The three hagiographies differ on the point at which Ahrar eventually becomes Yaʿqub's disciple. Safi and Samarqandi give the more detailed version reproduced above (Safi, *Rashahat*, 2:430, Samarqandi, *Silsilat al-ʿarifin*, 126–27), while Nishapuri states only that Ahrar was repulsed when Yaʿqub extended his hand and then took it when the shaykh said that Naqshband had said that his hand was like that of the earlier master (Nishapuri, *Malfuzat-i Ahrar*, 188). Nishapuri thus highlights the significance of the chain rather than the individual master.

23. Karaki, *Malfuzat-i Ahrar*, 512–13. The idea that the master has to be able to make himself into a beloved is repeated in the same work in a different context (537).

24. Ibid., 513. For a similar sentiment in another hagiography devoted to Ahrar, see Safi, *Rashahat*, 2:466.

25. Bukhari, *Anis at-talibin*, 379.

26. Kirmani, *Tazkira dar manaqib-i Hazrat Shah Niʿmatullah Vali*, 76.

27. The only manuscript of the work available to me gives no date of composition or copying. However, the last event the author mentions with a specific time component occurred eighteen lunar years after the death of his own shaykh in 1487. This means that the work was composed in 1504–1505 at the earliest (Kurani, *Rawzat as-salikin*, 169a).

28. The subject of this hagiography is a relatively little known master from the fifteenth century. His chain of affiliation goes through Saʿd ad-Din Kashghari, Nizam ad-Din Khamush, and ʿAlaʾ ad-Din ʿAttar (d. 1400) to Naqshband himself. In Naqshbandi history this line represents a minor tradition compared to the much more influential chain represented by Khwaja Ahrar and Yaʿqub Charkhi. For other sources on this master's life see Tosun, *Bahâeddin Nakşbend*, 141–42, 236.

29. Kurani, *Rawzat as-salikin*, 23a–b.

30. Ibid., 78a–79a. The "copy" mentioned in the last part refers to the physical body made from the mold of the species.

31. Masters' power to make their disciples long for them uncontrollably is reflected in other stories related in this hagiography as well (cf. Kurani, *Rawzat
as-salikin*, 24b–25a, 27b–28a).

32. Bukhari, *Anis at-talibin*, 244.

33. Badakhshi, *Khulasat al-manaqib*, 119.

34. Kurani, *Rawzat as-salikin*, 127b–128b.

35. Bukhari, *Anis at-talibin*, 177–78.

36. Badakhshi, *Khulasat al-manaqib*, 74.

37. Ibid., 58.

38. Lowry and Nemazee, *A Jeweler's Eye*, 144–55. This image is based on a motif
quite popular in painting from the fifteenth century. The basic story here is
substantially the same as the one being depicted in figures 2.1 and 6.1.

39. For details of the manuscript that contains this image see Martin, *Les miniatures de Behzad*, plate 9.

40. One work advocates this strategic deployment of love directly as a part of the
etiquette of a master (Samarqandi, *Silsilat al-'arifin*, 81).

41. This point is discussed more extensively in chapters 6 and 7.

42. Ardabili, *Safvat as-safaʾ*, 132.

43. Ibid., 135. Another text relates a similar story where a master is unable to get
warm no matter how much anyone tries because the extreme cold being experienced by a person traveling through a rough terrain is transferred to his body
(Safi, *Rashahat*, 1:193).

44. Ardabili, *Safvat as-safaʾ*, 100–101. The same idea of one person acting as mirror for another is described also in Farghanaʾi, *Hasht hadiqa*, 50a; Samarqandi,
Silsilat al-'arifin, 156.

45. Badakhshi, *Khulasat al-manaqib*, 222–23.

46. Kirmani, *Tazkira dar manaqib-i Hazrat Shah Ni'matullah Vali*, 25–26;
Ni'matullahi, *Risala*, 141.

47. Samarqandi, *Silsilat al-'arifin*, 264.

48. Shihab ad-Din, *Maqamat-i Amir Kulal* , 43b.

49. Kirmani, *Tazkira dar manaqib-i Hazrat Shah Ni'matullah Vali*, 22; Badakhshi,
Khulasat al-manaqib, 30–33.

50. Badakhshi, *Khulasat al-manaqib*, 58–59.

51. For the rivalry between Nurbakhsh and Barzishabadi and its representation
in hagiographical sources, see Bashir, *Messianic Hopes and Mystical Visions*,
45–54.

52. Nurbakhsh, *Risalat al-huda*, 130.

53. For general information about this work and its author see Shiro Ando, "Gazor-
gahi, Mir Kamal al-Din Husayn," s.v. *EIr*.

54. For the details of this particular manuscript, see Richard, *Splendeurs persanes*,
197. For this work's remarkable run as a subject for illustrated manuscripts in

the sixteenth century, see Uluç, *Turkman Governors, Shiraz Artisans, and Ottoman Collectors*, 183–223.

55. Gazurgahi, *Majalis al-ʿushshaq*, 148–50.

5. ENGENDERED DESIRES

1. For references to explications of these terms in classical Arabic Sufi sources,
see ʿAjam, *Mawsuʿat mustalahat*, 867–68, 876–88. For a summary of these
views in the original literature I am reviewing, see Samarqandi, *Silsilat al-
ʿarifin*, 63–65.

2. For a recent set of sophisticated methodological discussions in this arena
within Islamic studies, see Babayan and Najmabadi, *Islamicate Sexualities*.

3. For recent studies that discuss homoerotic desire in Islamic contexts, see
Zeʾevi, *Producing Desire*; Sprachman, "*Le beau garçon san merci*"; Andrews and
Kalpaklı, *Age of Beloveds;* and El-Rouayheb, *Before Homosexuality in the Arab-
Islamic World.*

4. Cf. Ingrid Mattson, "Law: Family Law, 7th–Late 18th Centuries," *EWIC*
(Brill Online, September 17, 2009, http://www.brillonline.nl/subscriber/
entry?entry=ewic COM-0113).

5. Hamadani, "Risala-yi zikriyya," 531–32.

6. Farghanaʾi, *Hasht hadiqa*, 68b.

7. For the texts of both the narrative poem and the prose summary, along with
French translations, see Fattahi, *Coeur et Beauté ou Le livre des amoureux*. For
the author's background and the work's enduring influence in later centuries
see Tahsin Yazıcı, "Fattahi-Nisaburi, Mohammad Yahya Sibak," s.v. *EIr.*

8. For details of this manuscript, see Titley, *Miniatures from Persian Manuscripts*,
41 (no. 104).

9. For a detailed assessment of this theme in a more recent period, see Najmabadi,
Women with Mustaches and Men Without Beards. My assessment of love and desire in Sufi narratives agrees with the comment of one reviewer of this book who
suggests that Najmabadi's overall concern with showing the transition to modernity makes her minimize the thoroughly hierarchical nature of the premodern discourse (cf. Norma Claire Moruzzi, "Review," *IJMES* 39 [2007], 128–30).

10. Kurani, *Rawzat as-salikin*, 155a–b.

11. Badakhshı, *Manqabat al-javahir*, 352a–b.

12. Kurani, *Rawzat as-salikin*, 148b–149a.

13. Safi, *Rashahat*, 1:339–40.

14. Ibid., 1:205. It is, of course, possible to read more into this story than the desire
of touching hands. I leave the matter at the actual textual representation in
order to convey the inhibitions reflected in the discourse.

15. For the incident involving Hurufis, see the various historians cited in detail in Sa'id Nafisi's introduction in *Kulliyat-i Qasim-i Anvar*, 5–48.

16. Safi, *Rashahat*, 2:417.

17. Jami, *Nafahat al-uns*, 591–91.

18. Safi, *Rashahat*, 2:420–21. For another comment in this work relating to the deficiencies of Qasim's followers, see 2:487.

19. Ibid., 2:453. The idea of using young men as muses has a long history in Persianate literatures, although it is inadequately explored as a research area. For a collection that brings together a number of sources but has a tendentious and condemnatory attitude, see Shamisa, *Shahidbazi dar adabiyyat-i Farsi*.

20. Safi, *Rashahat*, 2:555–56.

21. Murshidi, *Ma'dan ad-durar*, 70.

22. For a detailed examination of the relationship implied between women's voices and sexuality in a different Islamic context, see Malti-Douglas, *Woman's Body, Woman's Word*.

23. Mahmud b. 'Usman, *Miftah al-hidayat*, 61. For another case like this, see Samarqandi, *Silsilat al-'arifin*, 242.

24. Bukhari, *Anis at-talibin*, 184–85.

25. Samarqandi, *Silsilat al-'arifin*, 282.

26. Ardabili, *Safvat as-safa'*, 643–44.

27. Nishapuri, *Malfuzat-i Ahrar*, 312. Of course, the fact that this woman is old puts her in a different category for the purposes of male-female interactions than would be the case for a young woman.

28. Bukhari, *Anis at-talibin*, 92.

29. Parsa, *Risala-yi qudsiyya*, 120. The "bird coming out of an egg" reference here echoes Parsa's general explanation of the significance of shari'a discussed in chapter 2 on the basis of his work *Fasl al-khitab* (309–10).

30. Safi, *Rashahat*, 1:91–92; Karaki, *Malfuzat-i Ahrar*, 522. Along with other slight differences in the way the story is given in the two texts, Karaki gives the name of the master in question as Amir Kulal Vashi.

31. Anonymous, *Malfuz-i Hazrat Zayn ad-Din Taybadi*, 28a–29b. Sufi masters' miraculous ability to protect people from afar, as in this case, is discussed in chapter 7.

32. The theme of male religious authority figures acting as mothers is a notable feature of Christian hagiography as well in certain periods. For details, see Bynum, *Jesus as Mother*.

33. Ishaq, *Khwabnama*, 20a–22a.

34. Ishaq, *Mahramnama*, 32, 33, 39.

35. Sources for Kalimatallah's life are discussed in Mihrabi, *Kalimatallah Hiya al-'Ulya*.

36. Farghana'i, *Hasht hadiqa*, 35b–37a.

37. Ibid., 75a.

38. Ibid., 24a, 34a, 65b.

39. Ibid., 30b.

40. Ibid., 67a.

41. Safi, *Rashahat*, 2:372.

42. Kurani, *Rawzat as-salikin*, 93b–94a.

43. Ibid., 94b–95b.

44. Nishapuri, *Malfuzat-i Ahrar*, 166; Samarqandi, *Silsilat al-ʿarifin*, 187–88.

45. Samarqandi, *Silsilat al-ʿarifin*, 65.

46. For a comparative perspective on this theme from Sufism in a different region, see Marín, "Images des femmes dans les sources hagiographiques maghrébines."

47. Ardabili, *Safvat as-safaʾ*, 170–71. It is noteworthy that both Shaykh Safi and Shaykh Ahmad Bashiri are shown married to women named Fatima, hinting at a relationship to the Prophet through marriage.

48. Safi, *Rashahat*, 1:163. The fourth daughter is said to have died before Naqshband himself. This information is provided in a marginal note in a manuscript of the *Rashahat*. For other sources on this issue see Tosun, *Bahaeddin Nakşbend*, 112.

49. Safi, *Rashahat*, 2:603–4.

50. Murshidi, *Maʿdan ad-durar*, 46.

51. Shihab ad-Din, *Maqamat-i Amir Kulal*, 68a–b.

52. Ibid., 69b–70a.

53. As far as I am aware, only one such group of Sufi women finds mention in premodern Islamic sources. The so-called Sisters of Anatolia are said to have been a corporate social group parallel to the male guild called the Brothers. For historical evidence regarding this group, see Bayram, *Bâciyân-i Rum*. For literature pertaining to women's authoritative roles in another Islamic context, see Pemberton, *Women Mystics and Sufi Shrines in India*.

54. Safi, *Rashahat*, 2:374; Samarqandi, *Silsilat al-ʿarifin*, 114–15.

6. MIRACULOUS FOOD

1. Farghanaʾi, *Hasht hadiqa*, 56b.

2. Ibid., 2a–b.

3. I use the term *economy* here with some trepidation given its particular connotation as a concept used to explain patterns in the economic organization of modern states. As such, to call the types of work one sees as being interconnected in Sufi hagiographic texts an economy is necessarily an approximation for the sake of convenience. To do so is heuristically valuable, nev-

ertheless, because it allows us to see how, in this context, various types of work were exchanged on the basis of values imagined through the fact of their interdependency.

4. The literature on miracles in religious understandings is too huge to describe here in summary fashion. For some scholarship outside Islamic studies that parallels what I am attempting, see Kee, *Miracle in the Early Christian World*; Mullin, *Miracles and the Modern Religious Imagination*; Aigle, *Miracle et Karama*.

5. For summary information regarding the discussion of prophetic miracles in Islamic thought, see Denis Gril, "Miracles," s.v. *EQ*. A dense theological exploration of the theme can be found in Baqillani, *Miracle and Magic*. For a recent exploration of various facets of the development of Muhammad's life story as a religious exercise, see Brockopp, ed., *Cambridge Companion to Muhammad*.

6. For more details regarding the types of miracles one can encounter in Sufi texts, see Renard, *Friends of God*; Gramlich, *Die Wunder der Freunde Gottes*; Badran, *Adabiyyat al-karama as-sufiyya;* Ford, "Constructing Sanctity."

7. A partial exception to this statement is to be found in the opinion that when it comes to heavenly journeys called *mi'raj*, only the one attributed to Muhammad is to be seen as having been with the body. Such miraculous journeys attributed to Sufi masters are said to be in the spirit alone. This opinion is reported in one hagiographic text with citation to a work entitled *al-Minhaj fi l-mi'raj* by the early Sufi author Abu l-Qasim Qushayri (cf. Murshidi, *Ma'dan ad-durar*, 84–85).

8. Jami, *Nafahat al-uns*, 22.

9. For explorations of this theme based on Islamic materials, see Benkheira, *Islam et interdits alimentaires*; van Gelder, *God's Banquet*. Bynum's *Holy Feast and Holy Fast* is the classic work to explore this issue in a religious context.

10. Shihab ad-Din, *Maqamat-i Amir Kulal*, 3a-b; Safi, *Rashahat*, 1:75.

11. Farghana'i, *Hasht hadiqa*, 7b.

12. Anonymous, *Malfuz-i Hazrat Zayn ad-Din Taybadi*, 2a.

13. Safi, *Rashahat*, 2:391.

14. Shihab ad-Din, *Maqamat-i Amir Kulal*, 35b–36a.

15. Farghana'i, *Hasht hadiqa*, 65a, 89a.

16. Mahmud b. 'Usman, *Miftah al-hidayat*, 9. Asceticism is discussed in greater detail in chapter 2.

17. Ibid., 62.

18. Ibid., 137.

19. Safi, *Rashahat*, 1:346–47. The author attributes this view to a certain Yemeni master named Shaykh 'Abd al-Kabir and speculates that this meant that he was one among the Abdal, a major station in the ever-existing hierarchy of God's

friends. The Abdal's rejection of meat is attributed here to the fact they were responsible for channeling life to all living beings.

20. Farsi, *Manaqib-i Jamal ad-Din Savi*, 53–54.

21. Shihab ad-Din, *Maqamat-i Amir Kulal*, 22b.

22. Ibid., 28a. The term *halal* in this context means food acquired through just means rather than simply meat killed according to Islamic legal prescriptions. The two meanings of halal (and haram or forbidden food or acts) are often invoked intermingled in Islamic literatures.

23. Ibid., 32a–b.

24. Ibid., 55b.

25. Kirmani, *Tazkira dar manaqib-i Hazrat Shah Ni'matullah Vali*, 124.

26. Va'izi, *Risala dar siyar-i Hazrat Shah Ni'matullah Vali*, 303.

27. Bukhari, *Anis at-talibin*, 185–86.

28. Anonymous, *Malfuz-i Hazrat Zayn ad-Din Taybadi*, 31b–32a.

29. Ibid., 12a.

30. Ibid., 34b.

31. Bukhari, *Anis at-talibin*, 244–45.

32. Mahmud b. 'Usman, *Miftah al-hidayat*, 57. A *jigarband* is the combination of heart, liver, and lungs of the body of an animal.

33. Shihab ad-Din, *Maqamat-i Amir Kulal*, 30a–31a.

34. Ni'matullahi, *Risala*, 165.

35. For a listing of Ahrar's properties, which were sources of agricultural produce that satisfied countless people, see Safi, *Rashahat*, 2:404–5.

36. Safi, *Rashahat*, 2:399–401; Samarqandi, *Silsilat al-'arifin*, 205.

37. Nishapuri, *Malfuzat-i Ahrar*, 211.

38. Murshidi, *Ma'dan ad-durar*, 91.

39. Shihab ad-Din, *Maqamat-i Amir Kulal*, 5.

40. Shihab ad-Din, *Maqamat-i Amir Kulal*, 25a–b. The presence of Amir Kulal and Naqshband in each other's hagiographies makes for interesting comparison. Their lineages are interlaced, but by the time the texts were produced the two were anchoring figures in rival collateral lines within the Khwajagani tree. Consequently, the mention of one in a work dedicated to the other carries a begrudging tone.

41. Ibid., 40b.

42. Ibid., 45a–b. The case of Mary is invoked in theoretical Sufi literature as well in order to prove that individuals other than prophets can perform miracles (cf. Parsa, *Fasl al-khitab*, 384). The woman who speaks in this story was the mother of Kalan Khatun, the daughter of Amir Hamza discussed at the end of chapter 5.

43. Bukhari, *Anis at-talibin*, 117–18. In a similar instance reported in the *Rashahat*, the ever-living prophet Khizr refused to eat a piece of bread on the

grounds that the person who had leavened the dough for it had not been in a state of ritual purity (1:65). The necessity of ritual purity on the part of a cook is indicated from Shaykh Bashiri as well (Farghana'i, *Hasht hadiqa*, 66b–67a).

44. Bukhari, *Anis at-talibin*, 125. For a brief but illustrative work that lays out the proper etiquette while consuming food see ʿAla ad-Dawla Simnani, "Adab-i sufra," in *Musannafat-i Farsi*, 7–12. For a description of the etiquette of eating in the Persianate sphere see also Mahmud b. Muhammad, *Adab al-muzifin va zad al-akilin*.

45. Bukhari, *Anis at-talibin*, 172–74.

46. Ibid., 181.

47. Safi, *Rashahat*, 2:541; Samarqandi, *Silsilat al-ʿarifin*, 280.

48. Ibid., 2:559. For Qushchi, see Fazlur Rahman and David Pingree, "ʿAli Qusji (Qusju)," s.v. *EIr*. Ahrar's antipathy toward Qushchi probably reflects the fact that the latter was a dedicated partisan of the physical sciences versus Ahrar's claim of possessing hidden truths acquired through Sufi methodologies.

49. Safi, *Rashahat*, 2:643–44; Samarqandi, *Silsilat al-ʿarifin*, 280.

50. Safi, *Rashahat*, 2:403–404.

51. Ardabili, *Safvat as-safaʾ*, 143–44.

52. Farghana'i, *Hasht hadiqa*, 63b.

53. Ardabili, *Safvat as-safaʾ*, 344–45.

54. Ibid., 347–78.

55. Ibid., 350–53.

56. Badakhshi, *Manqabat al-javahir*, 385b–390a. The king is not identified in this text, but in later works where this story is cited he is taken to be Timur (cf. DeWeese, "Sayyid ʿAli Hamadani").

57. Badakhshi, *Manqabat al-javahir*, 391a–b.

58. Ibid., 378a–382b.

59. For details of the manuscript where this painting occurs, see Robinson, *Persian Paintings in the John Rylands Library*, 22, 94; the same theme occurs in figures 2.1 and 4.3.

7. CORPSES IN MORTICIANS' HANDS

1. Cf. Samarqandi, *Silsilat al-ʿarifin*, 74.

2. For a perceptive consideration of the process of transition from oral to written narratives, see DeWeese, "Ahmad Yasavi and the Dog-Men."

3. Bukhari, *Maslak al-ʿarifin*, 45a–b.

4. Shihab ad-Din, *Maqamat-i Amir Kulal*, 52a.

5. Ardabili, *Safvat as-safaʾ*, 146.

6. Farghana²i, *Hasht hadiqa*, 43a.

7. Bukhari, *Anis at-talibin*, 254–55.

8. Farghana²i, *Hasht hadiqa*, 24b.

9. Safi, *Rashahat*, 1:183–84, Samarqandi, *Silsilat al-ʿarifin*, 249.

10. Samarqandi, *Silsilat al-ʿarifin*, 89–90.

11. Mahmud b. ʿUsman, *Miftah al-hidayat*, 57.

12. Farghana²i, *Hasht hadiqa*, 86a–b.

13. Murshidi, *Maʿdan ad-durar*, 101. The text goes on to describe what ʿUmar did to alleviate other ailments and hardships such as the burden of loans.

14. Shihab ad-Din, *Maqamat-i Amir Kulal*, 12b–13a.

15. For some examples, see Ardabili, *Safvat as-safa²*, 306, 318; Anonymous, *Malfuz-i Hazrat Zayn ad-Din Taybadi*, 46b–47a, 51a–52a; Bukhari, *Anis at-talibin*, 169, 179–80; Badakhshi, *Manqabat al-javahir*, 409b; Kirmani, *Tazkira dar manaqib-i Hazrat Shah Niʿmatullah Vali*, 121–22; Niʿmatullahi, *Risala*, 153, 168; Farghana²i, *Hasht hadiqa*, 56a, 78a–79b, 90a.

16. For further details regarding this image, see Lowry and Nemazee, *A Jeweler's Eye*, 160–61. For the popular theme of Sufi masters' riding tigers, see van Bruinessen, "Haji Bektash, Sultan Sahak."

17. Cf. Urunbaev and Gross, *Letters of Khwaja ʿUbayd Allah Ahrar*. For Ahrar's political role, see Paul, *Die politische und soziale Bedeutung*, and Gross, "Khoja Ahrar."

18. A full consideration of Sufi masters' role in the political setup of Persianate societies in this period is beyond the scope of this book. Such a treatment would require expanding the base of sources to the many dynastic and regional historical narratives composed in the period, which is a task I aim to take up in the future. For existing studies in the arena that deal with relationships between particular masters and rulers, see studies on Khwaja Ahrar previously mentioned in this chapter, and Bashir, *Messianic Hopes and Mystical Visions*; Paul, *Doctrine and Organization*; Potter, "The Kart Dynasty of Herat."

19. Mahmud b. ʿUsman, *Miftah al-hidayat*, 47. This story is followed by the case of a man whose clothes become disheveled while sleeping, and the master comes and tucks them up correctly to keep his body properly covered from other eyes. On this theme see also Bukhari, *Anis at-talibin*, 162–63.

20. Murshidi, *Maʿdan ad-durar*, 49.

21. Bukhari, *Anis at-talibin*, 198–99.

22. Ibid., 164–66.

23. Shihab ad-Din, *Maqamat-i Amir Kulal*, 29b–30a.

24. Ibid., 19b–20a.

25. Ibid., 9b–10a. For other instances of the theme that involve Amir Kulal's successor Amir Hamza see Shams ad-Din, *Maqamat-i Amir Kulal*, 48a–50a.

26. Badakhshi, *Manqabat al-javahir*, 364b–365b. For an evaluation of ʿAli Hamadani's long-term legacy, see Elias, "A Second ʿAli."
27. Badakhshi, *Manqabat al-javahir*, 434a–435a.
28. Parsa, *Risala-yi qudsiyya*, 17–18.
29. Bukhari, *Anis at-talibin*, 177–78.
30. Ibid., 188–89.
31. Ibid., 226–27.
32. Ibid., 381.
33. Farghanaʾi, *Hasht hadiqa*, 18b.
34. For explicit evocation of this theme, see the discussion of ascetic practices and first meetings between masters and disciples in chapters 3 and 4 respectively. The notion of a second birth or resurrection after dying to worldly concerns could be connected to Jesus in particular as a prophet. This is articulated directly in one source that equates the Sufi desire for a living death with the death and resurrection of Jesus (Safi, *Rashahat*, 2:384–85).
35. For useful encapsulations of various perspectives on this issue, see Hallam, Hockey, and Howarth, *Beyond the Body*. For an extensive exploration of this theme using Islamic materials, see Halevi, *Muhammad's Grave*.
36. Kurani, *Rawzat as-salikin*, 159a–b. The public mourning of women has a long history as a debated practice in Islamic societies (cf. Halevi, *Muhammad's Grave*, 114–42).
37. Vaʿiz, *Maqsad al-iqbal-i sultaniyya*, 71.
38. The painting is attributed to the great master Bihzad (cf. Bahari, *Bihzad*, 86–89; Lukens-Swietochowski, "The Historical Background").
39. Ardabili, *Safvat as-safaʾ*, 970–71.
40. Ibid., 977–78.
41. Ibid., 973–75.
42. Ibid., 983–87.
43. Nishapuri, *Malfuzat-i Ahrar*, 323–24.
44. Shaykh, *Khavariq-i ʿadat-i Ahrar*, 633–34.
45. Safi, *Rashahat*, 2:655–58. Isfizari describes the scene at ʿAbd ar-Rahman Jami's death in quite similar terms (*Rawzat al-jannat fi awsaf madinat Herat*, 237).
46. In addition to his own work, Mawlana Shaykh is cited as the instigator behind Burhan ad-Din Samarqandi's hagiography devoted to Ahrar (Samarqandi, *Silsilat al-ʿarifin*, 54).
47. For other extended accounts relating to masters' deaths see: Badakhshi, *Khulasat al-manaqib*, 279–88; Murshidi, *Maʿdan ad-durar*, 103–24.
48. Subtelny's recent account of the shrine provides an overview and references to earlier discussions (*Timurids in Transition*, 208–12). The site's architectural history is discussed in Golombek, "Mazar-i Sharif."

49. Cf. Lari, *Takmilat nafahat al-uns*. This work formed the second part of Lari's commentary on the *Nafahat* that he wrote following a request by Jami's son.

50. Lari, *Tarikhcha-yi Mazar-i Sharif*, 20–31.

51. Ibid., 34.

52. Ibid., 35.

53. Cf. Subtelny, *Timurids in Transition*, 212–14. For an extensive exploration of the theme of gardens see also Subtelny, *Le Monde est un jardin*.

54. One can get a good sense for the density of funerary structures in a single city (Herat) by reading through a guidebook for shrines such as Va'iz, *Maqsad al-iqbal-i sultaniyya*, and Allen, *Timurid Herat*. For helpful scholarship in this regard that includes coverage of social issues in addition to formalistic architectural concerns, see Golombek, *The Timurid Shrine at Gazur Gah*; Golombek and Wilber, *The Timurid Architecture of Iran and Turan*; Rizvi, *Safavid Dynastic Shrine*; DeWeese, "Sacred Places and 'Public' Narratives," and "Dog Saints and Dog Shrines in Kubravi Tradition"; Claus-Peter Haase, "Shrines of Saints and Dynastic Mausolea."

55. Samarqandi, *Silsilat al-'arifin*, 189.

56. For the details of this manuscript and another image of two facing pages showing a funeral procession, see Folsach, *For the Privileged Few*, 94–95. For the poet, whose work is infused thoroughly with Sufi ideas, see Shirazi, *Kulliyat-i ash'ar*, 1–79.

57. Kurani, *Rawzat as-salikin*, 53a. For another incident of this type in this source, see 168a–b.

58. Safi, *Rashahat*, 2:630–31.

59. Ardabili, *Safvat as-safa'*, 1002–1003.

EPILOGUE

1. Safi, *Rashahat*, 2:428.

BIBLIOGRAPHY

MANUSCRIPTS

Abū l-Ḥasan b. Khwāja Sayf ad-Dīn. *Maqāmāt-i Shaykh Nūr ad-Dīn Baṣīr*. MS. 3061/ II, Oriental Studies Institute, Tashkent, 50b–76b.

Anonymous. *Malfūẓ-i Haẕrat Shaykh Zayn ad-Dīn Tāybādī*. MS. Indian Inst. Pers. 46, Bodleian Library, Oxford, 1a–56b.

Anonymous. *Risala*. MS. Ali Emiri Farsça 993 (No. 14), Millet Library, Istanbul, 102b–104a.

Arzangī, Muḥammad b. Niẓām Khwārazmī. *Manāqib-i Khwāja ʿAlī ʿAzīzān Rāmītanī*. MS. 8743/II, Oriental Studies Institute, Tashkent, 167b–259a.

Astarābādī, Ghiyāṣ ad-Dīn Muḥammad. *Istivānāma*. MS. Persian 34, Vatican Library, 13b–128b.

Badakhshī, Ḥaydar. *Manqabat al-javāhir*. MS. India Office 1850, British Library, London, 346b–442b.

Bukhārī, Muḥammad b. Asʿad. *Maslak al-ʿārifīn*. MS. Or. 6490, British Library, London.

Charkhī, Yaʿqūb. *Kitāb-i maqāmāt va silsila yi Naqshbandī*. MS. e. 37, Bodleian Library, Oxford, 145a–168b.

Farghānaʾī, Naṣīr b. Qāsim Turkistānī. *Hasht ḥadīqa*. MS. 1477, Oriental Studies Institute, Tashkent, 1a–128a.

Hamadānī, ʿAlī. *Risāla dar bayān-i adab-i mubtadī va ṭālibān-i haẕrat-i ṣamadī*. MS. Add. 1684, British Library, London.

Isḥāq, Khwāja Sayyid. *Khwābnāma*. MS. Ali Emiri Farsça 1042, Millet Library, Istanbul, 1a–69b.

―――― *Risala*. MS. Ali Emiri Farsça 993 (No. 10), Millet Library, Istanbul, 71b–81b.

Kūrānī, ʿAlī b. Maḥmūd al-Abīzī. *Rawżāt as-sālikīn*. MS. India Office Ethé 632, British
Library, London, 1a–174b.

Nāfajī, Majd ad-Dīn Ḥasan. *Khwābnāma*. MS. Persian 17, Vatican Library, 1a–94b.

Nūrbakhsh, Muḥammad. *Kitāb-i insān-nāma (Risāla-yi Nūrbakhsh fī ʿilm al-firāsa)*.
MS. Lala Ismail 115, Süleymaniye Library, Istanbul.

Shihab ad-Din. *Maqāmāt-i Amīr Kulāl*. MS. c.1562, Russian Academy of Sciences,
Saint-Petersburg Branch, Institute of Oriental Studies, 1b–74a.

PUBLISHED LITERATURE

Abarqūhī, Shams ad-Dīn Ibrāhīm. *Samāʿ dar khānqah*. In *Andar ghazal-i khvīsh nihān
khvāham gashtan: Samāʿ-nāmahā-yi Fārsī*, ed. Najīb Māyil Hiravī, 290–301. Tehran: Nashr-i Nay, 1993.

Abīvardī, Ḥusayn. "Kitāb-i anīs al-ʿāshiqīn." Ed. Īraj Afshār. *FIZ* 15 (1969): 85–160.

Abrahamov, Binyamin. *Divine Love in Islamic Mysticism: The Teachings of al-Ghazâlî
and al-Dabbâgh*. London: RoutledgeCurzon, 2003.

Aigle, Denise, ed. *Miracle et Karama: Hagiographies médiévales comparées*. Turnhout,
Belgium: Brepols, 2000.

ʿAjam, Rafīq al-, ed. *Mawsūʿat muṣṭalaḥāt at-taṣawwuf al-Islāmī*. Beirut: Maktabat
Lubnān Nāshirūn, 1999.

Algar, Hamid. "Éléments de provenance Malamati dans la tradition primitive Naqshbandi." In *Melâmis-Bayrâmis: Études sur trois mouvements mystiques musulmans*,
ed. Nathalie Clayer, Alexandre Popovic, and Thierry Zarcone, 27–36. Istanbul:
Isis, 1998.

―――― *Nakşibendîlik*. Ed. A. Cüneyd Köksal. Istanbul: İnsan Yayınları, 2007.

―――― "Reflections of Ibn ʿArabi in Early Naqshbandî Tradition." *Journal of the Ibn
ʿArabi Society* 10 (1991): 45–66.

―――― "Silent and Vocal Dhikr in the Naqshbandi Order." In *Akten des VII Kongresses
für Arabistik und Islamwissenschaft*, 39–46. Göttingen: Vandenhoeck and Rupre-
cht, 1976.

―――― "The Naqshbandi Order: A Preliminary Survey of Its History and Significance." *SI* 44 (1976): 123–52.

Allen, Terry. *Timurid Herat*. Wiesbaden: Reichert, 1983.

Amri, Nelly. *Les saints en islam, les messagers de l'espérance: Sainteté et eschatologie au
Maghreb aux XIVe et XVe siècles*. Paris: Cerf, 2008.

Amri, Nelly, and Denis Gril, eds. *Saint et sainteté dans le christianisme et l'islam: Le
regard des sciences de l'homme*. Paris: Maisonneuve and Larose, 2007.

Andrews, Walter, and Mehmet Kalpaklı. *The Age of Beloveds: Love and the Beloved in Early-Modern Ottoman and European Culture and Society*. Durham: Duke University Press, 2005.

Anvār, Shāh Qāsim-i. *Kulliyāt-i Qāsim-i Anvār*. Ed. Saʿīd Nafīsī. Tehran: Kitābkhāna-yi Sanāʾī, 1958.

Arberry, A. J. "The Biography of Shaikh Abu Ishaq al-Kazaruni." *Oriens* 3, no. 2 (1950): 163–82.

Ardabīlī, Ibn Bazzāz. *Ṣafvat aṣ-ṣafāʾ*. Ed. Ghulām Riżā Ṭabāṭabāʾī Majd. Tehran: Zaryāb, 1998.

Arjomand, Saïd Amir. "From the Editor: Defining Persianate Studies." *Journal of Persianate Studies* 1, no. 1 (2008): 1–4.

Atalay, Besim. *Bektaşilik ve Edebiyati*. Istanbul: Matbaʿa-i Amira, 1922.

Aubin, Jean. "L'avènement des Safavides reconsidéré (Études safavides)." *Moyen Orient et Océan Indien* 5 (1988): 1–130.

Aubin, Jean, ed. *Matériaux pour la biographie de Shâh Niʿmatullâh Walî Kermânî*. Tehran: Institut Français d'Iranologie de Téhéran, 1956.

Awbahī, Sulṭān ʿAlī. *Farhang-i tuḥfat al-aḥbāb*. Ed. Farīdūn Taqīzāda Ṭūsī and Nuṣrat az-Zamān Riyāżi Hiravī. Mashhad: Muʾassassat-i Intishārāt-i Āstān-i Quds-i Rażavī, 1986.

——— "Risāla-yi muṣāfaḥa." In *Maqālāt-i ʿĀrif (Daftar-i duvvum)*, ed. ʿĀrif Nawshāhī, 473–81. Tehran: Bunyād-i Mawqūfāt-i Duktur Maḥmūd Afshār, 2007.

Azmeh, Aziz Al-. *The Times of History: Universal Topics in Islamic Historiography*. Budapest: Central European University Press, 2007.

Babayan, Kathryn. *Mystics, Monarchs, and Messiahs: Cultural Landscapes of Early Modern Iran*. Cambridge: Harvard Center for Middle Eastern Studies, 2002.

Babayan, Kathryn, and Afsaneh Najmabadi, eds., *Islamicate Sexualities: Translations Across Temporal Geographies of Desire*. Cambridge: Harvard Center for Middle Eastern Studies, 2008.

Badakhshī, Jaʿfar. *Khulāṣat al-manāqib*. Ed. Sayyida Ashraf Ẓafar. Islamabad: Markaz-i Taḥqīqāt-i Fārsī-yi Īrān va Pākistān, 1995.

Badrān, Muḥammad Abū l-Faḍl. *Adabiyyāt al-karāma aṣ-ṣūfiyya: Dirāsa fī sh-shakl wa-l-maḍmūn*. al-ʿAyn, United Arab Emirates: Markaz Zāyid li-t-Turāth wa-t-Tārīkh, 2001.

Bahari, Ebadollah. *Bihzad: Master of Persian Painting*. London: I. B. Tauris, 1996.

Bākharzī, ʿAbd al-Vāsiʿ. *Maqāmāt-i Jāmī: Gūshah'hāyī az tārīkh-i farhangī va ijtimāʿī-yi Khurāsān dar ʿaṣr-i Tīmūrīyān*. Ed. Najīb Māyil Hiravī. Tehran: Nashr-i Nay, 1992.

Ballanfat, Paul. "Théorie des organes spirituels chez Yûsuf Hamadânî." *SI* 87, no. 2 (1998): 35–66.

Balyānī, Amīn ad-Dīn. "Maktūb-i Amīn ad-Dīn Kāzarūnī beh Darvīsh ʿAlī Ḥājjī Rashīd." In *Twenty Philosophical-Mystical Texts in Persian and Arabic*. ed. Ali Muhaddis. Uppsala: Acta Universititatis Upsaliensis, 2008.

Bāqillānī, Abū Bakr Muḥammad b. aṭ-Ṭayyib. *Miracle and Magic: A Treatise on the Nature of the Apologetic Miracle and Its Differentiation from Charisms, Trickery, Divination, Magic and Spells.* Ed. Richard J. McCarthy. Beirut: Librairie Orientale, 1958.

Baqqālī, ʿAbd as-Salām al-. *At-Taṣmīm al-jasadī fī l-Islām.* Casablanca: Dār Qurṭuba, 1998.

Barry, Michael. *Figurative Art in Medieval Islam and the Riddle of Bihzad of Herât (1465–1535).* Paris: Flammarion, 2004.

Bashir, Shahzad. "Between Mysticism and Messianism: The Life and Thought of Muḥammad Nūrbakš (d. 1464)." PhD diss., Yale University, 1998.

———— "Body." In *Key Themes for the Study of Islam*, ed. Jamal Elias, 72–92. Oxford: Oneworld, 2009.

———— *Fazlallah Astarabadi and the Hurufis.* Oxford: Oneworld, 2005.

———— *Messianic Hopes and Mystical Visions: The Nūrbakhshīya Between Medieval and Modern Islam.* Columbia: University of South Carolina Press, 2003.

———— "Muhammad in Sufi Eyes: Prophetic Legitimacy in Medieval Iran and Central Asia." In *The Cambridge Companion to Muhammad*, ed. Jonathan Brockopp. Cambridge: Cambridge University Press, 2010.

———— "Narrating Sight: Dreaming as Visual Training in Persianate Sufi Hagiography." In *Dreams in Islamic Societies: Exploring the Muslim Subconsciousness*, ed. Alexander Knysh and Özgen Felek. Albany: State University of New York Press, forthcoming.

———— "Shah Ismaʿil and the Qizilbash: Cannibalism in the Religious History of Early Safavid Iran." *HR* 45, no. 3 (2006): 234–56.

———— "The Imam's Return: Messianic Leadership in Late Medieval Shiʿism." In *The Most Learned of the Shiʿa*, ed. Linda Walbridge, 21–33. New York: Oxford University Press, 2001.

———— "The *Risālat al-hudā* of Muḥammad Nūrbakš: Critical Edition with Introduction," *RSO* 75, nos. 1–4 (2001): 87–137.

Bayram, Mikâil. *Bâciyân-i Rum: Selçuklular zamanında genç kızlar teşkilâti.* Konya: n.p., 1987.

Bell, Joseph Norment. *Love Theory in Later Hanbalite Islam.* Albany: State University of New York Press, 1979.

Benkheira, Mohammed Hocine. *Islam et interdits alimentaires: Juguler l'animalité.* Paris: Presses universitaires de France, 2000.

Bernardini, Michele. *Mémoire et propagande à l'époque timouride.* Paris: Association Pour l'Avancement des Études Iraniennes, 2008.

Black, Deborah L. "Psychology: Soul and Intellect." In *The Cambridge Companion to Arabic Philosophy*, ed. Peter Adamson and Richard C. Taylor, 308–26. Cambridge: Cambridge University Press, 2005.

Bouchrara, Traki Zannad. *Les lieux du corps en Islam.* Paris: Publisud, 1994.

Bourdieu, Pierre. *Outline of a Theory of Practice*. Trans. Richard Nice. Cambridge: Cambridge University Press, 1977.

Brockopp, Jonathan, ed. *Cambridge Companion to Muhammad*. Cambridge: Cambridge University Press, 2010.

Brown, Peter. *The Body and Society: Men, Women, and Sexual Renunciation in Early Christianity*. New York: Columbia University Press, 1988.

Bukhārī, Ṣalāḥ b. Mubārak. *Anīs aṭ-ṭālibīn va ʿuddat as-sālikīn*. Ed. Khalīl Ibrāhīm Sarīoghlū. Tehran: Kayhān 1992.

Butler, Judith. "Sexual Ideology and Phenomenological Description: A Feminist Critique of Merleau-Ponty's *Phenomenology of Perception*." In *The Thinking Muse: Feminism and Modern French Philosophy*, ed. J. Allen and I. M. Young, 85–100. Bloomington: Indiana University Press, 1989.

Bynum, Caroline Walker. *Holy Feast and Holy Fast: The Religious Significance of Food to Medieval Women*. Berkeley: University of California Press, 1987.

——— *Jesus as Mother: Studies in the Spirituality of the High Middle Ages*. Berkeley: University of California Press, 1982.

Chabel, Malek, ed. *Encyclopédie de l'amour en Islam: Érotisme, beauté et sexualité dans le monde arabe, en Perse et en Turquie*. Paris: Payot and Rivages, 1995.

Chih, Rachida, and Denis Gril, eds. *Le saint et son milieu ou comment lire les sources hagiographiques*. Cairo: Institut français d'archéologie orientale, 2000.

Chittick, William. "Sadr al-Din Qunawi on Oneness of Being." *International Philosophical Quarterly* 2 (1981): 171–84.

——— *The Self-Disclosure of God: Principles of Ibn al-ʿArabi's Cosmology*. Albany: State University of New York Press, 1998.

——— "Wahdat al-wujud in Islamic Thought." *Bulletin of the Henry Martyn Institute of Islamic Studies* 10 (Jan-Mar 1991): 7–27.

Chodkiewicz, Michel. *An Ocean Without Shore: Ibn Arabi, The Book, and the Law*. Albany: State University of New York Press, 1993.

——— *The Seal of the Saints*. Trans. Liadain Sherrard. Louisville, KY: Islamic Texts Society, 1993.

Clark, Elizabeth. *History, Theory, Text: Historians and the Linguistic Turn*. Cambridge: Harvard University Press, 2004.

——— "The Ascetic Impulse in Religious Life: A General Response." In *Asceticism*, ed. Vincent Wimbush and Richard Valantasis, 505–10. New York: Oxford University Press, 1995.

Coakley, Sarah, ed. *Religion and the Body*. Cambridge: Cambridge University Press, 2000.

Colby, Frederick. *Narrating Muhammad's Night Journey: Tracing the Development of the Ibn ʿAbbas Ascension Discourse*. Albany: State University of New York Press, 2008.

Corbin, Henry. *Alone with the Alone: Creative Imagination in the Ṣūfism of Ibn ʿArabī*. Princeton: Princeton University Press, 1998.

―――― *Spiritual Body and Celestial Earth: From Mazdean Iran to Shiʿite Iran*. Trans. Nancy Pearson. 2d ed. Princeton: Princeton University Press, 1977.

Cornell, Vincent. *The Realm of the Saint: Power and Authority in Moroccan Sufism*. Austin: University of Texas Press, 1998.

Dale, Stephen. "The Legacy of the Timurids." *JRAS*, 2d ser., 8, no. 1 (1998): 43–58.

Dāya, Najm ad-Dīn Rāzī. *Mirṣād al-ʿibād min al-mabdaʾ ilā l-maʿād*. Ed. Muḥammad Amīn Riyāḥī. Tehran: Shirkat-i Intishārāt-i ʿIlmī va Farhangī, 2005.

―――― *The Path of God's Bondsmen from Origin to Return*. Trans. Hamid Algar. Delmar, NY: Caravan, 1982.

Daylami, Abu ʾl-Hasan ʿAli b. Muhammad. *A Treatise on Mystical Love*. Trans. Joseph Norment Bell and Hassan Mahmood Abdul-Latif el-Shafie. Edinburgh: Edinburgh University Press, 2005.

de Bruijn, J. T. P. *Persian Sufi Poetry: An Introduction to the Mystical Use of Classical Persian Poems*. Richmond, Surrey: Curzon, 1997.

de Certeau, Michel. *The Writing of History*. Trans. Tom Conley. New York: Columbia University Press, 1988.

De Jong, Frederick, and Bernd Radtke, eds., *Islamic Mysticism Contested: Thirteen Centuries of Controversies and Polemics*. Leiden: Brill, 1999.

DeWeese, Devin. "Ahmad Yasavi and the Dog-Men: Narratives of Hero and Saint at the Frontier of Orality and Textuality." In *Theoretical Approaches to the Transmission and Edition of Oriental Manuscripts*, ed. Judith Pfeiffer and Manfred Kopp, 147–73. Beirut: Ergon Verlag Würzburg in Kommission, 2007.

―――― *An "Uvaysi" Sufi in Timurid Mawarannahr: Notes on Hagiography and the Taxonomy of Sanctity in the Religious History of Central Asia*. Bloomington, Ind.: Research Institute for Inner Asian Studies, 1993.

―――― "Dog Saints and Dog Shrines in Kubravi Tradition: Notes on a Hagiographical Motif from Khwarazm." In *Miracle et Karama: Hagiographies médiévales comparées*, vol. 2, ed. Denise Aigle, 459–97. Turnhout: Brepols, 2000.

―――― "Khojagani Origins and the Critique of Sufism: The Rehtoric of Communal Uniqueness in the *Manāqib* of Khoja ʿAlī ʿAzīzān Rāmītanī." In *Islamic Mysticism Contested: Thirteen Centuries of Controversies and Polemics*, ed. Frederick De Jong and Bernd Radtke, 492–519. Leiden: Brill, 1999.

―――― "Sacred Places and 'Public' Narratives: The Shrine of Ahmad Yasavi in Hagiographical Traditions of the Yasavi Sufi Order, 16th–17th Centuries." *MW* 90, 3–4 (2000): 353–76.

―――― "Sayyid ʿAli Hamadani and Kubrawi Hagiographical Traditions." In *The Legacy of Mediaeval Persian Sufism*, 121–58. Ed. Leonard Lewisohn. London: Khaniqahi Nimatullahi, 1992.

———— "The Eclipse of the Kubraviyah in Central Asia." *Iranian Studies* 21, nos. 1–2 (1988): 45–83.

———— "The Legitimation of Baha' ad-Din Naqshband." *Asiatische Studien/Études Asiatiques* 60, no. 2 (2006): 261–305.

———— "The Mashâ'ikh-i Turk and the Khojagân: Rethinking the Links Between the Yasavî and the Naqshbandî Sufi Traditions." *JIS* 7, no.2 (July 1996): 180–207.

Dodkhudoeva, Lola. "La bibliothèque de Khwâja Mohammad Pârsâ à Boukhara." *Cahiers d'Asie Centrale* 5/6 (1998): 125–46.

Dressler, Markus, Ron Geaves, and Gritt Klinkhammer, eds. *Sufis in Western Society: Global Networking and Locality*. New York: Routledge, 2009.

Druart, Thérèse-Anne. "The Human Soul's Individuation and Its Survival After the Body's Death: Avicenna on the Causal Relation Between Body and Soul." *Arabic Sciences and Philosophy* 10 (2000): 259–273.

During, Jean. *Musique et mystique dans les traditions de l'Iran*. Paris: Institut français de recherche en Iran, 1990.

Eaton, Richard. *Sufis of Bijapur, 1300–1700: Social Roles of Sufis in Medieval India*. Princeton: Princeton University Press, 1978.

Elias, Jamal. "A Second ʿAli: The Making of Sayyid ʿAli Hamadani in Popular Imagination." *MW* 90, nos. 3 and 4 (2000): 395–420.

Ernst, Carl. *Shambhala Guide to Sufism*. Boston: Shambhala, 1997.

———— "The Stages of Love in Early Persian Sufism, from Rabiʿa to Ruzbihan." In *The Heritage of Sufism*, ed. Leonard Lewisohn, 1:435–55. Oxford: Oneworld, 1999.

Ewing, Katherine. *Arguing Sainthood: Modernity, Psychoanalysis, and Islam*. Durham: Duke University Press, 1997.

Farahānī, Mahdī. *Payvand-i siyāsat va farhang dar ʿaṣr-i zavāl-i Tīmūrīyān va ẓuhūr-i Ṣafavīyān (873–911/1468–1505)*. Tehran: Anjuman-i Ās̲ār va Mafākhir-i Farhangī, 2002.

Fārsī, Khaṭīb. *Manāqib-i Jamāl ad-Dın Sāvī (Manakib-i Camal al-Din-i Savi)*. Ed. Tahsin Yazıcı. Ankara: Türk Tarih Kurumu Basımevi, 1972.

Fattahi, Yahya b. Sibak. *Coeur et Beauté ou Le livre des amoureux*. Trans. Manijeh Vossoughi Nouri. Paris: Dervy, 1997.

Ferhat, Halima. "Le saint et son corps: une lutte constante." *Al-Qantara: Revista de Estudios Árabes* 21, no. 2 (2000): 457–69.

Feuillebois-Pierunek, Ève. *A la croisée des voies célestes: Faxr al-Din-i ʿErâqi, poésie mystique et expression poétique en Perse médiévale*. Tehran: Institut Français de Recherche en Iran, 2002.

———— "La maîtrise du corps d'après les manuels de soufisme (x^e–xive siècles)." *Revue des mondes musulmans et de la Méditerranée* (online), 113-114 (2006). Consulted 27 September, 2010 (http://remmm.revues.org/index2969.html).

——— "Maîtres, disciples et compagnons d'après trois manuels d'obédience suhrawardie." *Luqman* 19, no. 2 (2003): 29–59.

Flood, Gavin. *The Ascetic Self: Subjectivity, Memory and Tradition.* Cambridge: Cambridge University Press. 2005.

Folsach, Kjeld von. *For the Privileged Few: Islamic Miniature Painting from the David Collection.* Copenhagen: Davids Samling, 2007.

Ford, Heidi A. "Constructing Sanctity: Miracles, Saints, and Gender in Yusuf ibn Isma'il al-Nabhani's *Jami' karamat al-awliya'*." PhD diss., Indiana University, 2000.

Gaborieau, Marc, Alexandre Popovic, and Thierry Zarcone, eds. *Naqshbandis: Cheminements et situation actuelle d'un ordre mystique musulman.* Istanbul: Isis, 1990.

Gāzurgāhī, Kamāl ad-Dīn. *Majālis al-'ushshāq.* Ed. Ghulām Riżā Ṭabāṭabā'ī Majd. Tehran: Intishārāt-i Zarrīn, 1997.

Glucklich, Ariel. *Sacred Pain: Hurting the Body for the Sake of the Soul.* New York: Oxford University Press, 2001.

Golombek, Lisa. *The Timurid Shrine at Gazur Gah.* Toronto: Royal Ontario Museum, 1969.

——— "Mazar-i Sharif—A Case of Mistaken Identity?" In *Studies in Memory of Gaston Wiet*, ed. Myriam Rosen-Ayalon, 335–43. Jerusalem: Institute of Asian and African Studies, Hebrew University, 1977.

Golombek, Lisa, and Maria Subtelny, eds. *Timurid Art and Culture: Iran and Central Asia in the Fifteenth Century.* Leiden: Brill, 1992.

Golombek, Lisa, and Donald Wilber. *The Timurid Architecture of Iran and Turan.* 2 vols. Princeton: Princeton University Press, 1988.

Grabar, Oleg. *Mostly Miniatures: An Introduction to Persian Painting.* Princeton: Princeton University Press, 2000.

——— *The Mediation of Ornament.* Princeton: Princeton University Press, 1992.

Gramlich, Richard. *Die Wunder der Freunde Gottes: Theologien und Erscheinungsformen des Islamischen Heiligenwunders.* Wiesbaden: Steiner, 1987.

Gribetz, Arthur. "The Sama' Controversy: Sufi vs. Legist." *SI* 74 (1991): 43–62.

Gronke, Monika. *Derwische im Vorhof der Macht: Sozial- und Wirtschaftsgeschichte Nordwestirans im 13. Und 14. Jahrhundert.* Stuttgart: Steiner, 1993.

Gross, Jo-Ann. "Khojar Ahrar: A Study of the Perceptions of Religious Power and Prestige in the Late Timurid Period." PhD diss., New York University, 1982.

Gruber, Christiane, and Frederick Colby, eds. *The Prophet's Ascension: Cross-cultural Encounters with the Islamic mi'raj Tales.* Bloomington: Indiana University Press, 2009.

Haase, Claus-Peter. "Shrines of Saints and Dynastic Mausolea: Towards a Typology of Funerary Architecture in the Timurid Period." *Cahiers d'Asie Centrale* 3–4 (1997): 217–27.

Hagen, Gottfried. "'He never took the Path of Pastime and Play': Concepts of Child-hood in Ottoman Hagiography." In *Scripta Ottomanica et Res Altaicae: Festschrift für Barbara Kellner*, ed. Ingeborg Hauenschild, Claus Schönig, and Peter Zieme, 95–118. Wiesbaden: Harrassowitz, 2002.

Halevi, Leor. *Muhammad's Grave: Death Rites and the Making of Islamic Society*. New York: Columbia University Press, 2007.

Hallam, Elizabeth, Jennifer Hockey, and Glennys Howarth. *Beyond the Body: Death and Social Identity*. London: Routledge, 1999.

Hamadānī, ʿAlī. "Risāla-yi darvīshiyya." In Muḥammad Riyāż, *Aḥvāl va āṯār va ashʿār-i Mīr Sayyid ʿAlī Hamadānī*, 489–500. 2d ed. Islamabad: Markaz-i Taḥqīqāt-i Fārsī-yi Īrān va Pākistān, 1991.

———— "Risāla-yi zikriyya." In Muḥammad Riyāż, *Aḥvāl va āṯār va ashʿār-i Mīr Sayyid ʿAlī Hamadānī*, Second Edition, 527–45. Islamabad: Markaz-i Taḥqīqāt-i Fārsī-yi Īrān va Pākistān, 1991.

Hannegraf, Wouter, ed. *Dictionary of Gnosis and Western Esotericism*. Leiden: Brill, 2006.

Heller-Roazen, Daniel. *The Inner Touch: Archeology of a Sensation*. Boston: Zone, 2007.

Hiravi, Najib Mayil, ed. *In barghā-yi pīr*. Tehran: Nashr-i Nay, 2002.

Hoyland, Robert. "Physiognomy in Islam." *Jerusalem Studies in Arabic and Islam* 30 (2005): 361–402.

Huart, Clément. *Anîs el-ʿochchâq: Traité des termes figures relatifs à la description de la beauté*. Paris: F. Vieweg, 1875.

Hujwiri, Ali. *Revelation of the Mystery*. Trans. Reynold Nicholson. Accord, NY: Pir, 1999.

Ibn al-ʿArabī. *Tanazzulāt al-Mawṣiliyya*. Ed. ʿAbd ar-Raḥmān Ḥasan Maḥmūd. Cairo: Maktabat ʿĀlam al-Fikr, 1986.

Ibn al-Karbalāʾī, Ḥāfiż Ḥusayn Tabrīzī. *Rawżāt al-jinān va jannāt al-janān*. Ed. Jaʿfar Sulṭān al-Qurrāʾī. 2 vols. Tabriz: Sutūda, 2005.

Ibn al-Munavvar, Muhammad. *Secrets of God's Mystical Oneness; or, The Spiritual Stations of Shaikh Abū Saʿīd*. Trans. John O'Kane. Costa Mesa, CA: Mazda, 1992.

Isfizārī, Muʿīn ad-Dīn Muḥammad. *Rawżāt al-jannāt fī awṣāf madīnat Herāt*. Ed. Sayyid Muḥammad Kāẓim Imām. Vol. 1. Tehran: Dānishgāh-i Tihrān, 1959.

Ishāq, Khwāja Sayyid. *Maḥramnāma*. In *Textes persans relatifs à la secte des houroûfîs*, ed. Clément Huart. Leiden: Brill, 1909.

Jackson, Peter, and Laurence Lockhart. *Cambridge History of Iran: The Timurid and Safavid Periods*. Cambridge: Cambridge University Press, 1986.

Jaghatāʾī, Badr ad-Dīn Hilālī. *Dīvān-i Hilālī Jaghatāʾī bā Shāh-o-darvīsh va Ṣifāt al-ʿāshiqīn-i u*. Ed. Saʿīd Nafīsī. Tehran: Kitābkhāna-yi Sanāʾī, 1958.

Jāmī, ʿAbd ar-Raḥmān. *Nafaḥāt al-uns min ḥażarāt al-quds*. Ed. Maḥmūd ʿĀbidī. Tehran: Intishārāt-i Iṭṭilāʿāt, 1996.

Kadkanī, Muḥammad Riżā Shafīʿī. *Qalandariyya dar tārīkh: Digardisihā-yi yak aydiulūzhī*. Tehran: Sukhan, 2007.

Karakī, Mullā Muḥammad Amīn. *Malfuẓāt-i Aḥrār*. In *Aḥvāl va sukhanān-i Khwāja ʿUbaydullāh Aḥrār*, ed. ʿĀrif Nawshāhī, 495–540. Tehran: Markaz-i Nashr-i Dānishgāhī, 2001.

Karamustafa, Ahmet. *God's Unruly Friends: Dervish Groups in the Islamic Later Middle Period, 1200–1550*. Salt Lake City: University of Utah Press, 1994.

Kāshānī, ʿAbd ar-Razzāq. *Laṭāʾif al-iʿlām fī ishārāt ahl al-ilhām*. Ed. Majīd Hādīzāda. Tehran: Mīrāṣ Maktūb, 2000.

Kāshānī, ʿIzz ad-Dīn Maḥmūd. *Miṣbāḥ al-hidāya va miftāḥ al-kifāya*. Ed. ʿIffat Karbāsī and Muhammad Riżā Bārzgar Khāliqī. Tehran: Zavvār, 2003.

Katz, Jonathan G. *Dreams, Sufism, and Sainthood: The Visionary Career of Muhammad al-Zawâwî*. Leiden: Brill, 1996.

Katz, Marion Holmes. *Body of Text: The Emergence of the Sunni Law of Ritual Purity*. Albany: State University of New York Press, 2002.

———— "The Study of Islamic Ritual and the Meaning of Wuduʾ." *Der Islam* 82, no. 1 (2005): 106–45.

Kay, Sarah, and Miri Rubin, eds. *Framing Medieval Bodies*. Manchester: Manchester University Press, 1994.

Kee, Howard. *Miracle in the Early Christian World: A Study in Sociohistorical Method*. New Haven: Yale University Press, 1983.

Kelly, Sean Dorrance. "Merleau-Ponty on the Body." In *The Philosophy of the Body*, ed. Michael Proudfoot, 62–76. Oxford: Blackwell, 2003.

Khabūshānī, Kamāl ad-Dīn Ḥājjī Muḥammad. "Ādāb-i darvīshī." In *Twenty Philosophical-Mystical Texts in Persian and Arabic*, ed. Ali Muhaddis. Uppsala: Acta Universititatis Upsaliensis, 2008.

Kirmānī, ʿAbd ar-Razzāq. *Taẕkira dar Manāqib-i Hażrat Shāh Niʿmatullāh Valī*. In *Matériaux pour la biographie de Shâh Niʿmatullâh Walî Kermânî*, ed. Jean Aubin, 1–131. Tehran: Institut Français d'Iranologie de Téhéran, 1956.

Knysh, Alexander. *Ibn ʿArabi in the Later Islamic Tradition: The Making of a Polemical Image in Medieval Islam*. Albany: State University of New York Press, 1999.

Koselleck, Reinhart. "Time and History." In *The Practice of Conceptual History: Timing History, Spacing Concepts*, trans. Todd Samuel et al., 100–14. Stanford: Stanford University Press, 2002.

Kugle, Scott. *Sufis and Saints' Bodies: Mysticism, Corporeality, and Sacred Power in Islam*. Chapel Hill: University of North Carolina Press, 2007.

Lāhījī, Shams ad-Dīn. *Mafātīḥ al-iʿjāz fī sharḥ-i Gulshan-i rāz*. Ed. Muḥammad Riżā Bārzgar and ʿIffat Karbāsī. Tehran: Zavvār, 1992.

Langer, Monika M. *Merleau-Ponty's "Phenomenology of Perception": A Guide and Commentary*. Tallahassee: Florida State University Press, 1989.

Lārī, ʿAbd al-Ghafūr. *Takmilah-i ḥavāshī-yi Nafaḥāt al-uns*. Ed. ʿAlī Aṣghar Bashīr Hiravī. Kabul: Anjuman-i Jāmī, 1964.

———. *Tarīkhcha-yi Mazār-i Sharīf*. Ed. Najīb Māyil Hiravī. Kabul: Anjuman-i Tārīkh va Adab, 1970.

Latimer, Joanna, and Michael Schillmeier, eds. *Un/knowing Bodies*. Hoboken, NJ: Wiley-Blackwell, 2009.

Lawrence, Bruce. *Notes from a Distant Flute: The Extant Literature of Pre-Mughal Indian Sufism*. Tehran: Imperial Iranian University of Philosophy, 1978.

Leder, Drew. "Flesh and Blood: A Proposed Supplement to Merleau-Ponty." In *The Body: Classic and Contemporary Readings*, ed. Donn Welton, 200–10. Oxford: Blackwell, 1999.

Le Gall, Dina. *A Culture of Sufism: Naqshbandis in the Ottoman World, 1450–1700*. Albany: State University of New York Press, 2005.

Lentz, Thomas. "Changing Worlds: Bihzad and the New Painting." In *Persian Masters: Five Centuries of Painting*, ed. Sheila Canby, 39–54. Bombay: Marg, 1990.

Lentz, Thomas, and Glenn Lowry. *Timur and the Princely Vision: Persian Art and Culture in the Fifteenth Century*. Los Angeles: Los Angeles County Museum of Art, 1989.

Lewis, Franklin. *Rumi Past and Present, East and West*. Oxford: Oneworld, 2000.

Lewisohn, Leonard. "The Sacred Music of Islam: Samāʿ in the Persian Sufi Tradition." *British Journal of Ethnomusicology* 6 (1997): 1–33.

Lock, Margaret, and Judith Furquhar, eds. *Beyond the Body Proper: Reading the Anthropology of Material Life (Body, Commodity, Text)*. Durham: Duke University Press, 2007.

Losesnsky, Paul. *Welcoming Fighani: Imitation and Poetic Individuality in the Safavid-Mughal Ghazal*. Costa Mesa, CA: Mazda, 1998.

Lowry, Glenn, and Susan Nemazee. *A Jeweler's Eye: Islamic Arts of the Book from the Vever Collection*. Seattle: University of Washington Press, 1988.

Lukens-Swietochowski, Marie. "The Historical Background and Illustrative Character of the Metropolitan Museum's *Mantiq al-Ṭayr* of 1483." In *Islamic Art in the Metropolitan Museum of Art*, ed. Richard Ettinghausen, 49–71. New York: Metropolitan Museum of Art, 1972.

McGregor, Richard. *Sanctity and Mysticism in Medieval Egypt: The Wafa Sufi Order and the Legacy of Ibn Arabi*. Albany: State University of New York Press, 2004.

Mcgregor, Richard, and Adam Sabra, eds. *Le développement du soufisme en Égypte à l'époque mamelouke*. Cairo: Institut français d'archéologie orientale, 2006.

Maghen, Ze'ev. "Much Ado About Wuduʾ." *Der Islam* 76, no. 2 (1999): 205–52.

———. *Virtues of the Flesh: Passion and Purity in Early Islamic Jurisprudence*. Leiden: Brill, 2005.

Maḥmūd b. Muḥammad, Sulṭān. *Ādāb al-muẓifin va zād al-ākilīn.* Ed. Īraj Afshār. Tehran: Mīrāš Maktūb, 2009.

Maḥmūd b. Uṣmān. *Vita des Scheich Abu Ishaq al-Kazaruni in der persischen Bearbeitung.* Ed. Fritz Meier. Leipzig: Brockhaus, 1948.

—— *Miftāḥ al-hidāyat va miṣbāḥ al-ʿināyat: Sīratnāma-yi Shaykh Amīn ad-Dīn Muḥammad Balyānī.* Ed. ʿImād ad-Dīn Shaykh al-Ḥukamāyī. Tehran: Intishārāt-i Rawzana, 1998.

Malamud, Margaret. "Gender and Spiritual Self-fashioning: The Master-Disciple Relationship in Classical Sufism." *JAAR* 64, no.1 (1996): 89–117.

Malti-Douglas, Fedwa. *Power, Marginality, and the Body in Medieval Islam.* Burlington, VT: Ashgate, 2001.

—— *Woman's Body, Woman's Word: Gender and Discourse in Arabo-Islamic Writing.* Princeton: Princeton University Press, 1992.

Manz, Beatrice Forbes. *Power, Politics and Religion in Timurid Iran.* Cambridge: Cambridge University Press, 2007.

Marín, Manuela. "Images des femmes dans les sources hagiographiques maghrébines: Les mères et les épouses du saint." In *Saint et sainteté dans le christianisme et l'islam: Le regard des sciences de l'homme,* ed. Nelly Amri and Denis Gril, 235–47. Paris: Maisonneuve and Larose, 2007.

Martin, F. R. *Les Miniatures de Behzad dans un manuscrit Persan daté 1485.* Munich: F. Bruckmann, 1912.

Masuzawa, Tomoko. *The Invention of World Religions.* Chicago: University of Chicago Press, 2006.

Mazzaoui, Michel. "A 'New' Edition of *Safvat al-safa.*" In *History and Historiography of Post-Mongol Central Asia and the Middle East: Studies in Honor of John E. Woods,* ed. Judith Pfeiffer and Sholeh Quinn, 303–10. Wiesbaden: Harrassowitz, 2006.

Meier, Fritz. *Essays in Islamic Piety and Mysticism.* Trans. John O'Kane and Bernd Radtke. Leiden: Brill, 1999.

—— *Meister und Schüler im Orden der Naqshbandiyya.* Heidelberg: Winter, 1995.

—— *Zwei Abhandlungen über die Naqshbandiyya.* Stuttgart: Steiner, 1994.

Meisami, Julie Scott. *Persian Court Poetry.* Princeton: Princeton University Press, 1987.

—— "The Body as Garden: Nature and Sexuality in Persian Poetry." *Edebiyat* 6 (1995): 245–74.

Merleau-Ponty, Maurice. *Phenomenology of Perception.* Trans. Colin Smith. 2d ed. London: Routledge, 2002.

Michot, Jean. *Musique et danse selon Ibn Taymiyya: Le Livre du samâʿ et de la danse (Kitâb al-samâʿ wa l-raqs).* Paris: Vrin, 1991.

Miḥrābī, Muʿīn ad-Dīn. *Kalimatallāh Hiya al-ʿUlyā (Dukhtar-i Fazlallāh Naʿīmī, bunyād-guzār-i junbish-i Ḥurūfiyya): Bānī-yi inqilābī va gumnān az qarn-i nahum.* Cologne: Nashr-i Rūyash, 1991.

Milstein, Rachel. "Sufi Elements in Late Fifteenth-Century Herat Painting." In *Studies in Memory of Gaston Wiet*, ed. Myriam Rosen-Ayalon, 357–69. Jerusalem: Institute of Asian and African Studies, Hebrew University, 1977.

Mitchell, Colin P. *The Practice of Politics in Safavid Iran: Power, Religion, and Rhetoric.* London: Tauris Academic Studies, 2009.

Moayyad, Heshmat, and Franklin Lewis, trans. *The Colossal Elephant and His Spiritual Feats: Shaykh Ahmad-e Jam.* Costa Mesa, Calif.: Mazda, 2004.

Molé, Marijan. "Autour du Daré Mansour: l'Apprentissage mystique de Baha' al-Din Naqshband." *Revue des Etudes Islamiques* 27, no.1 (1959): 35–66.

Molé, Marijan, ed. "Quelques traités naqshbandis (naqshbandiyyat)." *FIZ* 7 (1959): 273–323.

——— "La danse extatique en Islam." In *Les danses sacrées*, 145–280. Paris: Seuil, 1963.

Morris, James. "Ibn al-ʿArabi and His Interpretors." *JAOS*, 106 (1986): 539–51 (part 1), 733–56 (part 2); 107 (1987): 101–19 (part 3).

Mourad, Youssef. *La Physiognomonie arabe et le* Kitab al-firasa *de Fakhr al-Din al-Razi.* Paris: Librairie Orientaliste Paul Geuthner, 1939.

Muhaddis, Ali, ed. *Twenty Philosophical-Mystical Texts in Persian and Arabic.* Uppsala: Acta Universititatis Upsaliensis, 2008.

Mullin, Robert. *Miracles and the Modern Religious Imagination.* New Haven: Yale University Press, 1996.

Muminov, Ashirbek, and Shavasil Ziyadov. "L'horizon intellectuel d'un érudit du xvᵉ siècle: Nouvelles dècouvertes sur la bibliothèque de Muhammad Pârsâ." *Cahiers d'Asie Centrale* 7 (1999): 77–98.

Murshidī, Shams ad-Dīn Muḥammad ʿUmarī. *Maʿdan ad-durar fi sirat ash-Shaykh Ḥājjī ʿUmar.* Ed. ʿĀrif Nawshāhī and Muʿīn Niẓāmī. Tehran: Nashr-i Kāzarūniyya, 2005.

Musallam, Basim. "The Human Embryo in Arabic Scientific and Religious Thought." In *The Human Embryo: Aristotle and the Arabic and European Traditions*, ed. G. R. Dunstan, 32–46. Exeter: University of Exeter Press, 1990.

Najmabadi, Afsaneh. *Women with Mustaches and Men Without Beards: Gender and Sexual Anxieties of Iranian Modernity.* Berkeley: University of California Press, 2005.

Nawshāhī, ʿĀrif. *Aḥvāl va sukhanān-i Khwāja ʿUbaydullāh Aḥrār.* Tehran: Markaz-i Nashr-i Dānishgāhī, 2001.

——— "Dū risāla dar isnād-i muṣāfaḥa." In *Maqālāt-i ʿĀrif (Daftar-i duvvum)*, ed. ʿĀrif Nawshāhī, 460–91. Tehran: Bunyād-i Mawqūfāt-i Duktur Maḥmūd Afshār, 2007.

Netton, I. R. *Sufi Ritual: The Parallel Universe.* Richmond, Surrey: RoutledgeCurzon, 2000.

Newman, Andrew. "Tašrih-i Mansuri: Human Anatomy Between the Galenic and Prophetic Medical Traditions." In *La science dans le monde iranien à l'epoque islamique*, ed. Z. Vesel, H. Beikbaghban, and B. Thierry de Crussol, 253–71. Louvain: Peeters, 1998.

Niṣārī, Sayyid Ḥasan Khwāja Naqīb al-Ashrāf Bukhārī. *Muẕakkir-i aḥbāb.* Ed. Najīb Māyil Hiravī. Tehran: Nashr-i Markaz, 1999.

Nishāpūrī, Mīr ʿAbd al-Avval. *Malfūẓāt-i Aḥrār.* In *Aḥvāl va sukhanān-i Khwāja ʿUbaydullāh Aḥrār*, ed. ʿĀrif Nawshāhī, 98–494. Tehran: Markaz-i Nashr-i Dānishgāhī, 2001.

Niʿmatullāhī, Ṣunʿullāh. *Risala.* In *Matériaux pour la biographie de Shâh Niʿmatullâh Walí Kermânî*, ed. Jean Aubin, 133–268. Tehran: Institut Français d'Iranologie de Téhéran, 1956.

Norris, H. T. "The *Mirʾat al-talibin* by Zain al-Din al-Khawafi of Khurasan and Herat." *BSOAS* 53, no. 1 (1990): 57–63.

Nūrbakhsh, Muḥammad. *Risālat al-hudā.* See Bashir

Ocak, Ahmet Yaşar, ed. *Sufism and Sufis in Ottoman Society.* Ankara: Türk Tarih Kurumu, 2005.

Ökten, Ertuğrul. "Jāmī (817–898/1414–1492): His Biography and Intellectual Influence in Herat." PhD diss., University of Chicago, 2007.

Palāspūsh, Muḥammad al-Bāqī Balkhī. "Risāla-yi muṣāfaḥa." In *Maqālāt-i ʿĀrif (Daftar-i duvvum)*, ed. ʿĀrif Nawshāhī, 482–89. Tehran: Bunyād-i Mawqūfāt-i Duktur Maḥmūd Afshār, 2007.

Papas, Alexandre. "Shaykh Succession in the Classical Naqshbandiyya: Spirituality, Heredity, and the Question of Body." *Asian and African Area Studies* 7, no. 1 (2007): 36–49.

Pārsā, Khwāja Muḥammad. *Faṣl al-khiṭāb.* Ed. Jalīl Misgarnizhād. Tehran: Markaz-i Nashr-i Dānishgāhī, 2002.

―――― *Risāla-yi qudsiyya (Kalimāt-i Bahāʾ ad-Dīn Naqshband).* Ed. Aḥmad Ṭāhirī ʿIrāqī. Tehran: Kitābkhāna-yi Ṭahūrī, 1975.

Paul, Jürgen. *Die politische und soziale Bedeutung der Naqshbandiyya in Mittelasien im 15 Jahrhundert.* New York: Walter de Gruyter, 1991.

―――― *Doctrine and Organization: The Khwajagan/Naqshbandiya in the First Generation after Baha'uddin.* Berlin: Das Arabische Buch, 1998.

―――― "Forming a Faction: The Himâyat System of Khoja Ahrar." *IJMES* 23 (1991): 533–48.

―――― "Hagiographische Texte als historische Quelle." *Saeculum* 41 (1990): 17–43.

―――― "Maslak al-ʿārifīn: Ein Dokument zur frühen Geschichte der Hwajagan-Naqšbandiya." *Hallesche Beitrage zur Orientwissenschaft* 25 (1998): 172–185.

——— "Solitude Within Society: Early Khwājagānī Attitudes Towards Spiritual and Social Life." *Princeton Papers: Interdisciplinary Journal of Middle Eastern Studies* 15 (2006): 137–64.

Pemberton, Kelly. *Women Mystics and Sufi Shrines in India*. Columbia: University of South Carolina Press, 2010.

Potter, Lawrence. "The Kart Dynasty of Herat: Religion and Politics in Medieval Iran." PhD diss., Columbia University, 1992.

Radtke, Bernd, and John O'Kane. *The Concept of Sainthood in Early Islamic Mysticism*. Surrey: Curzon, 1996.

Rahman, Fazlur. "Dream, Imagination, and ʿAlam al-mithal." In *The Dream and Human Societies*, ed. G. E. von Grünebaum and Roger Caillois. Berkeley: University of California Press, 1966.

Reinhart, A. Kevin. "Impurity/No Danger." *HR* 30, no. 1 (1990): 1–24.

Renard, John. *Friends of God: Islamic Images of Piety, Commitment, and Servanthood*. Berkeley: University of California Press, 2008.

Renard, John, ed. *Tales of God's Friends: Islamic Hagiography in Translation*. Berkeley: University of California Press, 2009.

Richard, Francis. *Splendeurs persanes: Manuscrits du XIIᵉ au XVIIᵉ siècle*. Paris: Bibliothèque nationale de France, 1997.

Rizvi, Kishwar. *Safavid Dynastic Shrine: Architecture, Religion and Power in Early Modern Iran*. London: I. B. Tauris, (forthcoming 2011).

Robinson, B. W. *Persian Paintings in the John Rylands Library*. London: Sotheby Parke Bernet, 1980.

Robinson, B. W., and Basil Gray. *Persian Art of the Book*. Oxford: Bodleian Library, 1972.

Rouayheb, Khaled El-. *Before Homosexuality in the Arab-Islamic World, 1500–1800*. Chicago: University of Chicago Press, 2005.

Roxburgh, David. *The Persian Album, 1400–1600: From Dispersal to Collection*. New Haven: Yale University Press, 2005.

Ṣādiqī, ʿAlī Ashraf. "Āya Farhang-i tuḥfat al-aḥbāb az Ḥāfiẓ-i Awbahī ast?" *Nashr-i dānish* 19, no. 1 (2003): 38–46.

Ṣadrī, Bihnām, ed. *Kamāl ad-Dīn Bihzād: Majmūʿa-yi maqālāt-i hamāyish-i bayn al-milalī*. Tehran: Farhangistān-i Hunar, 2005.

Ṣafī, ʿAlī b. Ḥusayn Kāshifī. *Rashaḥāt-i ʿayn al-ḥayāt*. Ed. ʿAlī Aṣghar Muʿīniyān, 2 vols. Tehran: Majmūʿa-yi Mutūn-i Qadīm va Aḥvāl-i Dānishmandān va ʿIrfānān, 1977.

Samarqandī, Dawlatshāh. *Taẕkirat ash-shuʿarāʾ*. Ed. E. G. Browne. Tehran: Asāṭīr, 2004.

Samarqandī, Muḥammad b. Burhān ad-Dīn. *Silsilat al-ʿārifīn va taẕkirat aṣ-ṣiddīqīn*. Ed. Iḥsānullāh Shukrullāhī. Tehran: Kitābkhāna-yi Mūza va Markaz-i Isnād-i Majlis-i Shūrā-yi Millī, 2009.

Savage-Smith, Emilie. "Attitudes Toward Dissection in Medieval Islam." *Journal of the History of Medicine and Allied Sciences* 50 (1995): 68–111.

Scheper-Hughes, Nancy and Margaret Locke. "The Mindful Body: A Prolegomenon to Future Work in Medical Anthropology." *Medical Anthropology Quarterly* 1, no. 1 (1987): 6–41.

Schwarz, Florian. *"Unser Weg schließt tausend Wege ein": Derwische und Gesellschaft im islamischen Mittelasien im 16. Jahrhundert.* Berlin: Klaus Schwarz Verlag, 2000.

Shabistari, Mahmud. *The Garden of Mystery: The* Gulshan-i rāz *of Maḥmud Shabistarī.* Trans. Robert Abdul Hayy Darr. Bartlow, Cambridge: Archetype, 2007.

Shamīsā, Sīrūs. *Shāhidbāzī dar adabiyyāt-i Fārsī.* Tehran: Intishārāt-i Firdaws, 2002.

Shaykh, Mawlānā. *Khavāriq-iʿādat-i Aḥrār.* In *Aḥvāl va sukhanān-i Khwāja ʿUbaydullāh Aḥrār,* ed. ʿĀrif Nawshāhī, 573–705. Tehran: Markaz-i Nashr-i Dānishgāhī, 2001.

Shihāb ad-Dīn. *Maqāmāt-i Amīr Kulāl.* Bukhara, 1909.

Shīrāzī, Muḥammad Ahlī. *Kulliyāt-i ashʿār-i Mawlānā Ahlī-yi Shīrāzī.* Ed. Ḥāmid Rabbānī. Tehran: Kitābkhāna-yi Sanāʾī, 1965.

Shusterman, Richard. "The Silent, Limping Body of Philosophy." In *The Cambridge Companion to Merleau-Ponty,* ed. Taylor Carman and Mark B. N. Hansen, 151–80. Cambridge: Cambridge University Press, 2005.

Simnānī, ʿAlāʾ ad-Dawla. *Muṣannafāt-i Fārsī.* Ed. Najīb Māyil Hiravī. Tehran: Shirkat-i Intishārāt-i ʿIlmī va Farhangī, 1990.

Smith, Grace Martin, and Carl Ernst, eds. *Manifestations of Sainthood in Islam.* Istanbul: Isis, 1993.

Smith, Jonathan Z. *Relating Religion: Essays in the Study of Religion.* Chicago: University of Chicago Press, 2004.

Soucek, Priscilla. "The New York Public Library *Makhzan al-asrar* and Its Importance." *Ars Orientalis* 18 (1988): 1–37.

Soudavar, Abolala. *Arts of the Persian Courts.* New York: Rizzoli, 1992.

Spiegel, Gabrielle. "History, Historicism, and the Social Logic of the Text in the Middle Ages." *Speculum* 65, no. 1 (1990): 59–86.

Sprachman, Paul. *"Le beau garçon san merci:* The Homoerotic Tale in Arabic and Persian." In *Homoeroticism in Classical Arabic Literature,* ed. J. W. Wright and Everett Rowson, 192–209. New York: Columbia University Press, 1997.

Stchoukine, Ivan. *Les peintures des manuscrits Tîmûrides.* Paris: Imprimerie Nationale and Librairie Orientaliste Paul Geuthner, 1954.

Stern, Megan. "Dystopian Anxieties Versus Utopian Ideals: Medicine from Frankenstein to the Visible Human Project and Body Worlds." *Science as Culture* 15, no. 1 (2006): 61–84.

Strathern, Andrew. *Body Thoughts.* Ann Arbor: University of Michigan Press, 1996.

Subtelny, Maria. "A Taste for the Intricate: The Persian Poetry of the Late Timurid Period." *ZDMG* 136, no. 1 (1986): 56–79.

———— *Le Monde est un jardin: Aspects de l'histoire culturelle de l'Iran medieval*. Leuven: Peeters, 2002.

———— *Timurids in Transition: Turko-Persian Politics and Acculturation in Medieval Iran*. Leiden: Brill, 2007.

Suvorova, Anna. *Muslim Saints of South Asia: The Eleventh to Fifteenth Centuries*. Surrey: RoutledgeCurzon, 2004.

Szuppe, Maria. *L'Héritage timouride: Iran, Asie centrale, Inde XVe-XVIIIe siècles*. Aix-en-Provence: Édisud, 1997.

Tabrīzī, Abū l-Majd Muḥammad b. Masʿūd. "Munāẓara-yi samʿ va baṣr." In *Majmūʿa-yi rasāʾil-i Fārsī: Daftar-i haftum*. Mashhad: Bunyād-i Pizhuhishhā-yi Islāmī, 2007.

Thackston, Wheeler. *A Century of Princes: Sources on Timurid History and Art*. Cambridge, Mass.: The Aga Khan Program for Islamic Architecture, 1989.

Titley, Norah. *Miniatures from Persian Manuscripts: A Catalogue and Subject Index of Paintings from Persia, India, and Turkey in the British Library and the British Museum*. London: British Museum Publications, 1977.

Tosun, Necdet. *Bahâeddin Nakşbend: Hayatı, Görüşleri, Tarîkatı*. Istanbul: İnsan Yayınları, 2002.

Tourage, Mahdi. *Rumi and the Hermeneutics of Eroticism*. Leiden: Brill, 2007.

Trimingham, W. Spencer. *The Sufi Orders in Islam*. New York: Oxford University Press, 1971.

Turner, Bryan. "The Body in Western Society: Social Theory and its Perspectives." In *Religion and the Body*, ed. Sarah Coakley, 15–41. Cambridge: Cambridge University Press, 1997.

Uluç, Lale. *Turkman Governors, Shiraz Artisans, and Ottoman Collectors: Sixteenth-Century Shiraz Manuscripts*. Istanbul: Türkiye İş Bankası, 2006.

Urunbaev, Asom, and Jo-Ann Gross, eds. and trans. *Letters of Khwaja ʿUbayd Allah Aḥrar and His Associates*. Leiden: Brill, 2002.

Vāʿiẓ, Sayyid Aṣīl ad-Dīn. *Muqṣad al-iqbāl-i sulṭāniyya*. Ed. Mayil Hiravi. Tehran: Pizhuhishgāh-i ʿUlūm-i Insānī, 2007.

Vāʿizī, ʿAbd al-ʿAzīz b. Shīr Malik. *Risāla dar siyar-i Haẓrat Shāh Niʿmatullāh Valī*. In *Matériaux pour la biographie de Shâh Niʿmatullâh Walî Kermânî*, ed. Jean Aubin, 269–321. Tehran: Institut Français d'Iranologie de Téhéran, 1956.

van Bruinessen, Martin. "Haji Bektash, Sultan Sahak, Shah Mina Sahib and Various Avatars of a Running Wall." *Turcica: Revue d'Études Turcs* 21–23 (1991): 55–69.

van Gelder, G. J. H. *God's Banquet: Food in Classical Arabic Literature*. New York: Columbia University Press, 2000.

Vāṣifī, Zayn ad-Dīn. *Badāyiʿ al-vaqāyiʿ*. Ed. A. N. Boldyrev. 2 vols. Tehran: Bunyād-i Farhang-i Īrān, 1970–72.

Watenpaugh, Heghnar. "Deviant Dervishes: Space, Gender and the Construction of Antinomian Piety in Ottoman Aleppo." *IJMES* 37, no. 4 (2005): 535–66.

Wolper, Ethel Sara. *Cities and Saints: Sufism and the Transformation of Urban Space in Medieval Anatolia*. University Park: Pennsylvania State University Press, 2003.

Zarcone, Thierry. *Secret et sociétés secrètes en Islam: Turquie, Iran et Asie centrale, XIXe-XXe siècles*. Milan: Archè, 2002.

Ze'evi, Dror. *Producing Desire: Changing Sexual Discourse in the Ottoman Middle East, 1500–1900*. Berkeley: University of California Press, 2006.

INDEX

‘Ali Qushchi, Mawlana, 177

Alms tax (*zakat*), 55

Amputees, 15–16

Amulet (*ta‘viz*), 192

Annihilation (*fana’*), 41, 95–96, 128;
Naqshband on, 95

Antinomian asceticism, 64–68, 170; divi-
sions of, 65; miniature paintings of,
65, *66*; treating body as canvas, 67–68

Anvar, Shah Qasim-i, 97–98, *99*; Ahrar
on, 99–100, 145; on beloved, 113;
disciples of, 97, 144–48; as failure,
146; food and, 178; ghazal by, 111; on
heart, 43; Jami on, 145; on lovers,
113; on nobility, 29; sympathy for
Hurufi sect, 145

Appetite, lack of, 36

Ardabili, Shaykh Safi ad-Din: breaking
with mother, 116; dance of, 149–50;
death of, 204–5; early life of, 116;
gaze of, 190; Gilani and, first meeting between, 115–19; Gilani and,
melded bodies of, 128–29; last illness
of, 204–5; on love, 107; minimizing
senses, 117; punishment by, 211–12;
on ritual prayer, 56; on sama‘, 75;
sharing from mouth, 178–79; wet
dreams of, 117, 233*n*18; wife of, 159;
women and, 149–50

‘Arif, Mawlana, 172, 174–75

Aristotle, 221*n*4

Asceticism, 58–68; acquiring new bodies through, 63; of Ahrar, 62–63; ‘Ali
Hamadani and, 61–62; of Balyani,
63, 225*n*28; comfortable circumstances in old age reward for, 62;
contrastive nature of, 59; defined,
59; limited to early adulthood, 62;
of Master Morsel, 63; of ‘Umar
Murshidi, 63–64; of Vali, 63; *see also*
Antinomian asceticism

Astarabadi, Fazlallah, 32–33, 57; on
sexual relations, 155; wife of, 154–55

Astrology, 46

‘Attar, ‘Ala’ ad-Din, 54

‘Attar, Farid ad-Din, 202, *203*

‘Attar, Khwaja Yusuf, 71

Awbahi, Hafiz Sultan ‘Ali, 1; endowing
himself with power to intercede,
5–6; narrations of chains of handshakes, 7, 217*n*1; shaking hands with
Muhammad, 5

Awbahi, Mawlana Abu Sa‘id, 206

Azkani, Muhammad, 144

Badakhshi, Haydar, 179–84

Badakhshi, Ja‘far, 129; initiation of,
92–93; on pleasure of physical proximity to master, *93*

Balkhi, Husam al-Din Parsa, 233*n*21

Balyani, Amin ad-Din, 35; asceticism of,
63, 225*n*28; criticism of disciple desiring women, 149; on death, 35–36;
on food, 170; food miracles of, 172;
healing by, 192; initiation of, 91–92;
multilocation of, 195; poverty of, 63;
restricting rations, 63; on spiritual
bodies, 37–38

Barzishabadi, Sayyid ‘Abdallah, 130,
218*n*11

Bashiri, Shaykh Sayyid Ahmad, 39, 165,
184; as corpse, 201; food and, 168;
healing by, 192; on legal food, 169;
on love, 138–39; trance of, 94–95;
vocal zikr of, 191; wife of, 155–56, 164

Basir, Shaykh Nur ad-Din, 229*n*15

Batin, 20, 27, 55; ablutions pertaining
to, 55

Battle of the Trench, 4

Bayqara, Husayn, 103, 208

Beardless young boys (*pisaran-i amrad*),
146, *147*

Beauty (character in *Husn-o-dil*), 139, 140, 142

Being from God (*vujud-i mawhub-i haqqani*), 39

Bektashi Sufis, 223n41

Beloved: ʿAli Hamadani on, 125; Anvar on, 113; lovers and, contrast between, 111, 113; lovers as victims of, 110–11; lovers imprisoned by, 122–23; masters as lovers and, 124–28; miniature paintings depicting, 111, *112*, 125, *126*, *127*

Bihzad, Kamal ad-Din, *61*, *62*, 83, *84*, 101, *102*

Black dot (*suvayda'*), 44

Blood clot (*ʿalaqa*), 30, 32, 33

Bodies: acquired through asceticism, 63; acquisition of second, 39; as aspect of human imagination, 14; becoming present through social mediation, 15; as biological entity, 15; Bourdieu on, 16–17; as canvas, 67–68; connections between, 20; corresponding with alphabet, 45; as doorways, 27–28, 37, 47, 49; double meaning of, 28; elements composing, 34; food and, 168–69; God blowing his spirit into, 33; habitual, 15–17; heart as shadow, 43–44; Ibn al-ʿArabi on, 38; imaginal, 20; implicated in acts of deriving meaning, 14–15; individual/social, 101–4; interchangeability of, 129; intermingled with spirits, 39–41; as layered artifact, 16; to map systematic phenomena in cosmos, 14; master's control over, 81; Merleau-Ponty on, 15–17; molding, 21; origins in dust, 90; overlapping, 47–49; perfect, 12, 45; present, 15–17; as prism for sounds capable of inducing *samaʿ*,

76; readable, 45–47; restricted from thinking beyond immediate desires, 28; skepticism in analyzing, 14; spirit and, connection between, 28–29; spirit incarcerated in prison of, 35, 222n16; spiritual, 37–39, 44; studies concerning, 14; treated as corpse, 67; understanding human societies through, 16–17; women's, 21–22; zikr correlated with locations on, 69–70; *see also* Acquired body (*badan-i muktasab*); Melded bodies

Bones, 33

Bourdieu, Pierre, 15, 220n32; on body, 16–17

Breast (*sadr*), 44

Bukhari, Shams ad-Din, 202

Bustan (Saʿdi), 193, *194*

Certainty (*yaqin*), 75

Charkhi, Yaʿqub, 100; on ablutions, 55; Ahrar and, first meeting between, 119–21, 146, 233n22; on ritual purity, 54–55

Classes (*tabaqat*), 5

Companions (*sahaba*), 5

Conference of the Birds (ʿAttar, Farid ad-Din), 202, *203*

Contrition (*nadamat*), 75

Cosmos: bodies mapping, 14; division of, 221n1

Damghani, Khwaja Bayazid, 154

Dance, 51, 74–77; of Ardabili, 149–50; depicted in painting, *76*, 77

Dastur al-ʿushshaq (The Confidant of Lovers) (Fattahi), 139

Daʾud, Khwaja, 162

Daya, Najm ad-Din Razi, 43–44

Death, *48*, 129; of Abizi, 202; acting after, 211; of Ahrar, 205–7; of Ardabili,

Death (*continued*)
204–5; Balyani on, 35–36; Bukhari,
Shams ad-Din, preparing for, 202; of
Fatima (wife of Ardabili), 205; fear
of, 35–36; friends of God and, 86; of
Habashi, 2; of Kulal, 197–98; masters
power over life and, 198–201; memorialized after, 188; Naqshband power
over, 199–200; of Parsa, 161, 162;
preparing for, 59, 60; presence of,
202; successors after, 205–7
de Certeau, Michel, 18
Desire, 136, 143–51; of Balyani, 149;
beauty and, connection between,
144; disruptive, 21; interactions
involving, 137; of Kashghari, 144–45;
men as subjects/objects of, 144–48;
restricted from thinking beyond immediate, 28; shariʿa starving, 54; of
ʿUmar Murshidi, 148–49; of women,
148–50, 157
Devil, 71, 208; having intercourse with
itself, 222n13; Muhammad on, 70,
208
DeWeese, Devin, 96
Dimple (character in *Husn-o-dil*), 140,
142
Disciples, 11–13, 136; of Anvar, 97,
145–48; etiquette, 79, 80–85, 100;
fashioning themselves in image of
master, 82; fellowships of, 79; as lovers, 115; master eating, 27, 49; masters control over, 122–25, 190–92;
masters making themselves beautiful
to attract, 124–25; of, Khwafi, Zayn
ad-Din, 97–98; position of, 82; sub-
mitting to unconditional manipulation by, 187; wrongly infatuated, 127;
see also Melded bodies
Divan (Shirazi), 211, *212*
Doubt (character in *Husn-o-dil*), 139

Dreams, 38; initiation into lineage in,
94–96
Dust (*khak*), 90

Ear: Abizi on, 143; connected to heart,
74; corresponding with alphabet, 45
Earth, 34
Ecstasy (*vajd*), 75
Elias, 229n20
Embodiment, as analytical tool, 13–18
Embryo, 28, 29–33, 221n4; completed,
32; influence of heavenly spheres on,
32; in Quran, 30; as replication of
cosmogony, 32
Era of friendship, 85
Era of prophecy, 85
Etiquette, 78–79; Ahrar on, 81; disciple,
79, 80–85, 100; manual of, 80–81,
82; master, 79, 80–85; of Naqshband,
83; repercussions of proper, 83, 85;
Taybadi on, 83, 85; Vali on, 81; while
consuming food, 239n44
Eye: Abizi on, 143; corresponding with
alphabet, 45
Eyebrows, 45–46

Facial lines, seven, 33
Faith, profession of, 55, 69–70
Farsi, Khatib, 65–68
Fasl al-khitab (The Decisive Speech)
(Parsa), 34
Fasting (*sawm*), 55, 57; becoming
worldly fetish, 177; masters capacity
for, 57
Fatima, Bibi (wife of Ardabili), 159,
204–5; death of, 205
Fatima, Bibi (wife of Bashiri), 155
Fattahi, Muhammad Yahya b. Sibak,
139–43, 150
Fire, 34
Five pillars of Islam, 55

Flesh, 33

Followers' Followers (*tab'tabi'un*), 5

Followers of Muhammad's companions (*tabi'un*), 5

Followers of Savi, 65–67

Food: Ahrar and, 169, 173–74, 177, 178; 'Ali Hamadani detecting illegally acquired, 182–83; 'Ali Hamadani detecting legal status of, 179–82; Anvar and, 178; Balyani on, 170; Bashiri and, 168; Bashiri on legal, 169; bodies and, 168–69; boundaries and, 178–79; cats as, 181; complaints over not providing, 173; contamination of, 182–83; dogs as, 180; etiquette while consuming, 239*n*44; Gilani's favorite, 178; Kulal and, 168, 174–75; Kulal on pure, 169; masters control over, 166, 169–77; masters providing, 172–73, 183–84; Naqshband controlling, 175–77; pigs as, 181; religious valuations of, 168; restricting amount of, 169–70, 173–74; sharing v. not sharing, 178; as social resource, 174–77; source of, 182; Taybadi and, 168–69; 'Umar and, 173; Vali on, 173

Food miracles, 22; of Balyani, 172; of Hamza, 171; of Kulal, 170–71, 172; of Naqshband, 171–72; of Taybadi, 171; of Vali, 171

Friendship (character in *Husn-o-dil*), 140, *141*

Fusus al-hikam (Bezels of Wisdom) (Ibn al-'Arabi), 98–99

Gazurgahi, Kamal ad-Din, 131–34, 146

Ghijduvani, 'Ala' ad-Din, 152–53; mother of, 152–53

Ghijduvani, Khwaja 'Abd al-Khaliq, 70, 94

Gilani, Shaykh Zahid, 75; Ardabili and, first meeting between, 115–19; Ardabili and, melded bodies of, 128–29; daughter of, 159; favorite foods, 178; physical appearance of, 117, 118

God's direct epiphanies (*tajalliyat*), 53

God's friends (*awliya'*), 12, 59; Ahrar born as, 90; born as, 89–91; constructing religious authority, 12; death and, 86; as form of divine mercy, 85; hierarchy of, 79, 85–87; internal states and, 12–13; markers, 80; miracles performed by, 167; Naqshband born as, 89–90; Naqshband on, 80; power over organs, 80; reading bodies, 46; responsible for continuing existence of world, 85; rudeness to, 170–71; social relationships and, 12–13

Habashi, Sa'id, 1, 4; changing outward form, 6; death of, 2; identified as Mu'ammar, 6–7; longevity of, 1; meeting with 'Ali Hamadani, 6–7

Habitus, 16–17

Hafiz, Mawlana 'Abd ar-Rahman, 75

Hagiography, 18–20; forms of, 220*n*38; miracles and, 165; use of term, 18

Hajj, 51, 55, 57; Kulal on, 58; Parsa performing, 161; 'Umar Murshidi performing, 159–60; women performing, 159–60

Hamza, Sayyid Amir, 160; food miracles of, 171

Handshakes, chain of: Awbahi, Hafiz Sultan 'Ali, narrating, 7, 217*n*1; different, 4; establishing credentials, 7; limitation of cross-gender physical contact and, 6; Muhammad on, 1, 5, 217*n*1; physicality emphasized in, 3; Shari'a and, 6

Khizr, 140, 181; Elias and, interchangeability between, 229*n*20; on ritual purity, 239*n*43

Khulasat al-manaqib (The Summary of Virtues) (Badakhshi), 92–93

Khuttalani, Ishaq, 130

Khwafi, Rukn ad-Din, 82

Khwafi, Zayn ad-Din, 71–72; Ahrar on, 82, 99–100; disciples of, 97–98; on Ibn al-ʿArabi, 98–99; Samarqandi and, conflict between, 191; on zikr, 73

Khwajagani-Naqshbandi lineage, 88, *89*

Khwarazmi, Haydar, 59, *60*

Kitab-i maqamat va silsila-yi Khwaja Naqshband (Book of the Stations and Lineage of Khwaja Naqshband) (Charkhi), 54

Knowledge of numbers (*vuquf-i ʿadadi*), 70, 227*n*48

Kubravi-Hamadani lineage, 6, 130

Kubraviyya, 72

Kulal, Sayyid Amir, 57–58, 89–90, 152, 160; concern for food as resource, 174; death of, 197–98; extraterritorial influence of, 197; on food and intimacy, 174–75; food miracles of, 170–71, 172; on hajj, 58; healing by, 193; on Kaʿba, 58; multilocation of, 197–98; on pure food, 169; sensitivity to food, 168

Kurani, ʿAli b. Mahmud Abivardi, 122

Lahiji, Shams ad-Din, 30, 32

Lari, ʿAbd al-Ghafur, 208, 209

Limb (character in *Husn-o-dil*), 140, 142

Lineage, 87–96; born to God's friends, 89–91; charisma overshadowed by, 88; competition through, 79–80, 96–101; initiation in dreams/visions, 94–96; initiation of women, 156;

initiation rituals, 90–94; social cohesion through, 79–80; types of, 87; valuations of, 79; *see also specific lineages*

Love: affecting human body, 138–39; Ahrar on falling in, 121; ʿAli Hamadani on, 124; Ardabili on, 107; Bashiri on, 138–39; bringing turmoil/pain, 110, 124; cause/effects, 109–15; characters of, 109; consequences of falling in, 121–28; embodiment and, 130–34; as emotional attachment, 137; first meetings, 115–21; at first sight, 108; gripping heart, 122–24; as highly desirable state, 110; Ibn al-ʿArabi on, 133–34; masters as controllers of, 125, 127–28; masters of, 115; masters transforming to become object of, 115; Naqshband on, 121; necessity of human, 131; parameters of, 109–15; poetic discussion of, 109; Ruji falling in, 144; special capacity for, 131–34; ultimate object for, 107, 131; Vali on, 121; *see also* Desire; Melded bodies

Love (character in *Husn-o-dil*), 139, 140

Lovers: ʿAli Hamadani on, 125; Anvar on, 113; beloved and, contrast between, 111, 113; disciples as, 115; extraordinary, 131–34; imprisoned by beloved, 122–23; masters as beloveds and, 124–28; miniature paintings depicting, 125, *126, 127*; poets writing in voice of, 110–11; as victims of beloved, 110–11

Mafatih al-iʿaz fi sharh-i Gulshan-i raz (Miraculous Keys for Explaining The Secret Garden) (Lahiji), 30

al-Mahdi, Muhammad, 40

Mahmud (Sultan of Ghazna), 59, *60*

Servitude (*'ubudiyyat*), 200

Shabistari, Mahmud, 30

Shadows, casting, 82

Shahidbazi, 146, *147*

Shami, Muhammad, 182

Shari'a, 50, 51–58; 'Ali Hamadani on, 224*n*6; handshakes and, 6; influence of time period on, 52; intellect and, relationship between, 224*n*6; involuntary obedience to, 189; Naqshband on relationship between true reality and, 52; Parsa justifying, 52; perception and, 53; rationalizations of, 51, 52–53; starving desires, 54; validating, 55

Shaykh, Mawlana, 205–6, 207

Shaykh, Tunguz, 156

Shihab ad-Din, Amir, 160–61

Shi'ism, 221*n*1

Shirazi, Ahli, 211, *212*

Shrines, 188–89, 207–10; establishing, 210; guidebook for, 243*n*54; reputation and scale of, 210

Shunning society, 64–68

Sifat al-'ashiqin (The Qualities of Lovers) (Jaghata'i), 110

Sight (character in *Husn-o-dil*), 139, *141*, 142

Silsila, 79, 87, 109

Simnani, 'Ala' ad-Dawla, 130

Sin, protection from (*'isma*), 81

Singers (*qavvalan*), 75, 190–91

Sisters of Anatolia, 237*n*53

Smith, Jonathan Z., 219*n*16

Solitary retreat (*khalvat*), 82

Sperm (*nutfa*), 30, 221*n*4; receptor of, 33; residence of, 33

Spiegel, Gabrielle, 15; on texts, 17; on work of historian, 17

Spirit (*ruh*): 'Ali Hamadani on, 36; bodies intermingled with, 39–41; body and, connection between, 28–29; containing multiple, 40; diseased, 36; embodied, 34–37; as essence, 34; form of, 37–38; incarcerated in prison of body, 35, 222*n*16; manifestations of, 223*n*28; Parsa on, 34

Spiritual sight (*nazar-i basirat*), 146

Spiritual universalism, 10–11

Stature (character in *Husn-o-dil*), 140, 142

Subsistence (*baqa'*), 95, 128

Sufism: defining, 10; expansion of, 11–12; glossed as mysticism, 10; hide-and-seek and, 27; historical study v. popular culture associations of, 10; as Islamic heterodoxy, 11; Islamic history and, 9–11; marginalizing associations, 10–11; in relation to Shi'ism, 221*n*1; romanticizing associations, 10–11

Tabrizi, Muhammad Assar, 184, *185*

Tasawwuf: defined, 218*n*15; etymology of, 10; internal usage of, 10

Tashrih-i badan-i insan (Muhammad, Mansur b.), 30, *31*

Taybadi, Zayn ad-Din, 153; on etiquette, 83, 85; food and, 168–69; food miracles of, 171; on Ibnal-'Arabi, 98–99

Tazkira, 18–19

Temperament (*mizaj*), 75

Texts, 18–20; as descriptions of behavior, 23; generating social realities, 17; mirroring social realities, 17; occupying determinate social spaces, 17; paintings and, difference between, 19, 135; Spiegel on, 17

Tigers, riding, 193, *194*

Time, passage of, 5, 217*n*2

Trance (*ghaybat*), 72; of Bashiri, 94–95

Tress (character in *Husn-o-dil*), 140, 142